Lecture Notes of the Institute for Computer Sciences, Social Informatics and Telecommunications Engineering

542

The LNICST series publishes ICST's conferences, symposia and workshops.

LNICST reports state-of-the-art results in areas related to the scope of the Institute. The type of material published includes

- Proceedings (published in time for the respective event)
- Other edited monographs (such as project reports or invited volumes)

LNICST topics span the following areas:

- General Computer Science
- E-Economy
- E-Medicine
- Knowledge Management
- Multimedia
- Operations, Management and Policy
- Social Informatics
- Systems

Dragan Perakovic · Lucia Knapcikova
Editors

Future Access Enablers for Ubiquitous and Intelligent Infrastructures

7th EAI International Conference, FABULOUS 2023
Bratislava, Slovakia, October 24–26, 2023
Proceedings

 Springer

Editors
Dragan Perakovic ⓘ
University of Zagreb
Zagreb, Croatia

Lucia Knapcikova ⓘ
Technical University of Košice
Prešov, Slovakia

ISSN 1867-8211   ISSN 1867-822X (electronic)
Lecture Notes of the Institute for Computer Sciences, Social Informatics
and Telecommunications Engineering
ISBN 978-3-031-50050-3   ISBN 978-3-031-50051-0 (eBook)
https://doi.org/10.1007/978-3-031-50051-0

This Springer imprint is published by the registered company Springer Nature Switzerland AG
The registered company address is: Gewerbestrasse 11, 6330 Cham, Switzerland

Paper in this product is recyclable.

Preface

EAI FABULOUS 2023 - 7th EAI International Conference on Future Access Enablers of Ubiquitous and Intelligent Infrastructures (EAI FABULOUS 2023)

October 24–26, 2023, Bratislava, Slovak Republic

Dear authors, dear readers,

we are delighted to introduce the publication of EAI FABULOUS 2023-the 7th EAI International Conference on Future Access Enablers of Ubiquitous and Intelligent Infrastructures, which was the result of fruitful cooperation among the European Alliance for Innovation, Faculty of Transport and Traffic Sciences, University of Zagreb and Faculty of Manufacturing Technologies with a seat in Prešov of the Technical University of Košice.

The year 2023 was special because our conference was part of the worldwide Smart Life Summit, organized by the European Alliance for Innovation. This was an event uniting the brightest minds from academia, business, and municipal sectors for an extraordinary collaborative experience. The ambition was to establish channels of communication and disseminate knowledge among professionals working in manufacturing and related institutions.

Therefore, we cordially invited experts, researchers, academicians, and practitioners in relevant fields to share their expertise from the manufacturing systems management field at the conference. The themes of EAI FABULOUS 2023 were Teletraffic & Intelligent Networks, Internet of Things, Cyber Security, Artificial Intelligence, Machine Learning, Smart Environment Applications/Scenarios, and Multimedia.

The technical program of EAI FABULOUS 2023 consisted of 14 full papers in full conference format. We are grateful to all authors who prepared high-quality scientific presentations of their research work. We sincerely appreciate their constant support. Working with such an excellent organizing committee team was also a great pleasure. Full thanks for their hard work in organizing and supporting the conference. In particular, thanks go to the Technical Program Committee, led by our TPC Co-Chairs, Kim-Kwang Raymond Choo, Marko Periša, Aleksandar Jevremović, Anca D. Jurcut, and Annamaria Behunova. Thanks to Goran Marković (general co-chair), Web Chair Alexandru Vulpe, and Jozef Husar for all their support.

We are also grateful to the Conference Manager Katarina Antalova for her support and to all the reviewers who did excellent work. The 7th EAI FABULOUS provided a good network platform for all researchers, developers, and practitioners to discuss all science and technology relevant to Future Access Enablers of Ubiquitous and Intelligent

Infrastructures ecosystems. We strongly believe EAI FABULOUS 2024 will occur in Zagreb, Croatia, EU.

October 2023   Dragan Perakovic
                                                         Lucia Knapcikova

Organization

Steering Committee

Chair

Imrich Chlamtac   University of Trento, Italy

Co-chairs

Dragan Peraković   University of Zagreb, Croatia
Lucia Knapcikova   Technical University of Košice, Slovakia

General Chair

Dragan Peraković   University of Zagreb, Croatia

General Co-chairs

Goran Marković   University of Beograd, Serbia
Lucia Knapcikova   Technical University of Košice, Slovakia

Technical Program Committee Chairs

Kim-Kwang Raymond Choo   University of Texas at San Antonio, USA
Marko Periša   University of Zagreb, Croatia
Aleksandar Jevremović   Singidunum University, Belgrade, Serbia/
                                      Harvard University, USA
Anca D. Jurcut   University College Dublin, Ireland
Annamaria Behunova   Technical University of Košice, Slovakia

Web Chairs

Alexandru Vulpe   University POLITEHNICA of Bucharest,
                                      Romania
Jozef Husar   Technical University of Košice, Slovakia

Publicity and Social Media Chair

Petra Zorić   University of Zagreb, Croatia

Sponsorship and Exhibits Chair

Dragan Peraković   University of Zagreb, Croatia

Workshop Chair

Gordana Jotanović   University of East Sarajevo,
                                   Bosnia and Herzegovina

Publications Chairs

Lucia Knapcikova   Technical University of Košice, Slovakia
Dragan Peraković   University of Zagreb, Croatia

Posters and PhD Track Chair

Ivan Grgurević   University of Zagreb, Croatia

Local Chair

Ivan Cvitić   University of Zagreb, Croatia

Technical Program Committee Chairs

Marko Periša   University of Zagreb, Croatia
Marko Krstić   RATEL, Serbia
Anca D. Jurcut   University College Dublin, Ireland

Members

Alberto Huertas Celdrán   University of Murcia, Spain
Aleksandar Jevremović   Singidunum University, Serbia
Alessandro Ruggiero   University of Salerno, Italy
Alexandru Vulpe   University POLITEHNICA of Bucharest,
                                   Romania
Anca Delia Jurcut   University College Dublin, Ireland

Anna Otsetova	University of Telecommunications and Post, Sofia, Bulgaria
Annamária Behúnová	Technical University of Košice, Slovakia
Arcangelo Castiglione	University of Salerno, Italy
Arianit Maraj	Telecom of Kosovo and AAB College, Kosovo
B. Gupta	National Institute of Technology Kurukshetra, India
Dalibor Dobrilovic	University of Novi Sad, Serbia
Dharma Agrawal	University of Cincinnati, USA
Dražan Kozak	University of Osijek, Croatia
Dušan Šimšík	Technical University of Košice, Slovakia
Goran Marković	University of Belgrade, Serbia
Goran Jauševac	University of East Sarajevo, Bosnia and Herzegovina
Gordana Jotanovic	University of East Sarajevo, Bosnia and Herzegovina
Imran Razzak	Deakin University, Australia
Ivan Pavlenko	Sumy State University, Ukraine
Ivan Cvitic	University of Zagreb, Croatia
Ivan Grgurević	University of Zagreb, Croatia
Jakub Kaščak	Technical University of Košice, Prešov, Slovakia
Jan Pitel	Technical University of Košice, Prešov, Slovakia
Janusz Grabara	Czestochowa University of Technology, Poland
Jerzy Winczek	Czestochowa University of Technology, Poland
Jozef Husár	Technical University of Košice, Slovakia
Katarzyna Huk	University of Zielona Góra, Poland
Marcel Behún	Technical University of Košice, Slovakia
Marko Krstic	Regulatory Agency for Electronic Communications and Postal Services, Serbia
Marko Matulin	University of Zagreb, Croatia
Marko Periša	University of Zagreb, Croatia
Martin Straka	Technical University of Košice, Slovakia
Michael Herzog	Technical University of Applied Sciences Wildau, Germany
Milan Čabarkapa	University of Belgrade, Serbia
Mirjana Stojanović	University of Belgrade, Serbia
Miroslav Vujić	University of Zagreb, Croatia
Natalia Horňáková	Comenius University, Slovakia
Pavel Necas	Matej Bel University, Slovakia
Peter Kolarovszki	University of Žilina, Slovakia
Petr Skřehot	Occupational Safety and Health Expert Institute, Czechia

Contents

Smart Environment Applications/Scenarios

Future Access Networks

Currently, high costs of building blocks in a quantum network, which consist of devices such as Entangled Photon Source (EPS), Superconducting Nanowire Single-photon Detector (SNSPD), Single-photon Avalanche Detector (SPAD) and dark optical fibers, as well as the high expenses associated with the physical implementation of such network represents challenges in physical implementation. To address those challenges, simulations of such networks are of great importance as they provide insights into the events and processes occurring within the network. By exploring different sets of input parameters, simulations allow us to understand their impact on the functioning of the network as a whole. These results have the potential to serve as a foundation and reference for further research and decision-making regarding the feasibility of physically implementing a quantum communication network. Despite the clear significance of simulations in the field of quantum communications, there is a noticeable lack of research and analysis on software platforms and tools designed for such narrow purpose. This lack of research is further exacerbated in the area of network simulations for quantum key distribution, which is a subset of quantum communications. The reason for this is the extremely limited number of research groups working on this and similar research problems.

As the research field of quantum communications and QKD increasingly gains significance and demonstrates growing applications, the need for simulating events and processes occurring in such networks becomes more apparent. This highlights the necessity of synthesizing knowledge about existing simulation tools and platforms, as well as identifying their capabilities, characteristics, functionalities, and observed limitations. The results of this research will provide support to researchers in selecting appropriate simulation tools for future investigations. Additionally, they will underscore the need and importance of enhancing existing tools in terms of functionality, capabilities, and applicability across different scenarios.

The structure of this paper is organized as follows. Section 2 presents previous research on quantum network simulators. These research papers consist of relevant simulation tools, and comparison based information. The simulators were compared based on the programming language in which they were written, are they open sourced, do they have implemented noise models, are they modular, and do they have implemented QKD protocols. Section 3 provides an explanation of quantum key distribution (QKD) and describes the architecture of QKD networks. The architecture of these networks consists of quantum links, classical links and quantum nodes as elementary components that enable the transmission of entangled photons and accompanying classical information. Section 4 provides an overview and general information on the available simulation platforms for quantum networks. Section 5 presents a detailed analysis of simulators in the context of simulating QKD networks. This section compares simulators based on functionality and capabilities, such as: error modelling, programming interface, size of simulated network, node types, etc.

2   Previous Research

Researchers in [1] presents a survey of the latest, at the time of writing, simulation frameworks which are used to simulate different types of QKD protocols and QKD quantum networks. These simulation frameworks are used to develop and implement efficient and practical quantum cryptographic schemes and network protocols. This paper contains comparisons of the simulation frameworks based on a number of characteristics. Authors performed comprehensive, systematic analysis of experimental simulation frameworks and their functionalities with the ultimate goal of paving the way for a future, universal quantum testbed. Authors analyzed simulation frameworks designed to simulate only the QKD protocols and frameworks designed to simulate QKD networks and protocols within that network. Table 1 presents a summary of the main characteristics and functionalities of researched simulation frameworks.

Modularity was described as one of the most important characteristics of a QKD simulator, because it makes the development and modeling of proprietary networks and protocols easier [1]. Modularity enables the developer to take already implemented functionalities and change them or build on them.

Table 1. Comparison of characteristics of QKD simulation frameworks [1]

Simulators	Simulation Environment	Supported protocols	Modularity	Available publicly
QuCCs [2]	Java, Matlab, MySQL	BB84, B92	Yes	No
qkdSim [3]	Python	B92	Yes	No
EnQuad [4]	Matlab	BB84	Yes	Yes
Fan-Yuan et al. [5]	C++, OMNet++	BB84, MDI-QKD	No	No
Kreinberg et al. [6]	VPItransmissionMaker OpticalSystems	Weak Coherent Prepare-and_Measure CV-QKD	No	No
SeQUeNCe [7]	N/A	BB84, Cascade, Teleportation Based Protocols	Yes	Yes
QuNetSim [8]	Python	All generic Protocols	No	Yes
NetSquid [9]	Python	All generic protocols	Yes	Yes
Wu et al. [10]	N/A	BB84	No	No

With this paper, authors emphasized the importance of continuous development of quantum network simulators, since the practical deployment of these networks is still complex and expensive. The ideal simulator was described as modular and universal [1]. Research [11] is mainly focused on distributed quantum computing. This paper provides an overview of the main challenge and problems of distributed quantum computing. Distributed quantum computing will be enabled with the implementation of Quantum Internet, as such authors have provided a detailed analysis of simulation tools that are used to simulate quantum networks. Analysis is done from the perspective of distributed quantum computing, and tools are categorized within three classes: hardware-oriented, protocol-oriented and application-oriented.

Table 2 consists of distributed quantum communication simulation tools, their characteristics and categorization according to classes. These simulation tools can also be used to simulate quantum networks.

Table 2. Comparison of distributed quantum communication simulation tools [11]

Simulation tool	Language	Noise models	Open source	Class
SQUANCH	Python	Yes	Yes	HW
NetSquid	Python	Yes	No	HW
SimulaQron	Python	No	Yes	PR
SeQUeNCe	C++ /Python	Yes	Yes	PR
QuISP	C++	Yes	Yes	PR
QuNetSim	Python	No	Yes	PR
NetQASM SDK	C++ /Python	Yes	Yes	AP
QNE-ADK	C++ /Python	Yes	No	AP

Hardware-oriented simulation tools allow the developer to model noise and physical entities with high accuracy. Main examples of hardware-oriented simulation tools are SQUANCH and NetSquid. Protocol-oriented simulation tools are described as focused on design and evaluation of general-purpose quantum protocols. As such, noise modeling is usually limited or not implemented. Protocol-oriented simulators are SeQUeNCe, QuISP and QuNetSim. Application-oriented simulation tools are made to ease the process of designing and implementing quantum network applications [11]. This paper also highlights the need for ideal quantum network or distributed quantum computing simulation tools.

Research [12] describes quantum networks in great detail, it also contains analysis of the quantum network simulation platforms which were available at the time of writing. Simulation platforms introduced in this paper are: SimulaQron, QuNetSim, SQUANCH, QuISP, SeQUeNCe and NetSquid.

QuNetSim and SimulaQron are described as geared towards network application development. QuNetSim is focused on ease of implementation of network applications. QuNetSim has simplified the process of synchronization and the logic at the node because it simulates the joint arrival of the quantum payload together with a corresponding classical header. QuNetSim was used to explore routing schemes in networks. SimulaQron is a simulation platform that can be run physically distinct machines to create a quantum computer network. SimulaQron was used to investigate entanglement verification schemes and various quantum protocols. SQUANCH is a platform designed to simulate quantum information protocols in large networks with realistic noise models. SQUANCH is based on agents, which are connected to other agents using quantum and classical channels, this type of agent based modeling enables parallelization [12].

Authors describe three discrete event simulators: QuISP, SeQUeNCe and NetSquid. QuISP. QuISP is a module developed on OMNeT++ classical network simulator. QuISP is described as a simulator used to better understand emergent behavior in large, interconnected quantum networks. SeQUeNCe is designed to simulate physical layer accurately and is highly modular. SeQUeNCe was used to simulate BB84 QKD protocol, Cascade protocol, quantum teleportation, and quantum network with nine nodes. NetSquid is also designed to enable physically accurate modeling. Nodes in NetSquid are modeled on NV centers in diamond. This simulation tool is also highly modular allowing developers to combine and change already existing components. NetSquid was used to evaluate a quantum router architecture [12]. The authors of this paper also highlight the need for continuous development of quantum network simulation tools, and their importance in scenarios of complex quantum networks.

3 The Role of QKD Network in Secure Communication

3.1 Distinguishing Characteristics of QKD and Classics Key Distribution

Quantum communication networks are built upon the principles of quantum mechanics to facilitate the transmission and manipulation of information. The foundational concepts and technologies employed in quantum communication networks encompass QKD, quantum teleportation, and quantum repeaters. QKD is a cryptographic key distribution technique that ensures secure transmission through the utilization of quantum mechanical principles. This approach relies on the inherent property that measuring a quantum system inevitably disrupts its state, thereby rendering any attempted interception of the key by eavesdroppers detectable. These concepts and technologies are currently undergoing active development and research aimed at enhancing their capabilities and exploring novel implementations in practical scenarios. The successful realization of these technologies is of utmost importance for the establishment of secure, high-capacity, and high-speed quantum communication networks.

Key distribution is a fundamental challenge in the field of cryptography, which involves securely sharing encryption keys between two parties. While a straightforward approach is to physically meet in a secure environment and exchange keys, modern cryptographic protocols utilize techniques such as public key cryptography, such as ciphers, RSA, Diffie-Hellman, to enable remote key exchange. However, conventional key distribution methods based on simple mathematical calculations are vulnerable to attacks by third parties. As such, developing secure and efficient key distribution protocols is a critical research area in cryptography [13].

3.2 QKD Network Parameters and Architecture

QKD enables two parties to produce and share a key that is then used for encrypting and decrypting messages. Specifically, QKD is a key distribution method that relies on the principles of quantum mechanics, and the working principal of QKD between two nods can be seen in Fig. 1 [14].

Currently, quantum network security does not appear as an independent application that provides complete protocols for secure communication. However, quantum key distribution techniques complement well-established internet technology. They are used in conjunction with the public internet or, more likely, with private networks that use a set of internet protocols to build secure communication systems. Such private networks are currently widely used worldwide by users who require secure and private communication, e.g. financial institutions, government organizations, militaries, etc., and that the integration of QKD technology with these types of private networks may prove feasible and immediately attractive in certain contexts [15]. Today, secure communication between cryptographic endpoints or even between individual computers on the Internet is enabled by a well-defined IPsec architecture. It defines the protocols, algorithms, databases, and policies necessary for secure communication. Therefore, it would be optimal to integrate QKD technology with the currently well-established internet security architecture. This joint effort would guarantee secure internet traffic via quantum cryptography.

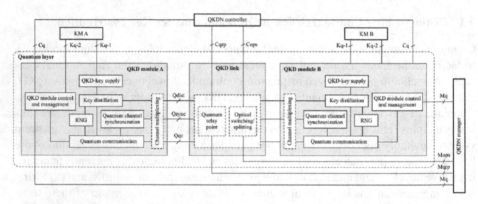

Fig. 1. The architecture of a system for QKD communication between two nodes [14]

Figure 2 elaborates one of possible scenarios of realizing QKD network as an upgrade to existing communication network infrastructure.

Quantum key distribution network consists of several key elements and characteristics that can become part of the simulation model. Fundamental element of a QKD network is a QKD link, representing logical connections between QKD nodes.Nodes are connected through quantum channel for entangled photons transmission and classical channel for synchronization and data exchange [15].

QKD network is represented by set of QKD links and QKD nodes and can be distinguished three layers, quantum layer, key management layer and communication layer [16]. QKD network has several specific requirements but also, as need to be integrated in existing environment it should meet several additional criteria. Link length is the criteria that defines the generation and transmission of secure key material. In current implementation with optical fibers (e.g. ITU-T G.652) the limitation distance for QKD links implementation is considered to be approximately 100 km [5, 17].

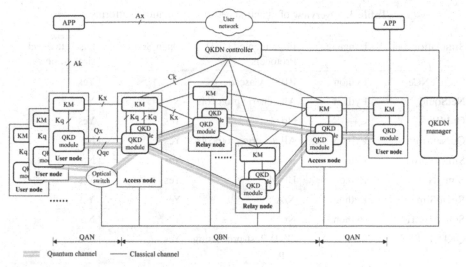

Fig. 2. QKD network implementation scenario [14]

The average key rate of a QKD link is a vital parameter that significantly impacts the performance of a QKD network as it determines the availability of key material for encryption and decryption operations. The competition between the rate of storing key material and its consumption directly affects network performance. Due to limited resources, communication within the network is minimized to conserve the previously established key material. To ensure security, communication typically occurs on the shortest routing path, reducing the number of nodes vulnerable to eavesdropping or abduction. Longer paths require more key material consumption. In cases of network congestion or communication issues, used key material is deliberately discarded, and new key material is applied for retransmission to mitigate the risk of leaks. Therefore, minimizing the number of hops is preferable to optimize network security [16].

The paramount interest in QKD arises from the need to ensure the privacy and uniqueness of the established key material, necessitating robust security measures at every level of the network architecture. This includes securing key material during its establishment, management, storage, and usage.

4 Overview of QKD Network Simulation Platforms

Based on the previous research and newly collected information, Table 3 contains currently available quantum network simulation platforms. Not all quantum network simulation platforms have the ability to simulate quantum key distribution, for that reason Table 3 contains implemented QKD protocols column which will be used to identify simulation platforms that enable QKD simulation.

Table 3. Overview of quantum network simulation platforms

Simulation tool	Language	Implemented QKD Protocols	Open Source	Discrete event simulation
SeQUeNCe	Python	BB84, Cascade	Yes	Yes
NetSquid	Python	All generic protocols	No	Yes
QuISP	C++	No	Yes	Yes
QuNetSim	Python	All generic protocols	Yes	No
SimulaQron	Python	N/A	Yes	No
SimQN	Python	BB84	Yes	Yes
ReQuSim	Python	N/A	Yes	Yes
SQUANCH	Python	No	Yes	No
QKDNetSim	C++	QKD Post-processing app	Yes	Yes
QNE-ADK	Python	Yes	No	No

4.1 Discrete-Event Simulation Platforms

Discrete-event simulation is a simulation paradigm that is used to model systems as a sequence of discrete events. It is based on events that define a change of state in the system – every individual event occurs at a specific time instance and records a change of state in the system. Discrete-event simulation allows for more accurate noise modelling since it depends on elapsed time. We give an overview of the following discrete-event simulation platforms.

SeQUeNCe is a scalable, modular, customizable, discrete-event quantum network simulator. It's open-source software that is available on GitHub [7]. SeQUeNCe has a modularized design that consists of six modules. First module is simulation kernel which enables discrete-event simulation. Second, hardware module consists of models of hardware components that are present in quantum networks, such as models of single-atom memories, light sources, single photon detectors, BSM nodes, quantum gates, quantum and classical channels. Third, entanglement management module enables high-fidelity end-to-end entanglement between network nodes. This module contains protocols for entanglement generation, purification and swapping. Fourth, resource management module is used to control local resources within one node. Resources are managed based on the commands issued by the network management module. Fifth, network management module provides quantum network services based on the requests from other modules. Sixth, the application module is designed to represent quantum network application and requests for resources. Examples of applications are quantum teleportation and quantum key distribution [7].

NetSquid is a simulation tool, developed at QuTech research center, designed for modelling and simulation of scalable quantum networks. NetSquid is freely available after registration, but it is not open-sourced. NetSquid is a software tool available as a

Python package, it is used to accurately simulate quantum networks and effects of physical non-idealities on them, such as networks where quantum entanglement is generated and utilized between nodes. Authors of this simulator implemented a discrete-event simulation engine – used to model delays during transmission and computation, specialized quantum computing library, framework for modelling of quantum hardware devices, and a framework for designing quantum protocols [6]. NetSquid is highly modular and as such it enables the use of already implemented hardware components as well as modification of said components.

QuISP is a discrete-event simulator that is designed to simulate and investigate behaviors of complex, large scale quantum networks with realistic noise models. QuISP is a module developed for OMNeT++ classical network simulator. Long term goal of this simulator is successful simulation of hundred networks, each containing hundred nodes. This simulation module was designed according to the following principles: realism – simulation needs to provide accurate information about the physical states that are distributed in the quantum network, scalability – complex, large scale quantum networks require high number of qubits, nodes and links between the nodes, flexibility – defined as high level of customizability which in turn ensures that QuISP will be able to accurately simulate present and future quantum hardware [18].

SimQN is a modular discrete-event network-layer simulation framework, packaged as Python library. This simulation framework is designed to facilitate large scale investigations of quantum networks. These simulations include QKD and entanglement distribution protocols, routing algorithms and resource allocation schemas. Authors of this simulation framework describe SimQN as general purpose, meaning it can be used to investigate QKD networks, entanglement distribution networks as well as other kinds of quantum networks [19]. As previously mentioned, goal of SimQN is to provide convenient way of simulating large scale quantum networks while balancing performance and functionality, this is achieved through modular design. Architecture of SimQN consists of several modules: a physical backend module, network utility module, network application module, quantum entities (nodes, quantum channel and classical channels) and other auxiliary modules [20].

ReQuSim is a simulation tool specifically designed to simulate quantum repeater networks. It is used to evaluate quantum repeater schemes to extend the distance of quantum key distribution and entanglement distribution protocols. ReQuSim enables entanglement purification, modeling of channel noise, multiple repeater links. ReQuSim is designed to combine realism and scale. ReQuSim can be used to model setups for quantum repeater, obtaining key rates for repeater protocols, evaluating effects of parameters on the performance of a repeater setup. This simulation tool is not designed to develop code that will be able to interface with future quantum hardware or simulate large scale networks containing thousands of nodes [21].

4.2 Non Discrete-Event Simulation Platforms

QuNetSim is a real time simulator written in Python and designed to ease the process of quantum network application development. Main goal of QuNetSim is to enable the users to quickly develop quantum networking protocols without having to invest time in implementation of low-level software related tasks, these protocols include QKD, quantum money, anonymous transmission. This simulator uses a layered architecture inspired by the OSI model, these layers include application, transport, and network. QuNetSim includes network nodes that can be linked using both quantum and classical connection. QuNetSim allows users to create a network configuration of nodes connected via classical or quantum links and then program the behavior of each node in the network as they want [8]. Current implementation of QuNetSim still uses simplistic channel models which are not good for large quantum network simulations, smaller scale simulations containing less than ten nodes [8].

SimulaQron is a simulator used to develop distributed software that can run on simulated or real classical and quantum nodes. Goal of this tool is ease of development of network applications and exploration of software engineering practices in the context of quantum Internet. SimulaQron is not developed to achieve efficient simulation of large scale quantum networks and effects of noise, error correcting codes and similar models on said network [22].

SQUANCH is an open-source Python framework designed to create parallelized simulations of distributed quantum information processing. SQUANCH contains features of a general purpose quantum computing simulator, but it is specifically optimized to simulate quantum networks. SQUANCH can simulate realistic noise models over large networks. This simulator allows users to design complex multi-party quantum networks and create classes for modeling of noisy quantum channels. SQUANCH is based on agents which can manipulate a subset of a distributed quantum state, simulations are parallelized and every node is running local processes mirroring the distributed structure of a quantum network [9].

QNE-ADK is an application development kit that allows the users to create applications and experiments and run them on a simulator. QNE-ADK offers the users a command line interface with implemented commands that are used to create necessary files that define applications or experiments, these files are templates that are used to develop custom applications. This development kit also offers the users to use already existing applications and experiments which are accessible by using the command line interface and clone command. When creating custom application or experiment, users can set custom parameters, different node roles, as well as which channels and nodes will be used in the simulation. Once the experiment is configured and ready to run, the experiment is parsed and sent to the NetSquid simulator [23].

5 Analysis of QKD Network Simulators Characteristics

Based on the overview of currently available quantum network simulation platforms and tools, following platforms and tools are chosen for further analysis of their capabilities in the context of quantum key distribution network simulation: SeQUeNCe, NetSquid, QuNetSim, SimQN, ReQuSim, QNE-ADK.

Modularity is one of the most important properties for a QKD simulator. It enables researchers to develop and model their own protocols and networks in the same way one constructs a network in the real world. If the simulation toolkit is modular, it becomes easier to add new modules or interchange the existing ones, making the toolkit viable in the future as well.

Table 4. Characteristics and functionalities of QKD network simulation platforms

Simulation tool	Modular	Error models	Size of simulated network	Node types	Programming interface	Layer
SeQUeNCe	Yes	Yes	Small (<15 nodes)	Multiple	Python	Physical
NetSquid	Yes	Yes	Very Large (>1000 nodes)	General	Python	Physical
QuNetSim	No	No	Small (<15 nodes)	General	Python	Application
SimQN	Yes	Yes	Large (>400)	General	Python	Network
ReQuSim	Yes	Yes	Medium (N/A)	Station	Python	Network
QKDNetSim	Yes	N/A	N/A	QKD node	C++	Network
QNE-ADK	No	Yes	Small (<15 nodes)	General	Python	Application

Programming interface describes the programming language that is used to configure and run simulations in the corresponding simulation tool. Every simulation tool enables the users to use python as an interface, except QKDNetSim which uses C++. QKD-NetSim also provides a graphical user interface through a web application that relays configuration settings to a simulator and displays simulation results.

Although quantum network simulators are developed with a focus on a specific layer, they also implement other layers to a varying degree of detail. Physical layer simulation tools are focused on detailed modeling of hardware components, while application layer tools leave the physical layer unspecified and focus on enabling the user to design and implement quantum network applications. Table 4 contains two application layer simulators – QuNetSim and QNE-ADK. Although the latter simulator is classified as an application layer, it communicates configuration settings to NetSquid that serves as a backend. QuNetSim also uses other simulators as a backend for physical simulation. User can configure which backend to use – SimulaQron [21], ProjectQ [24], or EQSN [25]. Network layer simulation tools are focused on enabling research focused on network management, entanglement distribution, routing in quantum networks, impact of different node configurations on the network, etc.

SeQUeNCe simulates hardware components with a high level of detail. It also provides the user with multiple types of network nodes. Network nodes can be general purpose, QKD node, quantum router, BSM node. QKD node contains protocol stack needed to create keys. SeQUeNCe implements BB84 and cascade QKD protocols – BB84 is used to generate a secure key between two nodes and cascade protocol is used to correct errors that occur while using BB84. Variety of nodes allows for high level of customizability needed to create a detailed simulation. Modular design of SeQUeNCe provides the access to hardware components such as light source, memory, optical channel, photon, BSM node, etc. Some of the optical channel parameters that can be configured include length, attenuation and polarization fidelity. Topology that will be used in simulation can be generated through JSON file. To successfully create a topology JSON file needs to contain nodes – their names, node type and size of memory; quantum channels – connected nodes, attenuation value, distance and type; classical channels – connected nodes and delay value. At the time of writing, SeQUeNCe is equipped with graphical user interface designed to create simulations that is not fully operational, but it does show great potential. SeQUeNCe was used to simulate Chicago quantum network which was the largest topology containing nine nodes [7].

NetSquid also simulates hardware components and physical properties of quantum devices – quantum gates, quantum memory, to a great level of detail. Nodes in NetSquid are created through a general node class that can hold and manage hardware subcomponents. By combining this node class and creating custom or using already implemented protocols that are run on nodes, users can create different simulation experiments such as repeater chains [25]. Another NetSquid functionality that allows precise simulation of quantum network is delay modeling. Already implemented delay models are fixed delay model – fixed timing delay model, gaussian delay model – channel delay model with a Gaussian distribution and fiber delay model – transmission delay model based on constant speed of photons through fiber. NetSquid also allows to user to create custom quantum error models or use already implemented models. Implemented quantum error models are depolarization noise model, dephasing noise model, T1T2 noise model – phenomenological noise model based on T1 and T2 times, and fiber loss model – model used for exponential photon loss in optical fiber channels, it is based on length of channel. Largest NetSquid simulation contained a topology consisting of 1025 nodes forming a quantum repeater chain.

QNE-ADK is an application layer simulator. Customization in QNE-ADK is comprised of predetermined networks with included channels and nodes. There are three networks that users can choose from that contain five nodes and varying number of links between nodes (4, 5 and 10 links) creating different topologies. Users can change parameters such as gate fidelity on nodes, elementary link fidelity on network channels. These quantum network components and parameters are used by an application that the user can develop. Entanglement based QKD is one of the examples of already implemented applications in QNE-ADK where users can specify the number of EPR pairs that Alice and Bob will generate. Results of this simulation contain number of pairs Alice and Bob measured in the same basis, number of pairs chosen to compare measurement outcomes for, QBER – fraction of compared measurement outcomes that are not equal, although they result from measurement in the same basis and raw keys that Alice and Bob possess. These simulations and results are visualized and displayed through a web application called quantum network explorer that contains graphical user interface.

QuNetSim is another application layer simulator that is not designed to simulate realistic physical models of quantum hardware and channels. This simulation tool is focused on enabling the users to develop and test protocols for quantum networks. QuNetSim doesn't use discrete event simulation engine which is necessary to model and track noise that is time dependent. Currently this simulation tool is used for smaller scale simulations consisting of five to ten nodes. Nodes in QuNetSim are called hosts and they can be configured to function as a quantum node, a relaying node or an eavesdropper.

SimQN is a network layer simulation tool that enables large scale simulations. One of the example use cases of SimQN is routing algorithm design for better QKD performance [26]. SimQN uses node class to describe quantum network nodes. Functionalities of these nodes can be changed by equipping them with ither devices like memories. SimQN contains already implemented error models such as dephasing and depolarization error models that can be applied to quantum memory, quantum channels. This simulation tool also allows access to delay models – normal, uniform, and constant delay models.

ReQuSim is another network layer simulation tool designed to investigate quantum repeater strategies. Nodes in ReQuSim are designed to be quantum repeater stations. Channels in this simulation tool can be equipped with noise models to simulate a network with higher level of detail.

QKDNetSim is a specialized simulation tool focused on simulating quantum key distribution, more specifically it is focused on key usage. QKDNetSim is designed with a simplified QKD link and focuses on network performance measurement and estimation, traffic management, key consumption, and routing protocols [27]. Simulation in QKD-NetSim can contain unlimited number of nodes. QKDNetSim is a module developed in the NS-3 simulator. As it was previously mentioned QKDNetSim can be accessed through a web interface where users can set up a simulation. Simulations consist of setting up QKD nodes on a desired location and connecting them with QKD links. These links contain changeable parameters: key rate, key size, packet size, etc. After placing the nodes and connecting them, users can place an applications that consume secret keys between two nodes. Parameters of applications are authentication type, encryption type, application packet size, application traffic rate, etc. Furthermore, application interface with key management service is described by ETSI GS QKD 014 and ETSI GS QKD 004 specifications. Results of simulation contain information about relayed, consumed and generated key pairs for each QKD link. Results also contain statistics about consumed key pairs for each added application and statistics about exchanged packets between application and key management service, application to application signaling packets and application to application data packets.

6 Conclusion

In the research presented in this paper we studied and analyzed currently available tools and platforms applicable for simulation of QKD networks. Simulation plays a crucial role in the design and pre-implementation stages of QKD networks. By utilizing simulation tools and platforms, researchers and engineers can gain valuable insights into the behavior and performance of these networks without the need for costly and time-consuming physical implementations.

The findings of this research have shed light on the limitations present in all the analyzed tools, which resulted from insufficient research engagement in this field. It is important to note that despite the numerous challenges and identified shortcomings, it is possible to establish a simulation model and conduct simulations at certain levels by combining the functionalities of multiple tools. However, it is evident that this area requires further research efforts and engagement in the development of existing tools, as well as the creation of new ones that would provide comprehensive functionality. The holistic approach is essential to facilitate the design and implementation of simulation models for QKD networks in the future.

References

1. Aji, A., Jain, K., Krishnan, P.: A survey of Quantum Key Distribution (QKD) network simulation platforms. In: 2021 2nd Global Conference for Advancement in Technology (GCAT), pp. 1–8. IEEE (2021). https://doi.org/10.1109/GCAT52182.2021.9587708
2. Zukarnain, Z.A., Buhari, A., Harun, N.Z., Khalid, R.: QuCCs: an experimental of quantum key distribution using quantum cryptography and communication simulator. In: The 6th International Cryptology and Information Security Conference, pp. 127–40 (2019)
3. Chatterjee, R., Joarder, K., Chatterjee, S., Sanders, Barry C., Sinha, U.: QkdSim, a simulation toolkit for Quantum Key Distribution including imperfections: performance analysis and demonstration of the B92 protocol using heralded photons. Phys. Rev. Appl. **14**(2) (2020). https://doi.org/10.1103/PhysRevApplied.14.024036
4. Abdelgawad, M.S., Shenouda, B.A., Abdullatif, S.O.: EnQuad: a publicly-available simulator for Quantum Key Distribution protocols. Cybern. Inform. Technol. **20**, 21–35 (2020). https://doi.org/10.2478/cait-2020-0002
5. Fan-Yuan, G.-J., Chen, W., Lu, F.-Y., Yin, Z.-Q., Wang, S., Guo, G.-C., et al.: A universal simulating framework for Quantum Key Distribution systems. Science China Inf. Sci. **63**, 180504 (2020). https://doi.org/10.1007/s11432-020-2886-x
6. Kreinberg, S., Koltchanov, I., Novik, P., Alreesh, S., Laudenbach, F., Pacher, C., et al.: Modelling weak-coherent CV-QKD systems using a classical simulation framework. In: 2019 21st International Conference on Transparent Optical Networks (ICTON), pp. 1–4. IEEE (2019). https://doi.org/10.1109/ICTON.2019.8840253
7. Wu, X., Kolar, A., Chung, J., Jin, D., Zhong, T., Kettimuthu, R., et al.: SeQUeNCe: a customizable discrete-event simulator of quantum networks. Quant. Sci. Technol. **6**, 045027 (2021). https://doi.org/10.1088/2058-9565/ac22f6
8. DiAdamo, S., Nötzel, J., Zanger, B., Beşe, M.M.: QuNetSim: A Software Framework for Quantum Networks (2020). https://doi.org/10.1109/TQE.2021.3092395
9. Bartlett, B.: A distributed simulation framework for quantum networks and channels (2018)
10. Wu, X., Zhang, B., Jin, D.: Parallel simulation of Quantum Key Distribution networks. In: Proceedings of the 2020 ACM SIGSIM Conference on Principles of Advanced Discrete Simulation, pp. 187–196. ACM, New York, NY, USA (2020). https://doi.org/10.1145/3384441.3395988
11. Caleffi, M., Amoretti, M., Ferrari, D., Cuomo, D., Illiano, J., Manzalini, A., et al.: Distributed Quantum Computing: a survey (2022)
12. Azuma, K., Bäuml, S., Coopmans, T., Elkouss, D., Li, B.: Tools for quantum network design. AVS Quant. Sci. **3**(1) (2021). https://doi.org/10.1116/5.0024062
13. Kozlowski, W., Dahlberg, A., Wehner, S.: Designing a quantum network protocol. CoNEXT 2020 - Proceedings of the 16th International Conference on Emerging Networking EXperiments and Technologies, pp. 1–16. Association for Computing Machinery, Inc (2020). https://doi.org/10.1145/3386367.3431293
14. ITU-T. Quantum key distribution networks – functional architecture (2020)
15. Mehic, M., Niemiec, M., Rass, S., Ma, J., Peev, M., Aguado, A., et al.: Quantum Key Distribution: a networking perspective. ACM Comput. Surv. **53** (2020). https://doi.org/10.1145/3402192

16. Tysowski, P.K., Ling, X., Lütkenhaus, N., Mosca, M.: The engineering of a scalable multi-site communications system utilizing Quantum Key Distribution (QKD). Quant. Sci. Technol. (2017). https://doi.org/10.1088/2058-9565/aa9a5d

17. Ribezzo, D., Zahidy, M., Vagniluca, I., Biagi, N., Francesconi, S., Occhipinti, T., et al.: Deploying an inter-European quantum network. Adv. Quant. Technol. **6**(2), 2200061 (2022). https://doi.org/10.1002/qute.202200061

18. Satoh, R., Hajdušek, M., Benchasattabuse, N., Nagayama, S., Teramoto, K., Matsuo, T., et al.: QuISP: a Quantum Internet Simulation Package (2021). https://doi.org/10.1109/QCE53715.2022.00056

19. Chen, L., Li, J., Xue, K., Yu, N., Li, R.: A discrete time scheduler designed for Quantum Network n.d. https://github.com/ertuil/SimQN. Accessed 30 May 2023

20. Chen, L., Xue, K., Li, J., Yu, N., Li, R., Sun, Q., et al.: SimQN: a network-layer simulator for the quantum network investigation. IEEE Netw. 1–8 (2023). https://doi.org/10.1109/MNET.130.2200481

21. Wallnöfer, J., Hahn, F., Wiesner, F., Walk, N., Eisert, J.: ReQuSim: faithfully simulating near-term quantum repeaters (2022)

22. Dahlberg, A., Wehner, S.: SimulaQron - a simulator for developing quantum internet software (2017). https://doi.org/10.1088/2058-9565/aad56e

23. Application Development Kit for Quantum Network Explorer n.d. https://github.com/QuTech-Delft/qne-adk. Accessed 30 May 2023

24. Steiger, D.S., Häner, T., Troyer, M.: ProjectQ: an open source software framework for quantum computing. Quantum **2**, 49 (2018). https://doi.org/10.22331/q-2018-01-31-49

25. Coopmans, T., et al.: Simulation of a 1025-node quantum repeater chain of NV centres with NetSquid, a new discrete-event quantum-network simulator (2019). https://ui.adsabs.harvard.edu/abs/2019APS..MARL28012C/abstract. Accessed 31 May 2023

26. Elliot Chen. SimQN (2022). https://ertuil.github.io/SimQN/introduction.html. Accessed 30 April 2023

27. Mehic, M., Maurhart, O., Rass, S., Voznak, M.: Implementation of quantum key distribution network simulation module in the network simulator NS-3. Quant. Inf. Process. **16**, 253 (2017). https://doi.org/10.1007/s11128-017-1702-z

A Blockchain Patient-Centric Records Framework for Older Adult Healthcare

Sheri Osborn$^{(\boxtimes)}$ and Kim-Kwang Raymond Choo

The University of Texas at San Antonio, San Antonio, TX 78249, USA
sheri.osborn@utsa.edu, raymond.choo@fulbrightmail.org

Abstract. Patient-centric medical record systems provide patients control over their health data versus electronic health record (EHR) systems that are health provider based and typically geared around bill presentment and payment. There are several limitations in current EHR systems, such as details of healthcare not making it into the system, the loss of out of network healthcare and potential for malicious cyber exploitations. This research effort posits the potential of utilizing blockchain to support a patient-centered personal health record (PHR) system focused on the healthcare needs of older adults. Such a system expands the data collected to include every source of healthcare provider from optometrists to chiropractors to oncologists. Blockchain technologies would provide architecture and security for such a system.

Specifically, we present the framework geared to track older adult health records including modules that provide early disease detection and drug-drug interaction for the top chronic diseases experienced by older adults using various machine learning classification algorithms. The algorithms evaluate the entirety of diagnoses and symptoms to find co-morbidities that may be an indicator of latent disease such as early signs of dementia and Alzheimer's diseases. The patient's health information is interpreted by a nurse practitioner or hospitalist who can determine if a specialist needs to be involved to evaluate the predicted disease. The proposed approach will provide a secure way to have a comprehensive view of the patient's health data and arm the patient with the most inclusive set of information for doctors to provide the best health care.

Keywords: Blockchain · Older Adults · Patient-Centric · Machine Learning · Proxy Re-encryption

1 Introduction

The objective of Electronic Health Record (EHR) systems is to deliver high quality and accessible patient care services, a better use of resources and improved outcomes. Additionally, healthcare records are supposed to meet strict Health Insurance Portability and Accountability Act (HIPAA) and the General Data Protection Regulation (GDPR) Act 2018 security and privacy guidelines. EHR records contain such personal data as names, addresses, social security numbers, insurance information and medical history.

D. Perakovic and L. Knapcikova (Eds.): FABULOUS 2023, LNICST 542, pp. 18–36, 2024.
https://doi.org/10.1007/978-3-031-50051-0_2

Unfortunately, any kind of third-party record repository can be corrupted by system failures, design failures, human mischief or errors. Hospital records are also becoming the target of cyber criminals. In 2021, for example, there were 686 healthcare data breaches during which 44,993,618 healthcare records were exposed or stolen [1]. As recently as August 2023, a cyberattack disrupted hospital computer systems across the United States which resulted in forced emergency room closure along with ambulances being diverted to other hospitals [2]. The healthcare processes of contemporary times particularly with chronic diseases require the collection of massive amounts of data so that doctors can make plausible healthcare decisions to care for their patients, manage patient care, communicate with partner organizations and meet regulatory standards.

1.1 Older Adults and Co-morbidities

Multimorbidity tends to be a common occurrence in older adults due to underlying conditions (e.g., physiological issues such as hypertension, atrial fibrillation and diabetes) and (unhealthy) behaviors (e.g., tobacco use, insufficient physical activity or an unhealthy diet). The relationships between multiple health problems and their impact on quality of life and life expectancy needs to be carefully studied and managed. Along with multiple health issues exists the problem of mood and anxiety disorders which are common in many older adults, particularly women, and are highly treatable at any age. Mental health disorders contribute to chronic diseases and vice versa and both need to be addressed. Health decline features typically present before the onset of a symptomatic disease.

There are many early warning symptoms of chronic disease that are so subtle that patients would not see a doctor when they occur until a dangerous, potentially deadly disease event occurs. For example, some of the early warning symptoms of coronary artery disease are fatigue, back pain, and shortness of breath. Early signs of chronic obstructive pulmonary disease, (COPD) include cough, wheezing or recurrent respiratory infection. The early warning symptoms of heart failure are breathlessness, fatigue and swollen limbs. Evidence suggests that when considering potentially early warning symptoms of disease, older adults tend to 1) discount them as normal or 2) reserve judgment as to the significance or 3) attribute them to other problems such as fatigue. Early symptoms of dementia would not necessarily require medical treatment such as aggression, depression, a personality change and sleep disturbances that taken together could lead to an earlier diagnosis and treatment. While research concerning the role of early treatment leading to a better dementia prognosis is limited, an early diagnosis could help the family make more informed decisions particularly about long-term care while the patient can contribute to the conversation. A more comprehensive view of patient care is particularly important in the case of dementia where co-morbidities may be mistaken for features of dementia. Unless the variety of features are understood to be early features of dementia and the general health declines addressed there could be an increased chance of poor outcomes and decreased quality of life [4]. Additionally, older adults with complex healthcare needs can get overwhelmed trying to determine which kind of doctor for them to see leading 22% of Americans to report that they avoid medical care of all kinds for either its high cost or because of the diseases that abound and inconvenience of the waiting room process.

1.2 EHR Gaps

The typical healthcare networks are composed of doctors, patients, medical and drug suppliers, insurance companies, third-party logistics (3PL) providers, and regulators. This leads to many and varied feature requirements. An EHR system focused only on delivering the best healthcare must be comprehensive and should include a formulation of the problem list, careful analysis of abnormal findings along with symptomology and diagnostics. Current EHR systems fall short of this standard and therefore have many problems delivering comprehensive healthcare data. One reason is that the healthcare data systems utilize non-standard data which is generally hard to comprehend, use and share. Another gap is that many EHR systems struggle when trying to share information across different states or to providers in rural areas that are not as computerized as larger suburban providers. Because patient records are typically stored in different databases across different service providers, it becomes difficult to get a comprehensive picture of the patient's health as control rests in the hands of each service provider [32]. Other problems involve getting the complete diagnostic dataset into the EHR system. Only the patient and/or their primary caregiver knows the breadth of their healthcare and treatment.

Physicians are so busy they do not use the online entry mode of the system so an assistant transcribes notes either from the doctor or as the doctor is speaking. These fragmented health records lead to uneven healthcare service delivery and to an inequitable allocation of resources. An even larger problem with network centric systems is that patients are given care typically only for their presenting problem and doctor visits are brief. Those with chronic versus acute disease may not receive instructions concerning how to care for their diseases on a day-to-day basis. A study of 516 patients found that EHR systems lack data as only 62.3% of diagnoses were recorded for the patients [5]. A different examination of 1347 breast cancer health records found either gaps in treatment or gaps in recording treatment as approximately 7% were missing the ejection fraction (EF) studies that are required for breast cancer chemotherapy treatment [6]. Healthcare systems today also do not provide a means for patients to control access to their health records.

1.3 A Case for Patient-Centric Healthcare

The typical doctor sees approximately 76 patients per week and spends approximately 13 to 24 min with each patient. Older adults with comorbidities do not normally offer the breadth of their health issues within the short time they have to spend with a doctor concerning the problem at hand. Many older adults are being treated by multiple subspecialists that each prescribe medicines, therapeutics and other treatments which cannot be conveyed within a single doctor's visit. Each doctor could deliver better health care if provided a more complete and comprehensive representation of the patient's health. Current clinical decision support tools have limited support for patients with co-morbidities. Comprehensive care is critical for the older adult patient as the effect of co-morbidities is generally related to mortality and/or a greatly diminished quality of life.

Nurse practitioners (NP) and hospitalists (HSP) are known to have the ability to deal with a breadth of medical issues and often coordinate the care of a variety of specialists. Both positions provide diagnosis, order labs, and prescribe medications. The nurse practitioner holds an advanced nursing degree and for many communities address the shortage of physicians and bring down healthcare costs [7]. The hospitalist treats an array of different medical conditions and rose in importance because primary care providers were not able to take time away from their offices to treat hospitalized patients. NPs working in conjunction with hospitalists have been able to close the healthcare gap particularly in rural communities where some hospitals are at risk of closing due to lower funding levels, lower patient volumes and decreased hospital revenue.

Wang et al., [8] identifies five capabilities of Big Data analytics implementations in healthcare: unstructured data analytical algorithms, care pattern analytics, predictive capabilities, decision support functionality and traceability. The proposed three-pronged technology solution for comprehensive care of older adults is 1) assemble a thorough collection of symptoms, therapeutics, all known diagnoses for the top ten health problems of older adults; 2) use analysis and predictive analytics to find potential problems from the breadth of patient data and 3) a trusted agent - nurse practitioner and/or hospitalist – who can review the output of the system, the symptoms/therapeutics that lead to a potential diagnosis and may then determine the next healthcare steps to take. The system acts as both an early warning system to healthcare problems along with providing a comprehensive health review of why the system believes there to be a problem. Additionally, to better prepare for a doctor visit, the patient can print out a report detailing their health history and prescribed drugs giving their physician a more complete view of their health status.

Blockchain has been described as a suite of technologies based on a means to get a network of computers to trust the state of a distributed ledger. The ledger is updated and maintained via a consensus protocol which is executed by the participants. It acts as a distributed transactional database which has the security of cryptography and a consensus mechanism as its authority. Blockchain provides transparency, security, and privacy using consensus-driven decentralized data management on top of peer-to-peer distributed computing systems. Blockchain solves many of the data requirements for health organizations including privacy, system security, authentication, interoperability, data sharing, data access, trust, visibility, and mobility. Each block can represent a variety of data types including currency, digital rights, identity, transactions of almost any kind and is said to disrupt all industries. Blockchain represents a structured approach to medical health records as it provides security and privacy for patients and an infrastructure for data collection and exchange.

This paper proposes a blockchain-based EHR system geared to the health needs of older adults. The features of the system are described in Sect. 3 including the framework, the workflow and the participants in the system. In Sect. 4, the prototype components and methods to evaluate each are defined. Contributions include a system focused on the healthcare needs of the most vulnerable members of our population who likely have the most healthcare problems and are prescribed more drugs than any other segment of the population – 85% of adults 60 years of age and older have used one or more prescription drugs in the past 30 days [10]. We will review the extant literature in the next section.

2 Review of Literature

This section presents the related works that are classified into five technology categories: blockchain applications in healthcare, blockchain frameworks and platforms, analytics and machine learning in healthcare, proxy re-encryption (PRE) and blockchain framework evaluation strategies.

2.1 Blockchain Applications in Healthcare

The underpinning technology of blockchain makes it valuable within a medical setting given the amount of coordination and data security that must be administered between various outside parties. Blockchain solves the trust problem between decentralized nodes via its verification and consensus mechanisms. Data can move from a single and proprietary siloed system to one that is distributed across many computers and servers. Data may be exchanged into or outside of the network EHR system without a trusted third party. One means that provides trust to data exchange within a blockchain-based system is a transaction-based smart contract - a means for multiple parties to stipulate that the terms of some agreement are met [11]. For the healthcare patient, smart contracts are regularly used to allow such events as patients providing permission to a third party to access their personal healthcare records. Blockchain healthcare use cases include electronic medical records (EMR), drug and pharmaceutical supply chain transactions, remote patient monitoring, health insurance claims and health data analytics with EMR representing the most common use case.

Some examples of healthcare applications built using blockchain technologies include solutions like MedRec EHR management system that offers patients some degree of control of their health data by providing a means for them to share data with professionals or not. MedRec is based on Ethereum, it uses proof-of-work as the consensus method (how all parties agree that the transaction is valid) which is extremely costly and energy inefficient [12, 13]. OmniPHR is a patient-centered application concerning electronic health records (EHR) storing records in blocks signed by the provider. FHIRChain is another blockchain solution geared around the need for standardized and secured shared clinical data with the goal of overcoming lack of trust relationships between healthcare entities and scalability concerns [14]. Both FHIRChain and MedRec store data off-chain. Data is accessible through pointers and smart contract-controlled access tokens.

2.2 Blockchain Frameworks and Platforms

Blockchain platforms provide the development environment for blockchain-based applications. Its plethora of technologies and implementation variations allow it to be used in finance, healthcare, governance, retail and more. The underlying principles of a BC framework are based on its application objective. However, some technologies lack a stable design and/or an established user base so there still is much research to be done [3]. Every part of the blockchain framework and development platform has different advantages and disadvantages. It is important for designers and developers to analyze each aspect of BC technology to determine its suitability for a specific application.

Table 1. Variety of Blockchain Framework Features

Application Category	Key Concern	Network	Consensus	Security /Privacy Protocol	Data Transfer	Citation
Secured Insurance	Fraudulent Transactions	Private Ethereum	PoA	Internal Validators	IPFS	Hassan et al. 2021
Diabetes Detection	Prediction/Security	BC Public key/PCCH	BC	PCA	IPFS	M. Chen et al. 2021
Patient Portal	Longitudinal Data Curation	Private	Hyper-ledger Fabric	Proxy Re-encryption (PRE)	FHIR	Hylock & Zeng 2019
Health Insurance	Fraudulent Transactions	Private – Invite Only	PBFT	Internal Validators	N/A	Ismail & Zeadally 2021
Health Oriented BC	Improve Scalability, Broader BC Adoption	Variable	Variable	Variable	OCSB	Miyachi & Mackey 2021
Transfer Patient Care	Scalability, Trust	Go Ethereum	PoA	DApp	DApp	Lo et al. 2019

This research effort includes a review of blockchain-based frameworks focusing specifically on healthcare applications. Depending on the application, the breadth of block chain technologies is varied. One blockchain-enabled system has been designed to detect diabetes in which blockchain utilizes a distributed ledger for storing smart contracts between the physician and the patient via the EHR system in combination with machine learning classification algorithms [15]. A different BC framework utilizes a decentralized application (DApp) for patients to interact with the national healthcare record system upon physician referral [16]. A blockchain based insurance application utilizes smart contracts and Proof of Authority (PoA) consensus algorithm to ensure secure fraud-free transactions covering client registration, policy issuance and refund settlement [17]. A similar blockchain based insurance fraud detection system, this one concerning healthcare, is a peer to peer private system with several layers of authorization and utilizes machine learning to detect fraud [18].

Other research efforts are designed to test various blockchain elements to ascertain their feasibility for use in any sort of application. One such research effort tested Hyper-Ledger Fabric using a variety of test scenarios to determine if it was a useful tool in the healthcare industry [12]. Off-Chain Blockchain Systems (OCBS) were similarly evaluated for healthcare records. Often a health record needs to move out of its home network and technologists were seeking a means to securely transport information without the need to pass the entire health record from one blockchain based system to another. The outcome provided a modular and flexible system architecture that allows secure data transfer - see Table 1: Variety of Blockchain Framework Features for comprehensive features of each blockchain application described above.

2.3 Analysis and Machine Learning in Healthcare

Machine learning (ML) and artificial intelligence (AI) algorithms have been used in a variety of ways in healthcare. For example, they allow hospitals to diagnose and customize medical care and follow-up plans to get better results. During the COVID-19 pandemic various ML models were used to predict symptomology and spread [19]. The diabetes detection system utilizes machine learning (ML) to classify diabetes using decision trees (DT), k-nearest neighbors (KNN), random forest (RF), linear regression (LR), and support vector machines (SVM) [15]. Natural Language Processing (NLP) has been used to find inconsistencies in surgical details or pathology reports [20]. Logistic regression and classification has been used to find care gaps within the treatment of cardiac patients, finding that 95.3% of the patients studied has one or more cardiometabolic care gaps during the period of the study [21]. Another combination of machine learning and blockchain technologies are used to model the risk of readmission across a variety of hospitals while the blockchain portion of the solution protected patient privacy [22]. Neural network algorithms have also been used to detect Parkinson's disease [17].

Drug contraindications (also called drug-drug interactions (DDI)) are problematic for older adults even with the wealth of information available about each drug. NLP techniques have been used in the past to consolidate such information for healthcare providers. Organizations like the World Health Organization (WHO), the Food and Drug Administration (FDA), the European Medicines Agency (EMA), and the Medicines and Healthcare products Regulatory Agency (MHRA) maintain a reporting system that enables individuals to spontaneously report any experienced adverse effects related to the use of medicines or healthcare products. Mei & Zhang report that DDI are typically uncovered using one of three methods: similarity-based methods, networks-based methods and machine learning algorithms [23]. Han et al. notes that DDI currently are found by two methods: 1) to summarize DDI from literature, electronic medical records, and spontaneous reports; 2) use known DDI to predict unknown DDI [24]. Disease information is typically organized by the pharmaceutics and often found to be queried together with Chemical/Drug or Gene/Protein information. Because the system described in this paper is focused only on the top ten diseases for older adults, the universe of drugs and potential interactions can be captured and contained from what is currently known with backup support from the NP/HSP.

2.4 Proxy Re-encryption

The Cloud computing paradigm has released data from legacy systems allowing the data to be securely held and accessed. Healthcare data are usually encrypted before uploading to the cloud server though this impedes data sharing between different medical institutions. The question becomes how to share patient data with outsiders in a secure manner without giving full access to all the patient data. How can the data stay secure as it passes from patient to nurse practitioner or hospitalist? The solution for this kind of data exchange is to be able to do so without a 3rd party encryption solution or exposing the encryption keys of the patient. Proxy Re-Encryption (PRE) provides a solution to this problem.

Proxy re-encryption allows a proxy to take Alice's ciphertext (the patient) into one that can be opened by Bob's (NP/HSP) secret key. PRE has been deployed in a variety of architectures including in the cloud, as part of a network storage system, in distributed file systems, as a function for email forwarding and in other various information exchange capacities. PRE has been found to be an important and secure scheme for handling IoT healthcare data such as data from glucose and blood pressure monitoring devices. It allows for off-chain data collection (regular glucose and BP statistics) while avoiding encrypting all of the data in the block which increases communication and computation costs over the cloud. Another solution for transferring patient records from one EHR system to another used PRE – it kept the disease itself invisible while transferring other data which protected the patient's privacy.

2.5   Blockchain Application Evaluation Strategies

Blockchain features in healthcare face a unique set of challenges compared to applications in other sectors of the economy [25]. One needs to consider all the participants of the block chain system, the feature set, the data flow, security needs, and in the case of healthcare governance and privacy – typically HIPPA and GDPR. In choosing the features of the framework, the individual elements of the system require an evaluation process appropriate for that feature of blockchain. The literature shows that both qualitative and quantitative methods have been used to evaluate frameworks [3] which varied based on the technology used within the framework.

Blockchain Technology Evaluation Strategies. One of the pressing problems with blockchain in general concerns performance. All transactions/every entry on a blockchain requires every node to process it and therefore not only slows down transactions but also creates scalability problems. Because of this, several researchers focused on performance and throughput to evaluate their frameworks. Another EHR solution first created a proof of concept then tested the system in a variety of configuration models to ascertain its performance within each configuration. Several research efforts added scalability and security to the list of evaluation measures [15, 18, 26]. Antwi added regulation compliance and flexibility given that many healthcare applications will need to connect with legacy applications [12]. Ateniese et al. evaluated Proxy re-encryption (PRE) by creating a suite of benchmark tests using a variety of types of content and measured functionality, performance and scalability [27].

Feature Function Evaluation Strategies. Other evaluation strategies focused more on features and functionality, even creating new evaluation frameworks. Miyachi & Mackay created a novel evaluation framework built on Yusif et al. [28] for performance features and evaluation topics to include technology purpose and accessibility and language to evaluate technology fit [29]. When evaluating permissioned blockchain framework solutions, Polge et al. started with a literature review then evaluated the technology based on the number of people using that particular technology (demand), community activity, adoption, privacy features along with scalability, throughput and latency [9]. Chowdhury used both qualitative and quantitative measures to evaluate a distributed ledger technology as a platform [26]. Peng et al. also evaluated on-chain/off-chain technology by creating an evaluation matrix of quantitative and qualitative features for permissionless blockchain [30].

Data-base Evaluation Strategies. Zhang used two different cancer patient databases to evaluate feature function and control logic along with technologies related to token retrieval and event logs. A fully functional system was developed that included a DApp and it was tested with actual patients in four hospitals measuring usage statistics [16]. Antwi utilized test cases to evaluate Hyperledger Fabric [12]. To ascertain performance of machine learning algorithms to detect diabetes, M. Chen used the Pima Indian Diabetes Disease Dataset (PIDDD) and the typical machine language performance measures of accuracy, precision, recall, Matthews Correlation Coefficient (MCC) and receiver operating characteristic curve (ROC) [15]. Another machine learning healthcare algorithm used 5-fold cross validation and ROC curve and Area Under The Curve (AUC) scores to determine performance of Drug Drug Interactions [23].

3 Proposed System

3.1 The Framework

The outcome for this proposed healthcare application is for the patient to be the owner of a comprehensive collection of their entire health landscape. Institution-centric EHRs introduce barriers that hamper patient engagement, data portability and information exchange [31]. The proposed blockchain architecture involves four distinct members (agents) of each patient's healthcare ecosystem with the patient being the chief administrator / data owner. The patient is in control of their own health data including requesting data from the disparate EHR systems to be added to their private patient healthcare record or adding any additional information which pertains to health even those not part of a diagnosis such as reading glasses or chiropractic visits. The choice of framework requires consideration of the feature and functionality of the system and the types of blockchain technology that best supports those features. Some of the technological issues to address are its decentralization features, transaction speed, security, auditability and control - see Fig. 1: Patient-Centric EHR System Framework.

3.2 The Agents

In this patient-based system, every kind of health event is entered into the care system as a transaction. The data is accessible by the patient and stored in unalterable blocks. Each new transaction is added to the system after approval by the patient. As new symptoms, prescriptions or treatments are added, the ML modules analyze all the data to determine if there are drug contraindications or signs of a new or alternative diagnosis not already in the system - see Table 2: Agents and Roles.

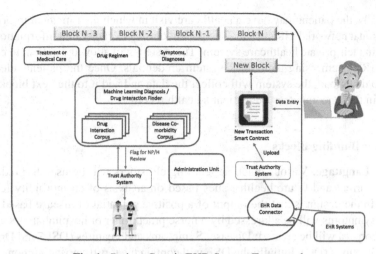

Fig. 1. Patient-Centric EHR System Framework

3.3 The Workflow

Data Collection Workflow. All system data entry is either manual entry by the patient or by a data connector from an EHR system. The data connector would have interoperability features for any kind of standard EHR system and convert the data to a standard format aligned with the patient's system.

Table 2. Agents and Roles.

Agent	Relevant System Data/Actions
Patient (or Caregiver)	Symptoms, Prior/current diagnoses, Therapeutics related to any diagnosis, Pharmaceuticals, supplements and drug regimens, Prior relevant heath concerns, Relevant diagnoses from family members
Network EHR	Relevant data to be added to the patient data such as Diagnoses, Prescriptions and Therapies by Category
Nurse Practitioner/Hospitalist	Receives reports from the system to be considered for future evaluation
External Health Data	Data outside of any EHR system (to be entered by the patient, caregiver, nurse practitioner / hospitalist including diagnostic testing such as auditory, chiropractic care, podiatrist, over the counter (OTC) medications, vitamins and supplements

Data Exchange. The patient desires to send some portion of their healthcare record to a NP/H. The system will give the patient the means to select one or more health records marked by a unique identifier and will transfer just that information to the NP/H.

Additionally, the patient may have a healthcare visit in which their medical information is in a hospital network EHR system. The patient desires to gather that information to be included in their private healthcare system. The system will allow the patient to connect to the EHR system using their EHR system credentials. Once the patient selects the records to download, the system will collect the data and add it to the next block of the blockchain that encompasses the patient's health records.

3.4 Other Building Blocks

Machine Language. Various machine learning classifiers will be used to predict and diagnose current and future health issues based on analysis of co-morbidity features. Included in the design is that the output of a positive potential of disease based on the patient's symptoms will be addressed by a nurse practitioner or hospitalist.

Two corpora will be created: Disease, Symptoms and Features (DSF) and Drug and Contraindications (DC). Initially the DSF will contain the top 10 most common chronic diseases in older adults, specifically: hypertension, lipid metabolism, diabetes, coronary artery disease, cancer, chronic obstructive pulmonary disease, heart failure, stroke, chronic kidney disease and osteoporosis [33]. All symptoms and features associated with each disease will be included in the corpus. The machine learning algorithm will process the patient's reported symptoms and diagnoses and deliver indications of undiagnosed disease in the patient. Should a new diagnosis be detected, the application will create a "potential diagnosis record" that includes the symptoms the patient has and the probability of the undiagnosed disease. The patient can decide if the information is to be sent to the NP/HSP.

The DC corpus will be created from existing drug databases and will only include contraindications at a very high-level rating each if it is a common occurrence or less common occurrence. It will also include over the counter drugs, vitamins and all contraindications of any combination of the drugs and therapeutics. Given that this is a patient-centric application, it shouldn't be considered a medical diagnostics and advice provider. The information is transferred to the NP/HSP to evaluate and determine the course of healthcare.

To evaluate the best algorithm the machine language performance measures of accuracy, sensitivity, specificity, precision, F1, recall, Matthews Correlation Coefficient (MCC) and receiver operating characteristic curve (ROC) will be used. To evaluate the disease or DDI prediction, 2000 dummy patient records will be created and processed with a variety of ML algorithms. The system will create a chart that lists the information (drug, symptoms, prior diagnoses) that ML found as an indication of disease and/or drug interaction. These will be studied independently by 20 experts including pharmacologists, hospitalists, chronic care doctors and geriatric care doctors to assess the accuracy of the system output.

Proxy Re-encryption (PRE) - The Security System. In the proposed system, the patient is the "authority" and chooses to whom and how much information to transmit to the nurse provider or hospitalist. A ciphertext transformation scheme is needed to transfer the owner's data into another ciphertext that the target user can decrypt [34]. For the proposed solution, the patient data is held in the cloud. The patient is prompted by the NLP system to alert the NP/HSP due to potential diagnosis or drug interaction. In this system, the patient desires to transfer some portion of their health record to the NP/HSP. The health record(s) along with a message is combined into a ciphertext. The NP/HSP requests a re-encryption key to facilitate decryption of the patient's ciphertext without exposing the party's private information. The NP/HSP can only see the subset of a patient's healthcare records – only the data that contributed to the alert message – the transferred data records, the output from the ML algorithms (the data that caused the alert) and any message(s) from the patient.

PRE-Summary for the Application

1. The patient desires to send a health record or a collection of health records to the NP/HSP. The data is encrypted with proxy-encryption.
2. The NP/HSP requests access to the patient's data using the patient's public key and their own private key that triggers the system to send the NP/HSP the re-encryption key and the encrypted data to the NP/HSP.
3. The NP/HSP uses the combination of their own private key and the re-encryption key to decrypt the patient's health record(s).

3.5 Security Analysis and Data Accuracy

We examine the patient-centric system based on proxy re-encryption method from integrity and confidentiality perspectives. The patient being the data owner and controller of the information within a private network eliminates many security issues.

Integrity. The nature of blockchain makes the system tamper-resistant and its records tracible. Should the patient detect invalid information such as incorrect data downloaded from a network EHR system, the patient can correct that information to maintain the integrity of the dataset.

Confidentiality. The system transfers data to the NP/H via a unidirectional use of static Diffie-Hellman exchange using a 2048-bit key. As Alice is sending a simple text file of new symptoms or potential diagnosis to NP Bob, it is unlikely that Eve would have a reason to try steal this limited information that is to go through the effort to solve the discrete logarithm that secures the data. The patient who is uploading their own health records would do so utilizing the network EHR system's security which would be very secure.

Privacy. The only identifying information is the patient record is the patient's name and birthdate which is used to identify the patient to the NP/H upon data transfer. This data remains encrypted within the system so privacy is preserved.

4 Prototype

As this application is designed to be used by older adults, the user interface (UI) should consider potential health limitations and disabilities. Older adults may struggle with blindness or low vision therefore the application interface should feature the ability to change text and font size and overall size of interface screen. Additionally, the system should limit any moving parts unless the speed can be controlled by the user [35]. Older adults who struggle through physical challenges to input data can be supported by Voice UIs (VUIs). Those who are deaf or hard of hearing should be supported by audio prompts that are always accompanied by another visual prompt or notification. Additionally, the application should include assistive technology such as interoperability with screen readers, screen magnifiers along with alternative input devices and work with Windows and Macintosh text-to-speech and speech recognition software.

The next step of the application is approval of the features by a hospital or geriatric medical practice. The goal is to find a group that could most benefit from such an application who will provide medical oversight and recommendations during the development process. With the medical team in place the application prototype can be developed. To evaluate the features, functions and UI, the system will be tested by 100 adults aged 60–75 who will receive training from an organization that specializes in teaching software applications to older adults such as OASIS or OATS. The class will last for one day. The instructors will walk the older adults through all the features of the product. The last class exercise is for each older adult, with the help and oversight of the trainers, to set up their own PHR system, import data from any hospital network EHR system and be shown how to add data and use the query and reporting system. Additionally, the students will be shown how to access the DDI and potential disease diagnostic algorithms though these will be tested with a dummy test set of health records for the sake of each person's privacy. Lastly, the research team will gather feedback from the older adults including feature satisfaction and recommendations, UI/user experience (UX) and desire to utilize such an application.

4.1 The Agent Panel and Features

The agent panel is how the patient accesses and controls the features of the application. There is a tiered menu system allowing access to features based on the kind of transaction desired. For example, to add a health record manually, the patient chooses the type of medical care from a drop-down box (or "Other" in the event the type of healthcare is not in the drop-down box). The patient is then provided a blank health record entry form customized to the type of healthcare or a generic form to be completed should the patient select the "Other" option.

4.2 Data Transfer

In the patient-centric healthcare record system, the patient is the governing authority for data moving to and from the system. The patient initiates the data transfer from their personal system to the NP/HSP and initiates the request for data transfer from any network that contains the patient's healthcare records. The patient selects the **Data Transfer** option from the home screen then chooses to send or receive health records. Every record in the system has a unique identifier. The patient chooses the records to send based on the unique identifier.

Send Information to NP/H for Evaluation. The patient is given a screen to help them choose which healthcare records to transfer to the NP/HSP. Additionally, the patient can add comments to each record or compose detailed instructions allowing them to communicate either the system findings or their own concerns. The patient is given a variety of ways to sort the health records or a search box to find individual records by word search or date.

Collect Information from Another EHR Network. The patient is given a screen to help them choose which EHR healthcare record system to connect with, then is taken to that EHR system's credential screen. From there the patient navigates to the specific health record(s) to be transferred. The patient selects the individual records, and the system transfers them by adding them to the blockchain with the next unique identifier for each record. This feature relies on the patient having credentials for a hospital network EHR system and uses Fast Healthcare Interoperability Resources (FHIR) standard for exchanging digital health data.

4.3 Algorithms

The purpose of the ML algorithm system is to act as an early warning system to the patient that there may be a health problem. Given the number of diseases experienced by older adults and the number of medicines and therapeutics older adults take, these features could alert the patient and their healthcare provider before the health problem harms the patient. Each time a new prescription, vitamin or other therapeutic is added to the healthcare system, the Drug Contraindications Algorithm (DCA) processes the patient's prescribed drugs, supplements and therapeutics through the drug contraindication corpus. The system then delivers a list of contraindications of the drugs prescribed to the patient.

Drug Contraindications. As the patient updates their medical record, the DDI algorithm will process the patient's current prescription list and generate a notice to the patient that there may be a DDI. The system will offer a screen to indicate which drugs are involved, some of the symptoms and if the patient should seek immediate medical care - see Fig. 2: Patient Notice of Drug Contraindication. Additionally, the patient can run the algorithm from the main menu. If the patient chooses to provide the information to the NP/HSP, the system will create a health record with the information required for an NP/HSP to provide further guidance such as a new prescription for a drug that doesn't have DDI.

Disease Prediction. As the patient updates their medical record, the Potential Disease algorithm will process the patient's current symptoms with all symptoms and diagnoses in the patient health record system. Should the system detect the symptoms of a disease not currently in the patient's health system, the application will generate a report like Fig. 3: Indication of Potential Disease Report. Additionally, the patient can run the algorithm from the main menu. The patient is given the option to send the health record to the Nurse Practitioner or the Hospitalist on that screen. If selected this information will be sent to the NP/HSP connected to the patient.

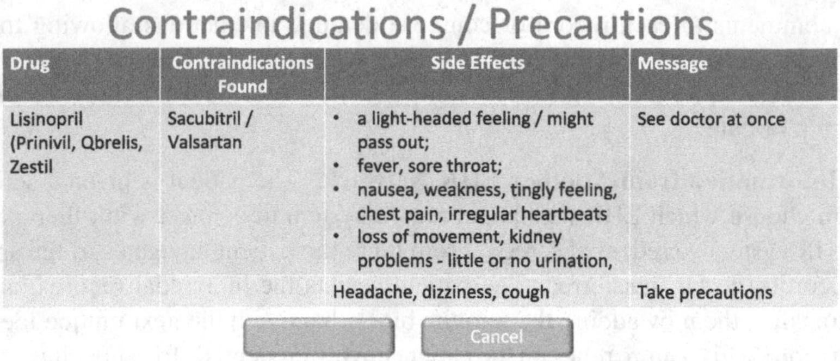

Contraindications / Precautions

Drug	Contraindications Found	Side Effects	Message
Lisinopril (Prinivil, Qbrelis, Zestil	Sacubitril / Valsartan	• a light-headed feeling / might pass out; • fever, sore throat; • nausea, weakness, tingly feeling, chest pain, irregular heartbeats • loss of movement, kidney problems - little or no urination,	See doctor at once
		Headache, dizziness, cough	Take precautions

Cancel

Fig. 2. Patient Notice of Drug Contraindication

Indications of Potential Disease

Patient Name: John Smith   Date of Birth: 6/10/1945

Current Symptoms: Low energy, dark patches on skin

Potential for **diabetes** based on the following symptoms and features:
1. Increase in volume of urination and frequency
2. Slow healing of skin wounds
3. Increase in thirst
4. Dark patches on skin
5. Visual changes
6. Weight loss unattributed to diet
7. Low energy level
8. Increased hunger

Next steps:
Send this health record to Nurse Practitioner or hospitalist assigned to your health. Click here

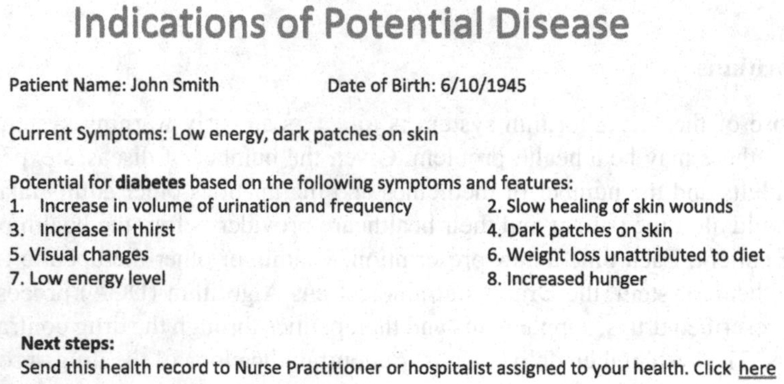

Fig. 3. Indication of Potential Disease Report

4.4 Queries

The query feature of the system is important to help patients provide doctors with a comprehensive review of their health status. To prepare for any doctor's appointment, the patient can choose Records & Reports and create a comprehensive report or filter the information between dates, by diagnosis, or by bodily organ.

The Medical Record Report will provide a complete history around the query topic that includes diagnoses, drugs, dates and symptoms. The patient will be given the opportunity to enter new symptoms to be added to the report see -Fig. 4: Sample Comprehensive Medical Report.

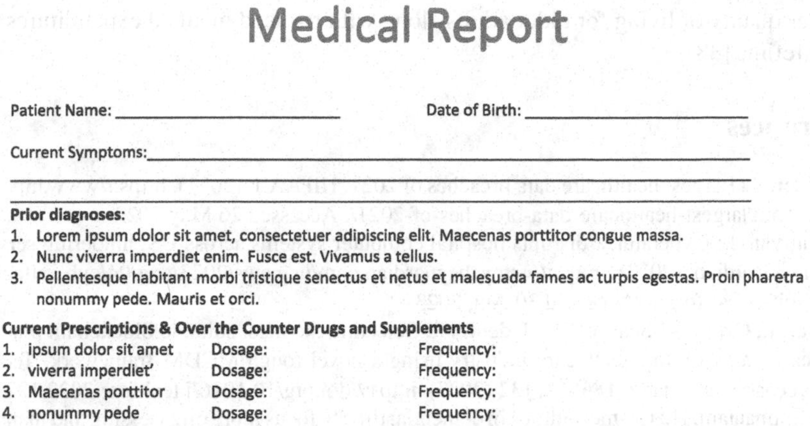

Medical Report

Patient Name: _____   Date of Birth: _____

Current Symptoms:_____
_____
_____

Prior diagnoses:
1. Lorem ipsum dolor sit amet, consectetuer adipiscing elit. Maecenas porttitor congue massa.
2. Nunc viverra imperdiet enim. Fusce est. Vivamus a tellus.
3. Pellentesque habitant morbi tristique senectus et netus et malesuada fames ac turpis egestas. Proin pharetra nonummy pede. Mauris et orci.

Current Prescriptions & Over the Counter Drugs and Supplements
1. ipsum dolor sit amet   Dosage: Frequency:
2. viverra imperdiet'   Dosage: Frequency:
3. Maecenas porttitor   Dosage: Frequency:
4. nonummy pede   Dosage: Frequency:

Fig. 4. Sample Comprehensive Medical Report

5 Conclusion

According to the Centers for Disease Control and Prevention, by 2040 the number of older adults is expected to reach 80.8 million [39]. The current US healthcare system reportedly struggles to accommodate the breadth of problems to properly care for older adults. For many diseases, early detection can bring about earlier treatment and less intrusive impact on health such as prolonging a patient's level of function in the case of Alzheimer's disease. Having a system that provides an early warning to health problems while providing doctors with a more complete picture of the patient's health for medical visits can provide many benefits for both the patients and the medical care givers. Further research efforts include expanding the number of diseases for the disease detection algorithm, to expand the predictive feature to include what is known for indications of disease for different demographics and to collect information such as weight, number of hours of sleep and mental state on a regular basis to add to disease prediction function. Lastly, the system could be evaluated for research purposes as such will have a substantial amount of health data for longitudinal studies of health needs for older adults.

Some of the barriers to success and wide adoption are matters concerning perception, the age and abilities of the patients and other EHR organizations will see this effort as competition. The current perception by EHR developers is that health records are the purview of the medical community. Patients and their caregivers are considered passive participants in personal healthcare data that should not have control over the information [36]. Another barrier evolves from the fragmented healthcare system of the United States with private practices, public and private hospitals and hospital networks creating a barrier for a standardized system of patient healthcare record. Another concern is both the technical prowess and medical understanding of the older adult leading to low quality data and the potential of misinterpretation [37]. Given that the expected number of people aged 60 years and over will reach 2.1 billion by 2050 and that some of these diseases share modifiable lifestyle-based risk factors, a systemic approach to early diagnosis and treatment of catastrophic disease could benefit families by providing a higher quality of living for older adults along with reduced medical expenditures over their lifetime [38].

References

1. Alder, S.: Largest healthcare data breaches of 2021. HIPAA J. (2021). https://www.hipaajour nal.com/largest-healthcare-data-breaches-of-2021/. Accessed 26 May 2023
2. Bhuiyan, J.: Cyberattack disrupts hospital computer systems across US, hindering services. The Guardian (2023). https://www.theguardian.com/us-news/2023/aug/04/cyberattack-us-hospitals-california. Accessed 30 Aug 2023
3. Erol, I., Oztel, A., Searcy, C., Medeni, IT.: Selecting the most suitable blockchain platform: a case study on the healthcare industry using a novel rough MCDM framework. Technol. Forecast. Soc. Chang. **186**, 122132 (2023). https://doi.org/10.1016/j.techfore.2022.122132
4. Subramaniam, H.: Co-morbidities in dementia: time to focus more on assessing and managing co-morbidities. Age Ageing **48**(3), 314–315 (2019). https://doi.org/10.1093/ageing/afz007
5. Poulos, J., Zhu, L., Shah, A.D.: Data gaps in electronic health record (EHR) systems: an audit of problem list completeness during the COVID-19 pandemic. Int. J. Med. Inform. **150**, 104452 (2021). https://doi.org/10.1016/j.ijmedinf.2021.104452
6. Philips, S., Willett, D., Das, S., Sara, E., Kannan, V., Zaha, V.: Use of an electronic health records registry to identify care gaps in cardiovascular care of cancer patients. J. Am. College Cardiol. **71**(11_Supplement), A698–A698 (2018). https://doi.org/10.1016/S0735-109 7(18)31239-7
7. Nurse Journal Staff. Nurse Practitioner (NP) Career Overview. American Association of Nurse Practitioners (2023). https://www.aanp.org/about/all-about-nps/whats-a-nurse-practi tioner. Accessed 3 April 2023
8. Wang, Y., Kung, L., Byrd, T.A.: Big data analytics: understanding its capabilities and potential benefits for healthcare organizations. Technol. Forecast. Soc. Chang. **126**, 3–13 (2018). https://doi.org/10.1016/j.techfore.2015.12.019
9. Polge, J., Robert, J., Le Traon, Y.: Permissioned blockchain frameworks in the industry: a comparison. ICT Express **7**(2), 229–233 (2021). https://doi.org/10.1016/j.icte.2020.09.002
10. Martin, C.B., Ogden, C.L., Hales, C.M., Gu, Q.: Prescription drug use in the United States, 2015–2016, NCHS Data Brief, no. 334, p. 8 (2019)
11. Vigliotti, M.G.: What do we mean by smart contracts? open challenges in smart contracts. Front. Blockchain **3** (2021). https://www.frontiersin.org/articles/https://doi.org/10.3389/fbloc.2020.553671. Accessed 7 May 2023
12. Antwi, M., Adnane, A., Ahmad, F., Hussain, R., Habib ur Rehman, M., Kerrache, C.A.: The case of HyperLedger Fabric as a blockchain solution for healthcare applications. Blockchain: Res. Appl. **2**(1), 100012 (2021). https://doi.org/10.1016/j.bcra.2021.100012
13. Ekblaw, A., Azaria, A., Halamka, J.D., Lippman, A.: MedRec: using blockchain for medical data access and permission management. In: 2016 2nd International Conference on Open and Big Data (OBD), pp. 25–30. IEEE , Vienna, Austria (2016). https://doi.org/10.1109/OBD.2016.11
14. Zhang, P., White, J., Schmidt, D.C., Lenz, G., Rosenbloom, S.T.: FHIRChain: applying Blockchain to securely and scalably share clinical data. Comput. Struct. Biotechnol. J. **16**, 267–278 (2018). https://doi.org/10.1016/j.csbj.2018.07.004
15. Chen, M., et al.: Blockchain-Enabled healthcare system for detection of diabetes. J. Inform. Secur. Appl. **58**, 102771 (2021). https://doi.org/10.1016/j.jisa.2021.102771
16. Lo, Y.-S., Yang, C.-Y., Chien, H.-F., Chang, S.-S., Lu, C.-Y., Chen, R.-J.: Blockchain-enabled iwellchain framework integration with the national medical referral system: development and usability study. J. Med. Internet Res. **21**(12), e13563 (2019). https://doi.org/10.2196/13563

17. Hassan, J., et al.: A lightweight proxy re-encryption approach with certificate-based and incremental cryptography for fog-enabled e-healthcare. Secur. Commun. Networks **2021**, e9363824 (2021). https://doi.org/10.1155/2021/9363824

18. Ismail, L., Zeadally, S.: Healthcare insurance frauds: taxonomy and blockchain-based detection framework (Block-HI). IEEE Commun. Mag. **23**(4), 36–43 (2021). https://doi.org/10.1109/MITP.2021.3071534

19. Aich,S., et al.: Protecting personal healthcare record using blockchain & federated learning technologies. In: 2022 24th International Conference on Advanced Communication Technology (ICACT), pp. 109–112 (2022). https://doi.org/10.23919/ICACT53585.2022.9728772

20. Moon, S., et al.: Identifying information gaps in electronic health records by using natural language processing: gynecologic surgery history identification. J. Med. Internet Res. **24**(1), e29015 (2022). https://doi.org/10.2196/29015

21. Yan, X., et al.: Persistent cardiometabolic health gaps: can therapeutic care gaps be precisely identified from electronic health records. Healthcare **10**(1), Art. no. 1 (2022). https://doi.org/10.3390/healthcare10010070

22. Kuo, T.-T., Ohno-Machado, L. : ModelChain: Decentralized Privacy-Preserving Healthcare Predictive Modeling Framework on Private Blockchain Networks (2018). https://doi.org/10.48550/arXiv.1802.01746

23. Mei, S., Zhang, K.: A machine learning framework for predicting drug–drug interactions. Sci. Rep. **11**(1), Art. no. 1 (2021). https://doi.org/10.1038/s41598-021-97193-8

24. Han, K., et al.: A review of approaches for predicting drug–drug interactions based on machine learning. Front. Pharmacol. **12** (2022). https://www.frontiersin.org/articles/https://doi.org/10.3389/fphar.2021.814858. Accessed 30 April 2023

25. Mackey, T.K., et al.: 'Fit-for-purpose?' - challenges and opportunities for applications of blockchain technology in the future of healthcare. BMC Med. **17**(1), 68 (2019). https://doi.org/10.1186/s12916-019-1296-7

26. Chowdhury, M.J.M., et al.: A comparative analysis of distributed ledger technology platforms. IEEE Access **7**, 167930–167943 (2019). https://doi.org/10.1109/ACCESS.2019.2953729

27. Ateniese, G., Fu, K., Green, M., Hohenberger, S.: Improved proxy re-encryption schemes with applications to secure distributed storage. ACM Trans. Inf. Syst. Secur. **9**(1), 1–30 (2006). https://doi.org/10.1145/1127345.1127346

28. Yusof, M.M., Kuljis, J., Papazafeiropoulou, A., Stergioulas, L.K.: An evaluation framework for Health Information Systems: human, organization and technology-fit factors (HOT-fit). Int. J. Med. Inform. **77**(6), 386–398 (2008). https://doi.org/10.1016/j.ijmedinf.2007.08.011

29. Miyachi, K., Mackey, T.K.: HOCBS: a privacy-preserving blockchain framework for healthcare data leveraging an on-chain and off-chain system design. Inf. Process. Manage. **58**(3), 102535 (2021). https://doi.org/10.1016/j.ipm.2021.102535

30. Peng, L., Feng, W., Yan, Z., Li, Y., Zhou, X., Shimizu, S.: Privacy preservation in permissionless blockchain: a survey. Digital Commun. Networks **7**(3), 295–307 (2021). https://doi.org/10.1016/j.dcan.2020.05.008

31. Hylock, R.H., Zeng, X.: A Blockchain framework for patient-centered health records and exchange (HealthChain): evaluation and proof-of-concept study. J. Med. Internet Res. **21**(8), e13592 (2019). https://doi.org/10.2196/13592

32. Agbo, C.C., Mahmoud, Q.H., Eklund, J.M.: Blockchain technology in healthcare: a systematic review. Healthcare (Basel) **7**(2), 56 (2019). https://doi.org/10.3390/healthcare7020056

33. Jacob, L., Breuer, J., Kostev, K.: Prevalence of chronic diseases among older patients in German general practices. Ger. Med. Sci. **14**, Doc03 (2016). https://doi.org/10.3205/000230

34. Wei, P., Zhu, S.: An improved secure unidirectional proxy re-encryption scheme. In: 2013 5th International Conference on Intelligent Networking and Collaborative Systems, pp. 681–684 (2013). https://doi.org/10.1109/INCoS.2013.130

35. Morris, J.M.: User interface design for older adults. Interact. Comput. **6**(4), 373–393 (1994). https://doi.org/10.1016/0953-5438(94)90009-4

36. Randeree, E., Whetstone, M.: Personal Health Records: Patients in Control. In: Health Information Systems : Concepts, Methodologies, Tools, and Applications, in "Contemporary Research in Information Science and Technology, vol. 4, , pp. 2111–2124. Medical Information Science Reference (an imprint of IGI Global), Hershey, PA (2010). https://www-igi-global-com.libweb.lib.utsa.edu/chapter/personal-health-records/49984. Accessed 13 May 2023

37. Suggs, L.S.: A 10-year retrospective of research in new technologies for health communication. J. Health Commun. **11**(1), 61–74 (2006). https://doi.org/10.1080/10810730500461083

38. Coley, N., et al.: Factors predicting engagement of older adults with a coach-supported ehealth intervention promoting lifestyle change and associations between engagement and changes in cardiovascular and dementia risk: secondary analysis of an 18-month multinational randomized controlled trial. J. Med. Internet Res. e32006 (2022). https://doi.org/10.2196/32006

39. Centers for Disease Control and Prevention: Promoting Health for Older Adults [Chronic Disease Fact Sheets]. Promoting Health for Older Adults, 8 September 2022. https://www.cdc.gov/chronicdisease/resources/publications/factsheets/promoting-health-for-older-adults.htm

Analysis of Serious Challenges Faced by the Aviation Industry

Peter Korba⬤, Edina Jenčová⬤, Samer Al-Rabeei(✉) ⬤, Martina Koščáková⬤,
and Ingrid Sekelová⬤

Faculty of Aeronautics, Technical University of Košice, Rampová 7, 041 21 Košice, Slovakia
{peter.korba,edina.jencova,samer.al-rabeei,martina.koscakova,
ingrid.sekelova}@tuke.sk

Abstract. Nowadays, we encounter significant technological progress in several areas and branches of industry. The aviation industry is no exception. Improvements are constantly being made in the area of airlines´ aircraft fleets and terminals are undergoing continuous development and modernization. As an example, we can cite the development of new, more modern and durable structural components and aircraft engines, which provide aircraft with better operational characteristics and contribute to more efficient use of aviation fuel. Control systems in aircraft cockpits are also undergoing a significant technological change. Over time, these are transitioning to fully computerized control without the need for significant intervention by the aircraft crew. The rapid introduction of new technologies due to the demand of the market also brings negative phenomena that can be the cause of air accidents. The aim of the article is to highlight the relevant challenges currently facing air traffic. The contribution is devoted to demographic factors that affect air transport, especially in economically developing regions of the world.

Keywords: digitalization · data collection · personalization

1 Introduction

Technologies in the digital space are an equally important area that not only airlines but also airport companies deal with. Their implementation or expansion can significantly facilitate the information of regular as well as occasional customers. It is not a problem to hear about situations where large global companies obtained information about customers or users of products, even though people were not informed about tracking in advance. The evidence that such activities also take place in aviation are, for example, pre-filled forms with your previous trip and personal data, which will significantly shorten your reservation time. The reality is that, even though such data collection can be undesirable, it is also beneficial for the functioning of the business and the facilitation of work.

Assurance of the safety and security of passengers, crew members, and the public is the number one priority of every airline worldwide. They maintain an unwavering

© ICST Institute for Computer Sciences, Social Informatics and Telecommunications Engineering 2024
Published by Springer Nature Switzerland AG 2024. All Rights Reserved
D. Perakovic and L. Knapcikova (Eds.): FABULOUS 2023, LNICST 542, pp. 37–49, 2024.
https://doi.org/10.1007/978-3-031-50051-0_3

commitment to safety and security despite workforce challenges and all the issues facing the airline industry [1].

The various response actions, that were adopted by organizations to overcome mega disturbances, must be studied and further implemented [1]. Additionally, the practices from these experiences should be incorporated into a knowledge base that can be transferred to the corresponding enterprise via a feedback loop [2].

Keeping flights up to schedule is highly dependent on the weather. Due to seasonality, airlines have historically been able to anticipate some cancellations. For example, hurricane season in Florida leads to some flights being cancelled, and snowstorms in the Northeast of US can impede trips in the middle of winter. Such events can be planned for and airlines can prepare themselves to mitigate the costs. In the recent years, long term planning, however, has become nearly impossible because of the effects of climate change [3].

Digitalization is shaping all fields today as with any other significant economic event. Since the airline industry relies heavily on security and is highly competitive, it participates actively in digital innovation to improve customer experience and financial performance [4].

2 Challenge of Big Data Management

The collection of large amounts of data by airlines, otherwise known as "big data", can take place in several ways and presents several benefits. In addition to faster and easier filling of reservation forms for passengers, there are other benefits, but from the airlines. One of the biggest advantages is the company's ability to react in real time to the changing demands of the market, customers and to quickly adapt to incoming changes, their planning and implementation. Systematic adherence and application of knowledge and data to operations can bring a reduction in operating costs, an increase in market competitiveness for a company and value for shareholders [5].

"Big data" can affect various business areas of airlines, such as:

- Increasing the revenue of airlines
- Intelligent maintenance
- Cost reduction
- Customer satisfaction
- Digital transformation
- Performance values
- Risk management
- Control and verification
- Predicting usability [5]

A detailed examination of the data collected from websites allows airlines to better adapt to customers and understand their preferences. The analysis of received ticket reservations helps entities to modify the offered products and services designed directly according to the personal preferences of customers, which brings them an increased number of reservations in a given time interval. Based on the information obtained directly from customers, airlines adjust the offered destinations or adjust marketing strategies for a specific market, which is reflected in different prices for identical products. From the point of view of passengers, the use of such data analysis results in more affordable prices [5].

Under the term "intelligent maintenance", we can imagine the analysis of data that is obtained directly from the aircraft during the flight itself using several modern technologies, sensors or chips. Like other technical industries, the aviation industry undergoes regular modernization. Just for comparison, the aircraft themselves have changed over the past decades not only in terms of design, but also in terms of technology. Nowadays, a lot of electronics and components are installed in aircraft, which provide airlines and engineers with a huge amount of valuable information and data. These are subsequently evaluated in a relatively short time by software that can inform the aircraft operator about technical problems, necessary maintenance, general repairs or, in the worst case, about the replacement of the aircraft. Proper identification, analysis and timely implementation of the necessary measures can reduce maintenance and repair budgets for airlines by up to 30–40% [6].

The reason why airlines currently invest considerable funds in data collection software is that unplanned maintenance causes considerable financial and operational problems for airlines. The most common problem in the occurrence and solution of unplanned maintenance is the subsequent financial compensation of affected passengers [6].

The care and maintenance of the aircraft fleet can be divided into active and reactive. Each form of maintenance has its own advantages and disadvantages. Reactive maintenance is performed additionally in the form of a reaction to a situation or problem that has already arisen. This may result in the aircraft being grounded for an extended period of time until the problem is resolved. Active maintenance is further divided into preventive and predictive. Preventive maintenance is generally defined by the aircraft manufacturer. We may encounter maintenance based on the number of hours flown, the number of landings performed or the age of use of individual components. The downside, but safety-wise, to this type of maintenance is that it is often done before significant wear and tear. Predictive maintenance is performed at the ideal time when specific conditions require it. Predictive maintenance provides airlines with a more convenient report on data obtained from sensors that monitor the technical condition of the aircraft. In most cases, these sensors are directly compatible with computers or other portable devices, so that technicians receive information in the form of notifications immediately and also with the possibility of viewing historical records [6] (Fig. 1).

The advantages of data collection are also reflected in the area of saving operating costs. According to available IATA data from 2019 [7], fuel costs accounted for up to 23.7% of total operating costs for airlines. Currently, with the help of software, airlines can calculate the amount of fuel consumed in real time and ensure its more efficient use. Artificial intelligence systems that work with built-in algorithms monitor the distance, flight level, weight of the aircraft or the surrounding weather during the flight. Based on the evaluation of these factors, the systems can inform the technical staff about the estimated amount of fuel for the next flight. The reduction of operating costs through these systems can also be achieved with passengers' checked luggage. A significant part of the costs of airlines is used in the form of refunds for lost or damaged luggage of passengers. Delta Airlines currently operates a mobile application that can show the

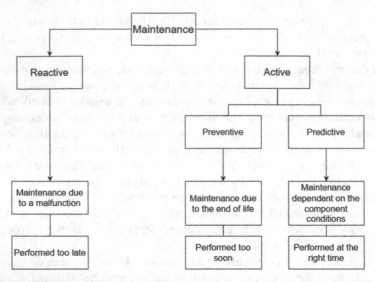

Fig. 1. The difference between preventive and predictive maintenance [6]

current location of luggage in real time and inform passengers about its status via their own smartphones. This app had a huge success immediately after its launch, as evidenced by more than 11 million downloads [5].

In addition to the private benefit from the collected information, airlines also take care to improve the travel experience of their customers. To increase passenger comfort and provide better services and products, airlines cooperate with external technology companies that provide them with tailor-made platforms and technologies. Such services include e.g. mobile applications containing virtual assistants who provide the passenger with basic information about the products offered, regarding flights, the current situation at the airport or help in filling out reservations. According to the annual report of the International Society for Aviation Telecommunications (SITA) from 2021 [8], several airlines are planning to engage in the field of artificial intelligence technologies to the extent that they will introduce technologies that facilitate the use of customer services. As an example, we can cite the cooperation of United Airlines with Amazon, which is developing its virtual bot Alexa. Miami International Airport already uses an application that provides passengers with a wide range of information about their flights [9].

Airlines also feel the benefits resulting from data collection in the area of operational performance measurement. While in the past airlines did not deal with operational indicators in such detail, today they devote considerable time and attention to this activity. Of course, constantly evolving software working with different analysis methods has the greatest impact on this. As stated by the website [5], "airlines usually operate in a globally competitive environment and therefore require fast and accurate measurement of business performance". Obtaining accurate and useful operational or financial information is a difficult activity in the aviation industry, as their variability differs not only in the method of data collection, the type of software used, but also in the different preferences of several airlines. The impact on different operating performance measures may be due to, for example, different business strategy, size and type of operating fleet or economic environment. Operational performance measures can be expressed in the form of physical or financial indicators. Natural operational indicators include distance flown, block hours, profitability point of aircraft capacity utilization, offered passenger kilometers, average seat capacity utilization and others. Financial operating indicators include the following indicators: total profit/loss of the company, operating profit/loss of the company, total revenues, operating costs, number of employees in the company or the number of aircraft that the company has. All these indicators inform airlines about the areas in which they achieve the highest goals or, on the contrary, where it is necessary to reevaluate the business strategy. Automating data collection gives airlines the opportunity to intervene in a timely and effective manner and minimize adverse impacts on the business [5].

Air transport is statistically one of the safest forms of transport, but even this does not guarantee a carefree way of doing business for airlines. The reason is the situations when air accidents and conflicts occur. The cause of an air accident may not only be the technical problems of the aircraft, but also the failure of the human factor in critical situations or overwork. In order to avoid such situations or to minimize their occurrence, airlines are currently focusing on developing and implementing models, simulators or choosing a risk management strategy. From this point of view, the analysis of the obtained data makes it easier for them, for example, to plan flight schedules for specific crews. Constantly flying through different time zones, long work shifts or unexpected changes in planning can negatively affect human health and concentration when performing work. Boeing's American business Jeppesen recently began integrating bio-mathematical fatigue models into operations to predict the level of exhaustion of crew members at specific times and reduce the risk of accidents resulting from human failure [5].

The aviation industry is currently facing massive development in the technical, economic and social spheres. From the point of view of constant adaptation to new regulations, directives or trends, it is important to apply knowledge and solutions in practice at the right time. The simplest method by which airlines can improve their offered services is to work on the personalization of products tailored to customers. The result can be an increase in potential and regular passengers.

By the term product personalization, we can understand the adaptation of offered services and products with regard to customer interest. Nowadays, people prefer variety and originality of purchased products and are looking for options and opportunities to differentiate themselves from others. The times when a uniform portfolio of products and services was on offer are on the wane and products of different price levels and features are coming to the fore. Airlines and entities operating in the field of aviation are currently able to meet customers and offer them various packages that customers can combine according to their own wishes [10].

Low-cost airlines, which began to appear on the aviation market to a large extent at the beginning of the 21st century, had a significant impact on the change in the way products and services are offered. The business model of low-cost airlines is aimed at reducing operating costs, which results in cutting down the offered product to the core and paying customers extra for additional services.

By additional services, we can understand any services that are available to the customer during different stages of the journey. Globally, we can divide them into services before the flight, services during the flight, i.e. on board the aircraft, and services available after arrival at the destination [10].

An additional service before the flight, for which the customer can pay, is, for example, an increase in the weight limit on the checked-in luggage, speeding up the security process directly at the airport or enabling priority boarding. A popular service, mostly among business travelers, is the provision of transportation from the hotel directly to the airport by airline. At the airport, customers will encounter additional services such as access to the business lounge, where drinks, meals and daily newspapers are available [11].

Alcoholic and non-alcoholic drinks, fast food and other snacks are available on board the aircraft. When traveling longer distances, passengers will appreciate the option to get pillows, blankets or headphones to privately enjoy multimedia content via the built-in screens in the seats. The availability of a WiFi connection is gradually becoming a matter of course [11].

After arriving at the destination airport, passengers can use services such as priority processing of travel documents, transfer from the airport by means of public transport, tracking of lost luggage using mobile devices or services of other business entities that cooperate with airports [11].

All the above examples of additional services are defined on the so-called ad-hoc basis, which means that they are bound to a given purpose. Individual airlines define these services based on their own business model, which differentiates them from their competitors. The aim of these aforementioned services is to expand the basic offer and provide passengers with greater comfort [11].

According to [12], additional services can be provided in two ways: in the form of "unbundling" or in the form of "added value". We can define unbundling as a puzzle of separately available services, which are already defined when booking and purchasing a ticket with a predetermined price. The customer's task is to assemble the final product according to their choice. In general, these are services that used to be part of the ticket and the customer paid for them, even if they did not actually use them [13].

The second form is the so-called "commission-linked products". Passengers encounter these services mainly after arriving at their final destination. This includes car rentals from the airport, hotel room reservations in partner hotels, various forms of travel insurance, currency exchange or the purchase of tickets for cultural events. The sale of such services by airlines means additional income for them from the provision of third-party services in the form of commissions [14].

Airlines have prepared for their regular and loyal customers various advantages resulting from frequent travel with their airline. One of them is the introduction of the so-called "partner programs". The purpose of these programs is to enable the customer to collect loyalty points, which can be used to apply discounts on new tickets up to 100% over time. These programs are mainly aimed at business travelers who travel around the world. While it may seem like it cannot be profitable for airlines, the opposite is true. Such loyalty points can also be purchased by other competing airlines or commercial companies, which subsequently provide them to their own customers. As an example, we can cite the cooperation of an airline with a food retail chain. By purchasing a ticket from an airline, the customer receives loyalty points of the grocery store chain, which can be used for the next purchase in its stores [11].

In today's era of technological boom, airlines use various information technologies for more detailed personalization of their products, through which they can collect a large amount of data and information about their regular and first customers. As an example, we can cite pre-prepared partially filled forms on the airlines' websites, which, in addition to collecting and storing passenger data from their previous flights, can speed up the reservation process for the passengers themselves. How it can look in real operation is shown in the following table [10] (Table 1).

Table 1. Customization of the product to the customer's needs

STANDARD PACKAGE OF SERVICES	PERSONALIZED SERVICE PACKAGE
The customer visits the website, chooses a date and completes the flight reservation	Websites detect repeat customers and offer them a pre-filled form, speeding up the process
The customer's flight is delayed - he will get the information on the airport information board	The customer will receive a personal SMS with an apology and further instructions
A frequent customer repeatedly orders the same whiskey but must inform the flight attendants of their preferences before each flight	When boarding the aircraft, the flight attendants greet the passenger by name and inform him that his drink is ready to be served

3   Challenge of B737 MAX Aircraft Grounding

The grounding of Boeing 737 MAX aircraft resulted in another challenge that has to be overcome by the aviation industry. The largest producers of commercial jet aircraft in the world include the French company Airbus, based in Toulouse, and the American company Boeing, based in Chicago. While they competed for the world market leadership in terms of the number of units sold, the year 2018 brought two aircraft crashes, which over time led to the suspension of Boeing 737 MAX machines.

The Boeing 737 MAX aircraft are among the latest models mainly of the Boeing company, which started their operations in January 2016. They are twin-engine narrow-body aircraft that are produced in four variants - MAX 7, MAX 8, MAX 9 and MAX 10. The differences between them are in size, seat capacity or maximum range [15].

Boeing 737 MAX aircraft differ from their predecessors with a new design of wings that are curved at their ends in the shape of >. The leading edge of the wing is covered with a coating of special materials that contribute to a natural laminar air flow. The developers also worked on the efficient use of fuel and engine performance, thereby achieving an increase in the maximum possible range by 19%. The very construction of the aircraft engines also underwent a change, on which the production materials were changed. In the cockpit, the latest model of display panels with larger displays are prepared for the pilots, which make it easier for the crew to search for the necessary data [15, 16].

The MCAS - Maneuvering Characteristics Augmentation System was a revolutionary technological system that was supposed to contribute to ensuring higher safety on flights. It is a computer-controlled aircraft stability system. This software helps the crew evaluate information from available sensors and prevents the so-called stopping the aircraft due to a steep climb. Sensors located in the nose of the aircraft's fuselage acquire data on the pitch angle. If this climb is too steep, the system can correct this angle by using the horizontal stabilizers in the rear of the fuselage and pushing the nose of the aircraft down. The risk may arise in the case of recording erroneous data from the aircraft sensor when the MCAS system applies its stabilization processes even at moments when the aircraft maintains a stable rate of climb. The disadvantage of this system can also be the fact that the data recorded through the built-in sensors are received continuously and this leads to the repeated switching on of the MCAS system. The solution in this case is a complete manual shutdown of the system by crew members. This cause could also be linked to two tragic crashes of Boeing 737 MAX aircraft [15, 16].

The first aircraft crash of a Boeing 737 MAX 8 aircraft, which belonged to the Lion Air airline took place in October 2018. It provided air connections between the cities of Jakarta and Pangkal Pinang in Indonesia. The aircraft fell into the Java Sea 13 min after takeoff. All 189 passengers on board, including the crew, did not survive the crash [16].

The second aircraft crash of the same type of Boeing 737 MAX 8 aircraft occurred in March 2019. Ethiopian National Airlines was operating a flight from the capital of Ethiopia, Addis Ababa, to the metropolis of Kenya - Nairobi. This aircraft crashed just 6 min after takeoff. There were 149 passengers and 8 crew members on board who did not survive the accident. The causes of both accidents are under investigation [16].

As a result of these accidents, the aviation authorities focused on the measures that need to be put into operation so that similar accidents do not happen again. This resulted in the immediate grounding of all Boeing 737 MAX aircraft until further notice. Several countries and airlines around the world have started applying these measures [17].

After the given decisions of the aviation authorities, the airlines had to immediately deal with the situation and look for solutions for the next few months to ensure further operation. As is generally known, the vast majority of airlines use one type of aircraft from a specific manufacturer when operating aviation activities, due to easier maintenance or repairs. Among the airlines with the most aircraft types at the time of the grounding order were Southwest Airlines (34 aircraft), Air Canada, American Airlines and China Southern (24 aircraft each), and Norwegian Air (18 aircraft) [17].

Immediately after its introduction, the Boeing 737 MAX became the fastest-selling aircraft type in Boeing's history, with approximately 5,000 units ordered from more than 100 companies worldwide [15].

According to Boeing's statistics, which are published on their website, 4,932 of 737 MAX aircraft were ordered by December 2019. However, only 387 aircraft were delivered [18].

Their biggest competitor, Airbus, could use the unpleasant situation on the aviation market to their advantage. Around the same time, it introduced a new class of twin-engine narrow-body aircraft called the A320neo Family. This "family" includes the A319neo, A320neo, A321neo aircraft. Since 2014, Airbus has received orders for 4,766 aircraft, while by the end of 2019, 1,186 aircraft were delivered to customers [19].

The following graphs illustrate the mutual comparison of the number of received orders and delivered pieces.

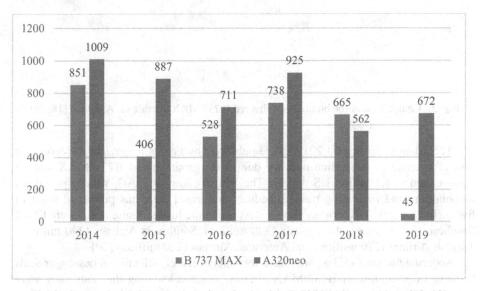

Fig. 2. Comparison of the number of received orders B 737 MAX vs. A32neo [18, 19]

As can be seen from Figs. 2 and 3, the competition between the two largest aircraft manufacturers moved in an almost identical range until the moment when two aircraft crashes occurred. After them, due to security measures, the airlines decided to suspend or cancel their orders, which resulted in a significant drop. While in 2014 Boeing received more than 800 orders, in 2019 there were only 45 of them. The situation became significantly more complicated for Boeing at the end of 2019, when the Federal Aviation Administration (FAA) announced that the lifting of restrictions would not take place before 2020. Thus, as of January 2020, Boeing stopped the production of new aircraft. In the same period, Airbus increased the number of its orders by more than 100, to more than 550 [16, 18].

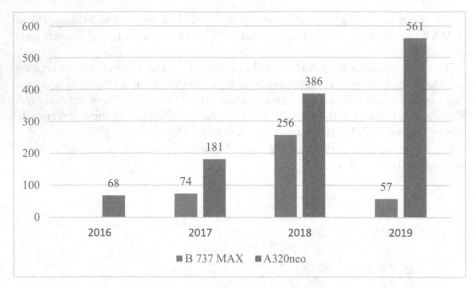

Fig. 3. Comparison of the number of delivered B 737 MAX aircraft vs. A330neo [18, 19]

According to an August 2019 article published by Forbes magazine, the economic loss of revenue in the airline industry due to the grounding of B737 MAX aircraft is estimated at 4.1 billion US dollars. The British company OAG, which specializes in obtaining and evaluating travel schedules and travel data, has published a list of five airlines that will experience the greatest economic losses. These airlines are China Southern (370 million), Air Canada (300 million), Southwest Airlines (290 million), Turkish Airlines (270 million) and American Airlines (220 million) [20].

According to the OAG airlines have lost approximately 41 million passenger seats because of grounding of B737 MAX aircraft. When calculating the seats, they were based on the chosen methodology, which expresses the difference between the planned capacity of individual airlines and the currently available capacity. A total of 387 aircraft operating for 43 different airlines were grounded [20] (Table 2).

In a public statement, Boeing apologized to all affected companies and passengers for the complications caused in air transport. The company expressed that safety is a priority and therefore they are working toward new updated software that would be certified and could ensure the return of 737 MAX aircraft back to service [20].

Airlines that experienced the greatest losses due to the grounding of aircraft confirmed that they had extensive conversations with Boeing regarding the damages caused and their refunds, but Boeing has not yet provided concrete solutions [20].

Table 2. The number of seats lost due to the grounding of the B737 MAX by individual airlines [20].

China Southern	3 653 816
Air Canada	3 268 291
Southwest Airlines	2 962 400
Turkish Airlines	2 706 367
American Airlines	2 186 292
Norwegian Air	2 178 036
Fly Dubai	2 136 420
SpiceJet	2 002 266
LOT	1 968 600
Jet Airways	1 578 180

Assistance to airlines in the given situation, whether financial or material, was provided by aircraft rental companies, which enabled airlines to reduce the amount of monthly flat-rate fees, or granted them exemptions from paying rental fees for a fixed period. According to some sources, even Boeing was supposed to participate in their introduction [17].

In addition to airlines, these problems also affected pilots and other carrier employees, who lost compensation for scheduled flights during the given period. American Airlines said that it will transfer the money received from Boeing in the form of compensation (up to $30 million) to the accounts of its employees [17].

However, according to experts from the field of air transport, this situation also brought positive effects, namely the reduction of the offered capacity of airlines. There has been a talk for a long time about a situation where the offered capacity of aircraft on the market was greater than the demand for air transport itself. This phenomenon was mostly reflected in airlines operating in North America, where it brought them higher revenues. However, the question remains how long this advantage will continue and whether it will change with the reintroduction of the B737 MAX aircraft into service [17].

The reintroduction of 737 MAX aircraft will not solve the situation immediately. The number of narrow-body aircraft in service will not be sufficient, although as Boeing reports, it currently has 400 manufactured aircraft ready to be shipped to customers. However, their delivery may take more than 6 months under optimal conditions. Experts agree on a duration of around three years [17].

Another challenge that either the aircraft manufacturer Boeing or the airlines themselves will have to face is to restore confidence in their aircraft among passengers and the general public. American Airlines, Southwest Airlines and United Airlines say they will conduct dozens of practice technical flights to assure passengers of their safety before returning their aircraft to service [17].

4   Conclusion

The benefit of new modern technological equipment is currently in great demand. It is no secret that when we give the customer a choice, his choice will be a newer and more modern model. And that is even in the case when the changes are minimal and often unimportant for a specific purpose. For this reason, but also for others, airlines approach the renovation of their aircraft fleets, which include more modern control systems, more economical aircraft engines or more aerodynamic construction materials. It is the rush to invent something newer and more modern that costs manufacturers, and subsequently airlines, considerable financial resources.

As a solution that could reduce unexpected operational problems, we consider slowing down the application of technological innovations and the introduction of more extensive safety tests, which would be carried out under specific laboratory conditions, thereby minimizing some errors that could otherwise have catastrophic consequences for the safety of passengers.

A similar situation is also taking place in the digital space, where companies apply new tools to their systems that help them get to know the passengers' requirements more closely, which the customers themselves often have no idea about. We see the application of support tools designed to improve commercial activities positively, but great attention must be paid to the security and degree of protection of the collected data. In general, this is the personal data of specific individuals, which in the wrong hands could cause serious problems for specific individuals. Therefore, it is advisable for airlines or airport companies to work closely with security companies and experts in the field of IT security when applying digital tools.

Acknowledgement. This work was supported by the Slovak Research and Development Agency within the "Research of an intelligent management logistics system with a focus on monitoring the hygienic safety of the logistics chain" project implemented under contract number 313011BWP9.

References

1. Jiang, Y., Wen J.: Effects of COVID-19 on hotel marketing and management: a perspective article. Int. J. Contemp. Hosp. Manage. **32**(8) (2020)
2. Williams, T., Gruber, D., Sutcliffe, K., Shepherd, D., Zhao, E.: Organizational response to adversity: fusing crisis management and resilience research streams. Acad. Manage. Ann. **11**(2) (2017)
3. Dwayer, K.: 8 Critical Risks Facing the Aviation Industry, Risk & insurance (2019). https://riskandinsurance.com/7-critical-risks-facing-the-aviation-industry/. Accessed 3 Nov 2022
4. Heiets, I., La, J., Zhou, W., Xu, S., Wang, X., Xu, Y.: Digital transformation of airline industry. Res. Transport. Econ. (92) (2022)
5. Zamiatina, A.: 9 incredible ways data analytics is transforming airlines, Business and Operational Analytics News. https://blog.datumize.com/9-incredible-ways-data-analytics-is-transforming-airlines. Accessed 15 nov 2022
6. Bree, S.: Big data in aviation - reduce costs trough predictive maintenance, EXSYN Aviation Solutions. https://www.exsyn.com/blog/big-data-in-aviation-predictive-maintenance. Accessed 18 Nov 2022

7. IATA. Fuel Fact Sheet. IATA (2019)
8. SITA. SITA Activity Report 2021 (2021). https://www.sita.aero/sita-activity-report-2021/. Accessed 23 Nov 2022
9. Choudhury, A.: 5 Ways Data Analytics is Transforming the Aviation Industry, Analytics India Magazine (2019). https://analyticsindiamag.com/5-ways-data-analytics-is-transforming-the-aviation-industry/. Accessed 28 Nov 2022
10. Dinsmore, J.: Personalizing the Passenger Experience: Are We There Yet?, guestlogix (2018). https://www.guestlogix.com/blog/personalizing-passenger-experience. Accessed 28 Oct 2022
11. Tourism Teacher. What are the categories of airline ancillary revenue? (2022). https://touris mteacher.com/categories-of-airline-ancillary-revenue/. Accessed 28 Nov 2022
12. Tourism Teacher. Why do airlines use a la carte ancillary products? (2020). https://tourismte acher.com/a-la-carte-ancillary-products/. Accessed 29 Oct 2022
13. Tourism Teacher. Unbudling: How airlines make a profit (2020). https://tourismteacher.com/ unbundling-how-airlines-make-profit/. Accessed 29 Oct 2022
14. Boeing. Boeing 737 MAX. https://www.boeing.com/commerce/737max/. Accessed 24 Nov 2022
15. EASA. Boeing 737 MAX Return to Service Report, European Union Aviation Safety Agency (2021)
16. FAA. Summary of the FAA's Review of the Boeing 737 MAX, Federal Aviation Administration (2020)
17. Dentons. The impact of the Boeing 737 MAX grounding (2020). https://www.dentons.com/ en/insights/alerts/2020/january/16/the-impact-of-the-boeing-737-max-grounding#:~:text= by%20the%20aircraft.-,Production%20cuts,52%20to%2042%20per%20month.   Accessed 21 Aug 2022
18. Boeing. Orders and Deliveries. http://www.boeing.com/commerce/#/orders-deliveries. Accessed 10 May 2022
19. Airbus. Orders and deliveries (2021). https://www.airbus.com/aircraft/market/orders-delive ries.html#past. Accessed 10 May 2022
20. Reed, T.: New report puts impact of Boeing 737 MAX grounding at $4.1 billion, Forbes Magazine (2019). https://www.forbes.com/sites/tedreed/2019/08/10/new-report-puts-impact-of-boeing-737-max-grounding-at-41-billion/. Accessed 25 Oct 2022

Internet of Vehicle Moving Objects Detection System for the Rural Road Networks

Gordana Jotanovic[1] ⓘ, Goran Jausevac[1](✉) ⓘ, Dragan Perakovic[2] ⓘ,
Zeljko Stojanov[3] ⓘ, Vladimir Brtka[3] ⓘ, and Dalibor Dobrilovic[3] ⓘ

[1] Faculty of Transport and Traffic Engineering, University of East Sarajevo,
Doboj, Bosnia and Herzegovina
{gordana.jotanovic,goran.jausevac}@sf.ues.rs.ba
[2] Faculty of Transport and Traffic Sciences, University of Zagreb, Zagreb, Croatia
dperakovic@fpz.unizg.hr
[3] Technical Faculty "Mihajlo Pupin", University of Novi Sad, Zrenjanin, Serbia
{zeljko.stojanov,dalibor.dobrilovic}@uns.ac.rs,
vbrtka@tfzr.uns.ac.rs

Abstract. The paper presents the concept of a system for detecting moving objects on rural road networks. Pedestrians, wild animals and domestic animals are the most common causes of traffic accidents on country roads. The system is designed to warn the driver in a timely manner about the possibility of the movement of living objects on the road, in order to protect the lives and ensure the health of living beings, as well as the driver's property on rural roads.

Keywords: Wildlife-Vehicle Collision (WVC) · Living Beings (LB) · Live Moving Objects (LMO) · Moving Object Detection (MOD) · Internet of Vehicles (IoV) · Roadside Unit (RSU) · Cooperative-connected Vehicle Communication Network (CVCN)

1 Introduction

Consequences of Wildlife-Vehicle Collision (WVC) cause incalculable damage to animals, people and property around the world. A large number of traffic accidents caused in this way lead to the fact that policy makers, road authorities, hunters and the resident population are forced to take protective measures. The topicality of the issue of WVC traffic accidents on a spatial and seasonal level is shown in studies dealing with hotspots [1, 2]. Factors such as traffic characteristics [3] and road infrastructure [4] help in spatiotemporal modeling of protection systems. Also, knowledge of these factors can provide a basis for mitigation measures. Unfortunately, an insufficient number of projects at the local and global level deal with this topic, so they cannot provide the information needed to reduce WVC risk at a higher level [5]. A comprehensive analysis of traffic factors and a strategic concept for mitigating the consequences are still missing.

The rural road network covers not only forest areas, but also pastures, arable land, and sparsely populated areas. Therefore, in addition to the lives of wild animals, the safety

D. Perakovic and L. Knapcikova (Eds.): FABULOUS 2023, LNICST 542, pp. 50–59, 2024.
https://doi.org/10.1007/978-3-031-50051-0_4

of people and then domestic animals is at risk. The priority in traffic on country roads is the safety of people and animals (Living Beings, LB). Early detection of pedestrians, animals and all living things in motion (Live Moving Objects, LMO) on the road and beside the road can save many lives [6]. Characteristic of LMO is sudden crossing of the road without clear signs of intention to cross, which affects the timely detection of moving objects on the road. Visibility in different weather conditions makes driving and spotting moving objects even more difficult for drivers.

The system presented in the paper is based on the timely detection of moving objects on rural roads in order to avoid potential accidents on the road. Rural roads are interesting to observe because of the unpredictable movement of wild animals, domestic animals and people (moving objects) on the road and poorly visible traffic signs. The aim of the research is to enable safe driving of the vehicle using the Internet of Vehicles (IoV) system in order to avoid accidents caused by moving objects. The research goal is to increase the safety of people and animals as well as to increase the safety of driving in rural areas.

The paper consists of the following chapters: Sect. 1 discusses the importance of research, Sect. 2 describes the concept of the Internet of Vehicles with accompanying communication methods. Section 3 presents an introduction to previous research. Potential hazards and protection of live objects on rural roads are explained in Sect. 4. Section 5 discusses the essence of the Internet of Vehicles concept based on LMO detection, and the conclusion is presented in Sect. 6.

2 Related Work

Current European Union rural development activities include environmental protection, agricultural landscape management and solutions for the protection of people, animals, plants, soil and water. Such activities are followed by the application of ecological projects and technological solutions related to the construction of rural roads. When designing rural road networks, many spatial analyzes and decision-making should be carried out within the framework of choosing the most appropriate infrastructure solutions.

A certain amount of research deals with the design of the network of rural roads with infrastructure adapted to the environment. Also, research deals with the connection of vehicles with road infrastructure and the observation of objects in the road environment.

2.1 Design of Rural Road Infrastructure

Management of rural roads is challenging task including several aspects such as social, institutional, technical, economic, and environmental [7]. However, all these aspects have not been usually considered, especially in developing countries. The authors presented development of a sustainable management system for rural road networks, which includes development of a framework with elements important for rural roads, as well as a computer tool that integrates elements from framework. Input data for the system are inventory data per road, present condition of network, and strategic level data. Modules in management system are condition performance module, network maintenance module, and long-term prioritization module, which strongly emphasis the importance of road condition performance monitoring. System output data include maintenance program, required budget, and network condition for analysis period. The system is implemented for management of rural roads in Chile and Paraguay.

Planning and development of rural road network assumes considering desired functions of the roads, technical layout and characteristics, and traffic characteristic [8]. This is very important due to the low quality of the roads, and existence of tractors and bikes, or even non - motorized traffic such as bicycles, pedestrians, or animals. Design of rural road network includes the following rural road inventory: road reference data, road geometric details, road pavement condition and surface type, terrain, and soil types. Efficient and effective rural road development should be based on a rural road plan that includes a database with details on all elements important for road design, usage and maintenance, which should be stored in a database withing a road information system with incorporated GIS.

The conceptual model of the development of the rural road network is described in the paper [9]. The model was designed on the basis of a spatial analysis using the analytical hierarchical process method. The results of the research suggest that the process of developing rural roads with the application of a multi-criteria spatial analysis model is more accurate and efficient than the traditional design method. The multi-criteria model enables solutions in the form of maps at the level of the rural community, and decision-making in real time.

Zhu et al. [10] proposed a road network model for rural road network planning. The model assumes the existence of large amount of data collected from the real conditions by using remote sensing technology. The authors proposed a framework diagram of the rural road network planning system with the following basic elements: socioeconomic forecast, traffic demand forecast, road network scale, and evaluation of road network structure performance. Evaluation of the proposed model indicates that it supports transport efficiency, leading to social and economic development of local communities.

Richter et al. [11] presented a project aimed at determining infrastructure and traffic-related variables that influence the occurrence and consequences of overtaking accidents, as well as the behavior of drivers during overtaking other objects in the traffic on two-lane rural roads. Accident analysis considers the influence of road markings and signage, the influence road design, the influence of existing overtaking sight. As a result, the authors provide recommendations for overtaking, with overall goal to increase safety in the traffic.

An integrated Advanced Driver Assistance System (ADAS) for rural and intercity environments was proposed by Jimenez et al. [12]. The system is based on perception techniques, communication between vehicles (V2V) and communication between vehicles and infrastructure (V2I). The system for avoiding collision is based on artificial intelligence, 3D-laser scanner, and wireless communication techniques. The system enables real time detection and classification of obstacles, as well as identification of potential risks. All necessary messages are delivered to the driver, while some information is broadcasted to other vehicles. The system also supports autonomous actions if the driver does not react in a proper way. The system was implemented on a passenger car, with satisfactory test results.

The study [13] was based on an emergency protocol. The protocol allows communication with nearby devices to transmit signals to a nearby emergency station, reducing wait times. The flow of information related to the traffic accident, the state of the vehicle is provided by Internet of Things (IoT). Through the transmitter, the signal is transmitted from the vehicle to a nearby vehicle or vehicle in motion, which receives the signal and transmits it to a nearby roadside assistance unit, fire department or ambulance.

3 Internet of Vehicles and Communications in the Traffic Environment

The development of vehicles and road infrastructure, whose main goal is road safety, requires the inclusion of modern technologies. The application of Internet technologies in the field of real-time communications could solve many traffic problems. The concept of IoV technology can serve as a network system for smart traffic management. Such a system unites pedestrians, animals, vehicles, things and the environment in order to solve many traffic problems. Systems based on the IoV concept could significantly reduce the number of human casualties in traffic and enable effective real-time traffic management. The network IoV concept includes: intra-vehicle networks, inter-vehicle networks and mobile Internet, whereby vehicles are considered as smart objects equipped with a multi-sensor platform and wireless communication interfaces that enable interaction with the environment.

Communications based on the IoV system consist of: Vehicle-Vehicle-Sensors (V2S), Vehicle-Pedestrian/Person (V2P), Vehicle-Roadside (V2R), as well as Vehicle-to-Network (V2N), or comprehensive Vehicle-to-everything (V2X).

Vehicle-to-vehicle (V2V) communication enables the transfer of data between at least two vehicles. Data exchange between vehicles and road infrastructure (traffic lights, warning signs for road works, road hazard signs, etc.) is denoted by V2R/I. Vehicle-to-Infrastructure (V2I) communications are: Infrastructure-to-Infrastructure (I2I) and Infrastructure-to-Vehicle (I2V), these types of communication support longer distances within the network [14]. The Roadside Unit (RSU) together with V2V and V2I communications plays a vital role in providing services in the vehicle network, [15].

The IoV system using V2X communication connects vehicles, road infrastructure, sensors, pedestrians (personal devices) to the Internet using different communication media and technologies. Communication between vehicles and between infrastructure and vehicles takes place mainly using wireless technology. The architecture of the IoV communication system consists of tablets, smartphones, sensors, etc. A large number of devices that exist in the system make the architecture more complex. The IoV vehicle communication system is important for flow management and vehicle tracking. It also provides a reliable communication platform for various types of software applications.

4 Potential Dangers and Protection of Living Moving Objects on Rural Roads

The appearance of LMOs on the road or on the side of the road is often the cause of traffic accidents that occur on rural road networks. The reason for this is usually the close interaction between the habitats of humans, wild and domestic animals. The most common factors of traffic accidents are proximity to forest, gentle topography with rare curves, road width and seasonal differences directly affect WVC, while traffic volume, distance to urban areas or accompanying road infrastructure are not clearly attributable factors that influence or do not influence [16].

Insufficiently developed vertical and horizontal traffic signaling on the rural road network is a big challenge compared to the road network in urban areas. Often, drivers on such roads develop high vehicle speeds, the driver's attention is weaker, and the visibility in relation to the road infrastructure is worse. Roadside infrastructure is usually poorly maintained, so there is vegetation along the road that prevents the driver from having good visibility on the road. Therefore, traffic accidents on rural roads are a frequent occurrence. Unfortunately, they most often happen due to unexpected stops on the roads by pedestrians, wild and domestic animals. Vertical traffic signaling in the form of traffic signs that exists on rural roads is insufficient to prevent traffic accidents. Road hazard signs that are most often placed on rural roads are shown in Fig. 1.

Fig. 1. Road Hazard Signs a) Wild animals on the road, b) Domestic animals on the road, c) Pedestrians on the road, e) Children on the road

However, vertical traffic signaling in the form of traffic signs that exists on rural roads is often not sufficient to prevent traffic accidents. Traffic accidents most often occur due to inappropriate speed, nighttime driving conditions, weather conditions, insufficient visibility of the road, etc. Road Hazard Signs are often not enough security to prevent traffic accidents. The system proposed in the paper has the function of additionally notifying the driver of potential danger in the form of living creatures on the road, regardless of the posted danger signs on the road. Timely detection of LMO allows, regardless of danger signs, additional safety on rural roads.

5 Internet of Vehicle Moving Objects Detection System Designed for the Rural Road Networks

Traffic accident prevention includes early of Moving Objects Detection (MOD) and driver warning due to the ability to react quickly in the moment of danger. Detection involves real-time tracking of LMOs near the road and on the road. The process of detecting people, wild animals and domestic animals can be very demanding in conditions of poor visibility, at night, when the weather is foggy, raining, snowing and with other aggravating meteorological factors. Therefore, the MOD system has the potential to protect the lives and health of all living beings, as well as the driver's property under difficult driving conditions [17].

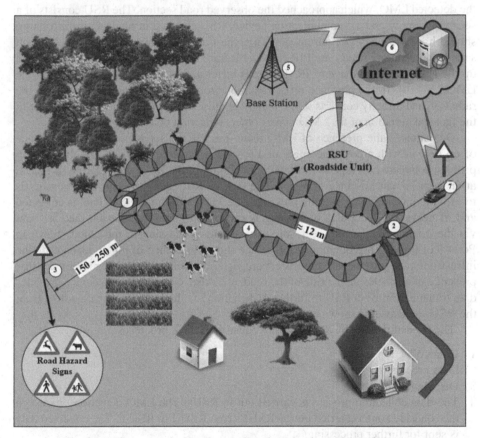

Fig. 2. MOD system for the observed road section in a rural environment

The proposed MOD system includes on-road and roadside units, a device responsible for local data processing and data distribution to a central data processing system. The IoV system is used for timely detection of the occurrence of LMO near a rural road. It also provides real-time communication between the LMO and the vehicle to prevent

direct contact. Figure 2 shows the section of the rural road between the Road Hazard
Signs, more precisely Point 1 and Point 2, which represent the starting and ending points
of the road section from different directions. On the observed section of the road, there is
a possible danger of the appearance of LMO near the road, which is marked with Road
Hazard Signs (Point 7 and Point 3, Fig. 2).

Point 1 and Point 2 are located at a distance of 150–250 m from the Road Hazard
Signs, but viewed from opposite directions. A distance of 150–250 m represents the
length of the vehicle's stopping distance in the event of an emergency. Between Point 1
and Point 2 in the roadside infrastructure, RSUs (Roadside Units) are distributed along
the entire length of the section between the mentioned points. Therefore, the RSUs
cover the entire length of the road section, even along the road at Point 1 and Point 2,
so that no LMO can enter the road without being detected beforehand. Point 4 shows
the detected LMO, which approached the observed road section. The RSU consists of a
sensor assembly and a communication device. RSUs located in roadside infrastructure
should have low energy requirements. The type of sensor installed in the RSU, which
satisfies low energy needs, are PIR (Passive Infrared) sensors. The two slots that make
up the PIR sensor are made of IR (Infrared) material that signals the movement of the
LMO [18, 19]. In the presence of IR radiation from the LMO, the sensor detects the
radiation and directly converts it into electrical pulses. Information about the change in
the thermal radiation of the LMO makes object detection possible.

Detection of the presence of LMO using the PIR sensor is possible at a distance
of up to 7 m with a coverage angle of 120° and an overlap angle of 10°. In order to
provide complete coverage of the zone of operation of the RSU, they need to be placed
at an approximate distance of 12 m. The task of RSU enriched with PIR sensors is
to provide information about the presence of LMO [20]. In the RSU, data is collected
and, if necessary, local data processing is carried out, then the relevant data are sent
via the communication device to the central data processing in the cloud shown in
Point 6 of Fig. 2. The communication device shown in Point 5 of Fig. 2 depends on the
infrastructure requirements, network coverage, terrain configuration, vegetation density,
presence of obstacles on the side of the road, etc. Also, communication device provides
data transmission from RSU to further distribution via the Internet. The data flow from
the RSU to the user is shown in Fig. 3.

The flow of data in the MOD system consists of three processes:

1) Data collection.
2) Data processing.
3) Distribution of data.
1. The data collection process is carried out in RSUs. The LMO detection process in
   the roadside zone is carried out by RSUs, from RSU 1 to RSU n. The collected data
   is sent for further processing.
2. Data processing is done in the cloud on a web server or in the vehicle itself, depending
   on the vehicle's architecture and the complexity of data processing. The collected
   data is processed in such a way as to prioritize when informing drivers and vehicles
   about potential road hazards. Therefore, each processed data will not have the same
   priority during the distribution process.

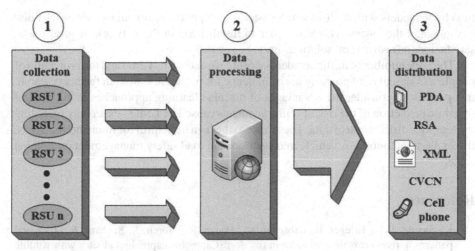

Fig. 3. Data flow of the MOD system

3. The data distribution process is directed towards the driver or directly towards the vehicle through mobile and web applications as well as software for managing autonomous vehicles. The distribution of data is carried out for the purpose of timely reaction of the driver or vehicle in order to avoid direct contact of the vehicle with LMOs.

Data processing and distribution processes should be completed in a short time to increase the time required for the driver and vehicle to react.

After the central processing of the data in the cloud is completed, the data is sent to the vehicle directly to a signal receiving device that enables audible and/or visual warning of the driver. Informing and warning drivers about the occurrence of LMO near the road can be realized with the help of a software application designed for the web environment. The MOD system is scalable and can be adapted to vehicles using multicast in Cooperative-connected Vehicle Communication Network (CVCN).

6   Conclusions

The MOD system is based on the concept of IoV with application on the network of rural roads, with the aim of protecting the lives of people and animals, as well as the protection of the property of drivers. MOD depends on timely detection of LMOs, speed of data processing, and rapid delivery of data, which is presented through a model for data collection, processing, and distribution. RSU-to-vehicle latency is crucial for timely driver-vehicle response to avoid a life-vehicle collision (LVC). However, latency was not considered in the research, but could be considered in future research. The system instead of PIR sensors, can include different types of sensors and technologies, which can also provide excellent results in data collection and processing. Internet of Vehicle Moving Objects Detection System for the rural road networks has advantages and disadvantages. The advantage of the system is scalability. The system can be adapted to vehicle models with built-in smart systems to support multimedia services. The disadvantage of the system is that in order to install RSU in the network of rural roads, satisfactory infrastructural solutions must be sought.

The large number of traffic accidents worldwide caused by LMO and the protection of people and animals and property are a challenge for further research. In further research, it is possible to consider the advantages of machine learning approaches in the form of dynamic prediction of the risk of traffic accidents caused by LMO - especially including the temporal distribution of data. These approaches can be helpful for future notifications, driver alerts, autonomous vehicle management and road safety management on a global scale.

References

1. Kämmerle, J.-L., Brieger, F., Kröschel, M., Hagen, R., Storch, I., Suchant, R.: Temporal patterns in road crossing behaviour in roe deer (Capreolus capreolus) at sites with wildlife warning reflectors. PLoS ONE **12**, e0184761 (2017). https://doi.org/10.1371/journal.pone.0184761
2. Gagnon, J.W., Theimer, T.C., Dodd, N.L., Manzo, A.L., Schweinsburg, R.E.: Effects of traffic on elk use of wildlife underpasses in Arizona. J. Wildl. Manag. **71**, 2324–2328 (2007). https://doi.org/10.2193/2006-445
3. Garriga, N., Franch, M., Santos, X., Montori, A., Llorente, G.A.: Seasonal variation in vertebrate traffic casualties and its implications for mitigation measures. Landsc. Urban Plan. **157**, 36–44 (2017). https://doi.org/10.1016/j.landurbplan.2016.05.029
4. Pagany, R., Dorner, W.: Do crash barriers and fences have an impact on wildlife–vehicle collisions?—an artificial intelligence and GIS-based analysis. ISPRS Int. J. Geo-Inform. **8** (2019). https://doi.org/10.3390/ijgi8020066
5. van der Ree, R., Jaeger, J.A.G., van der Grift, E.A., Clevenger, A.P.: Effects of roads and traffic on wildlife populations and landscape function. Ecol. Soc. **16** (2011)
6. Stjepanović, A., Ćurguz, Z., Kostadinović, M., Jotanović, G., Stojčić, M., Kuzmić, G.: Pedestrian detection in automated vehicles using ultrasonic and passive infrared sensors. Presented at the 21st International Symposium INFOTEH- JAHORINA , Jahorina March 16 (2022)
7. Chamorro, A., Tighe, S.: Development and application of a sustainable management system for unpaved rural road networks. Transp. Res. Rec. **2673**, 891–901 (2019). https://doi.org/10.1177/0361198119864908
8. Rajović, G., Bulatović, J.: Rural roads-issues and development: overview. J. Manage. Account. Stud. **4**, 70–77 (2016)
9. Krupowicz, W., Sobolewska-Mikulska, K., Burinskienė, M.: Modern trends in road network development in rural areas. Baltic J. Road Bridge Eng. **12**, 48–56 (2017)
10. Zhu, M., Wang, Z., Cui, H., Yao, S.: Rural road network planning based on 5g and traffic big data. J. Adv. Transp. **2022**, 1991757 (2022). https://doi.org/10.1155/2022/1991757
11. Richter, T., Ruhl, S., Ortlepp, J., Bakaba, E.: Causes, consequences and countermeasures of overtaking accidents on two-lane rural roads. Transport. Res. Procedia **25**, 1989–2001 (2017). https://doi.org/10.1016/j.trpro.2017.05.395
12. Jiménez, F., Naranjo, J.E., Anaya, J.J., García, F., Ponz, A., Armingol, J.M.: Advanced driver assistance system for road environments to improve safety and efficiency. Transport. Res. Procedia **14**, 2245–2254 (2016). https://doi.org/10.1016/j.trpro.2016.05.240
13. Dhanush, V.V.S., Reddy, T.S.K., Charan, M.S., Priya, K.H.: IoT based system for detecting and monitoring automobile accidents. Int. Res. J. Modern. Eng. Technol. Sci. **04**, 2029–2039 (2022)

14. Kouonchie, P.K.N., Oduol, V., Nyakoe, G.N.: Roadside units for vehicle-to-infrastructure communication: an overview. Presented at the Proceedings of the Sustainable Research and Innovation Conference (2022)
15. Mekala, M.S., et al.: Deep learning-influenced joint vehicle-to-infrastructure and vehicle-to-vehicle communication approach for internet of vehicles. Expert. Syst. **39**, e12815 (2022). https://doi.org/10.1111/exsy.12815
16. Pagany, R.: Wildlife-vehicle collisions - Influencing factors, data collection and research methods. Biol. Cons. **251**, 108758 (2020). https://doi.org/10.1016/j.biocon.2020.108758
17. Ma, H., Pljonkin, A., Singh, P.K.: Design and implementation of Internet-of-Things software monitoring and early warning system based on nonlinear technology **11**, 355–363 (2022). https://doi.org/10.1515/nleng-2022-0036
18. Wang, S., Wang, B., Wang, S., Tang, Y.: Feature channel expansion and background suppression as the enhancement for infrared pedestrian detection. Sensors **20** (2020). https://doi.org/10.3390/s20185128
19. Anson, G.A.J., Huplo, K.C.T., Marin, M.A.V., Rivera, J.A.C., Pinili, M.V.M., Dr. Eric, B.: Blancaflor: TAOAID: pedestrian assistance using car motion detection system. In: Proceedings of the International Conference on Industrial Engineering and Operations Management. pp. 706–714. Nsukka, Nigeria (2022)
20. Saeidi, M., Arabsorkhi, A.: A novel backbone architecture for pedestrian detection based on the human visual system. Vis. Comput. **38**, 2223–2237 (2022). https://doi.org/10.1007/s00371-021-02280-6

Sustainable Communications and Computing Infrastructures

Photogrammetry in a Virtual Environment

Jakub Kaščak[1]([✉]) [iD], Marek Kočiško[1] [iD], Rebeka Tauberová[2] [iD], Stella Hrehová[2] [iD], and Justyna Trojanowska[3] [iD]

[1] Faculty of Manufacturing Technologies with a Seat in Prešov, Department of Computer-Aided Manufacturing Technologies, Technical University of Košice, Štúrova 31/A, 080 01 Prešov, Slovak Republic
{jakub.kascak,marek.kocisko}@tuke.sk

[2] Faculty of Manufacturing Technologies with a Seat in Prešov, Department of Industrial Engineering and Informatics, Technical University of Košice, Bayerova 1, 080 01 Prešov, Slovak Republic
{rebeka.tauberova,stella.hrehova}@tuke.sk

[3] Faculty of Mechanical Engineering, Department of Production Engineering, Poznan University of Technology, Piotrowo Street 3, 61-138 Poznan, Poland
justyna.trojanowska@put.poznan.pl

Abstract. The use of photogrammetry is currently considered one of the most time-efficient ways of digitizing objects, the preparation of which does not require a high level of accuracy. It is generally known that the digitization of objects is demanding in terms of hardware and software, and it also requires a certain amount of skills and knowledge of this technology. Therefore, the use of photogrammetry in virtual environments makes the entire process significantly more efficient because it facilitates the process of digitizing physical objects from a digital model. This is achieved by the creation of an object, such as a classroom, that was used in this case by taking the photographs required during the scanning process to capture all the characteristics of the object. These images are combined to create a 3D model of the object that can be used in various software. A large number of special software can process point clouds and greatly simplify the reconstruction of objects. In this case, Rhinoceros software and its other extensions are used. Their combination enables the reconstruction of this data on an arbitrary scale using a VR headset.

Keywords: Virtual Reality · Reverse Engineering · CAD Modeling · Virtual Room · Education · Photogrammetry

1 Introduction

Virtual environment or interactive education in a virtual environment was a relatively significant trend due to the events of the past years. Since some parts of educational processes follow this trend and enrich it with new possibilities, even nowadays we quite often encounter the so-called virtual rooms. The presented article responds to this trend

© ICST Institute for Computer Sciences, Social Informatics and Telecommunications Engineering 2024
Published by Springer Nature Switzerland AG 2024. All Rights Reserved
D. Perakovic and L. Knapcikova (Eds.): FABULOUS 2023, LNICST 542, pp. 63–73, 2024.
https://doi.org/10.1007/978-3-031-50051-0_5

and presents the possibilities of digitizing objects, or digitalization of large-scale objects like a whole classroom or laboratory, and the creation of a virtual twin in which several users can participate in the educational process or other types of courses. In the first phase, elements of reverse engineering were implemented in the virtual reality (VR) environment to streamline the process necessary for the digitization of objects, in this case, the entire room. The purpose of this initiative was to create the so-called virtual laboratory, i.e. a virtual space that can serve as a tool used for distance education. For this purpose, a series of software and hardware solutions were used, which are part of the equipment of the faculty and are currently becoming relatively available and widespread in the commercial area as well.

1.1 Photogrammetry and Its Current State

Photogrammetry is a process of taking precise images of an object or scene from many different angles. Photogrammetry is widely used in a variety of industries, such as automotive manufacturing and product development. The data can be collected from both real objects and from models or prototypes manufactured using rapid prototyping technologies [1]. The data can then be used to create a 3D model of the object that can be analyzed and optimized for various purposes. Image-based modelling has emerged as a popular technique for generating 3D digital representations of objects or scenes. It typically involves collecting images of the object or scene from different viewpoints and then using computer algorithms to merge the multiple images to form a complete 3D model [2]. An example of this process can be seen in Fig. 1.

Fig. 1. Demonstration of digitization of interiors and objects [2]

Using this method, it is possible to create a highly accurate representation of the object or scene. However, it is also a computationally intensive process and requires a large amount of processing power to perform image merging accurately [3]. Currently, the use of Unmanned aerial vehicles (UAVs) in the field of reverse engineering is a fairly big trend. Especially when it comes to the digitization of exteriors and historical monuments. The use of devices such as lidar, or various types of videogrammetry and photogrammetry is currently on the rise. On the following Table 1 we can see selected types of available software, which are used for the aforementioned video or photogrammetry purposes.

Table 1 . General information on photogrammetry tools and techniques [3].

S No	Name	Developer	Mode of Operation	Free/Paid
1.	Python Photogrammetry Toolbox	Pierre Moulon, Alessandro Bezz/ Code provided by steve-vincent (GitHub)	Aerial, Close-Range	Free
2.	3DF Zephyr	3DFlow	Aerial, Close-Range	Free/Paid (Paid for more than 50 images)
3.	WebODM	OpenDroneMap	Aerial	Paid
4.	Agisoft Metashape	Agisoft LLC.	Aerial, Close-Range	Paid
5.	RealityCapture	Capturing Reality/ Epic Games	Aerial, Close-Range	Paid
6.	ReCap Pro	Autodesk	Aerial, Close-Range	Paid (provides free educational license)
7.	PhotoModeler	Eos Systems Inc.	Aerial, Close-Range	Paid
8.	SOCET GXP	BAE Systems	Aerial, Satellite	Paid

As mentioned in the publication "Evaluation of Photogrammetry Tools following Progress Detection of Rebar towards Sustainable Construction Processes" by A.H. Qureshi, 2022, not all available photogrammetry software achieves the expected results. For this purpose, several types of available software were selected from Table 1, and a series of measurements and data processing was subsequently performed. For this purpose, a model was used, which can be seen in Fig. 3. The image also shows the result in the form of a processed point cloud, which is usable in the next process [3].

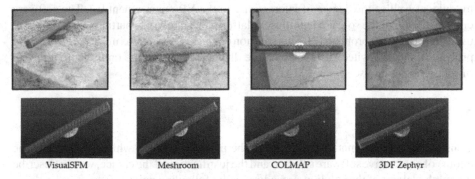

VisualSFM   Meshroom   COLMAP   3DF Zephyr

Fig. 2. The level of data processing from photogrammetry with different software [3]

Based on the results of the aforementioned analyzes and the rate of data processing, the 3DF Zephyr software was chosen for this article. In the area of data processing, intuitive software control, and the ability to supplement details with additional photos, it demonstrated superior and user-friendly properties [5].

The next step in this process is to digitize the input data in another series of software. For this purpose, based on the previous experiences mentioned in the publications "Virtual reality and its possible integration into the process of distance learning focused on technically oriented subjects" E. Franas, 2021, we can build on the already existing solution implemented using Rhinoceros and Mindesk software.

Fig. 3. The user interface of the Mindesk (Rhinoceros) software in a virtual environment [4]

As the presented publication states, the use of such a software solution allows us several solutions. The first is importing the required data formats [5]. Working with a cloud of points, creating planes, and surfaces, or working with a mesh is characteristic of this kind of software. In the second phase, it is necessary to state that this process takes place thanks to the Mindesk plugin simultaneously in CAD, and also a VR environment. By simply changing the input devices respectively keyboard and mouse for a VR Headset, the user can participate in a specific solution on a real scale and with full VR support. The third phase is the possibility to interactively intervene in this process through standard input devices and thus increase the degree of achieved accuracy of the reconstructed models, as well as the degree of interactivity in the VR environment [6]. The software enables the use of the so-called multiuser platform that allows the participation of several users in solving one problem [7]. This solution enables interventions in the reconstruction process of other "invited" users, which are displayed in real-time on the output device of all participating users.

2 Methodology

Considering the information presented in the previous chapter, which is related to the choice of an effective software solution and the justification of the choice, we can describe the methodology of the solution procedure in the following points:

- Creation of photo- documentation of individual parts of the VR classroom.
- Importing the obtained photos into the photometric software and creating a series of files containing information about the so-called point clouds.
- Importing the acquired data into Rhinoceros software and subsequent reconstruction of objects in the VR environment of one of his plugins called Mindesk.

- Reconstruction of partial scans of the classroom and their subsequent connection into one unit.
- Use of the Mindesk software interface, which allows connecting more users to the virtual environment.
- Creation of a virtual clone of the laboratory, also suitable for a virtual form of education.

As can be seen from the previous information, it is expected that such a solution will ultimately enable more than just the reconstruction of objects within the VR environment [9]. Due to the already mentioned interactivity of the environment with several users, in the case of reconstruction of objects, manipulation of virtual models, and full interactivity of the virtual environment, there is an opportunity to create and use a fully interactive VR room [10]. The use of such an environment in combination with available VR equipment can have a relatively large impact on further increasing the level of distance education.

2.1 Data Collection

The quality, level of processing, and accuracy achieved during data collection are practically the most important part of the entire process in this regard. Making a sufficient amount of photo documentation that captures as many details and views as possible is a key factor in this case [11].

In the first phase, the classroom as a whole was photographed using a 360° camera of the Fly 360 type, (Fig. 4b). The images from this process were subsequently supplemented with photo documentation created by the Canon EOS 2000D device, (Fig. 4c). For the digitization of objects in the virtual environment, the HTC Vive Pro 2 device was used in the final phase, which can be seen in Fig. 4a.

Fig. 4. Devices used (a- HTC Vive Pro2, b- Fly 360 camera, c- Canon EOS 2000D) [12]

The collection of data for the digitization of the model was quite simple. It consisted in placing the 360° camera in a suitable place to create a panoramic image that can capture the largest possible area of the digitized space. [13] Subsequently, these panoramic images were supplemented with detailed images created by a DSLR camera. All this collected data is imported into the Zephyr software.

As already mentioned, digitization using photogrammetry is undemanding in terms of the skill requirements of the implementer [14]. Compared to other equipment for digitization, which often requires e.g. treatment of glossy surfaces, use of position marks or other manual skills, using the camera is a relatively simple matter [15]. The negative side of this process is the relatively low geometric accuracy of digitized objects, as we can see in Fig. 2. However, this was trivial in the case of digitizing the room and not the functional components.

2.2 The Process of Creating a Virtual Room

After the successful creation of a cloud of points in the specialized software, this data was processed in the programs Rhinoceros and its Mindesk plugin. The Rhinoceros software and its plugins fulfil 3 basic conditions that are necessary for the successful creation of a functional version of the digital model.

First of all, as we can see in Fig. 5, Rhinoceros software allows importing and working with point clouds. This type of data is essential for the reconstruction of digitized objects. In Fig. 5 we can see the addition of data to the panoramic image, respectively photos that the comprehensive shot could not capture. This data is later added to the process and thus allows for capturing digitized objects with a higher degree of detail.

Fig. 5. Preview of the first part of the digitized classroom

The second important part is its plugin called Mindesk. This enables the import of this data into a virtual environment and the modification of CAD functions to suit the specific type of reconstructed parts. Using the HTC VIVE device and its full compatibility with the used software, it is possible for the user to fully immerse himself in the virtual space and work on the reconstruction on a 1:1 scale. The view of the user in VR and the palette and the reconstruction of simpler parts can be seen in Fig. 6.

Fig. 6. Point cloud import into the CAD and VR part of the software

3 Results

As c seen in Fig. 7, the drivers allow both a preview of the interface of the Grasshopper plugin functions, the use of the basic palette of CAD tools, and self-created functions that facilitate work in solving specific problems.

All these mentioned functions and the use of a VR headset require a certain amount of manual skills. Even after they were achieved, there were shortcomings and inaccuracies during modeling in CAD environment, which correlate with the already mentioned geometric deviations caused by digitization through photogrammetry.

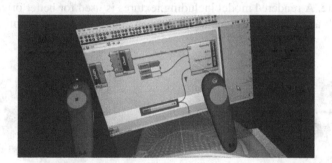

Fig. 7. Demonstration of editing the optimized tool palette

In Fig. 8, we can observe the work performed by the user in the VR environment in real-time and edit the CAD functions used by him to make the reconstruction process as efficient as possible. As we can see Fig. 8 also captures a preview of the tool palette that is available to the user in a virtual environment. This palette contains the basic CAD functions of Rhinoceros software. Its advantage is the possibility of modification, addition, or removal of functions due to the nature of the work performed by the user. Another advantage is full access to the Grasshopper plugin, also supported in the VR environment. This subsequently enables the creation of new functions, their combination, or the use of other generative algorithms. They enable a significant streamlining of work, especially in an environment with repetitive tasks.

Fig. 8. Demonstration of work in a virtual environment

It must be emphasized that working with a VR device and in a VR environment is difficult, less accurate compared to other input devices, and requires a certain form of skills that the user must acquire during this process. After literally getting used to using an alternative type of equipment, the reconstruction process becomes intuitive and the work efficiency is relatively high. Despite the possibilities of using different types of scales for digital models, this process cannot be considered sufficiently accurate, even in the case of data obtained by technologies other than photogrammetry. In Fig. 9 we can see the gradual reconstruction of the object as it is displayed in the CAD interface of the software. A rendered model including textures is used for better orientation. All data in the VR and CAD environment are updated in real-time for all connected users.

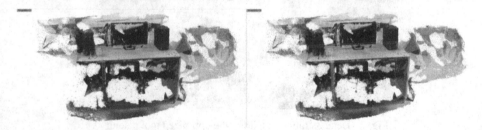

Fig. 9. Display of the rendered model and reconstruction progress in the CAD environment

As already mentioned, renovations and getting used to the new control method take quite a lot of time in the initial stages [17]. More than once it is necessary to supplement the VR activity with individual steps in the CAD interface. After getting used to the new way of controlling, the first advantages of its use appear. The possibility of being "directly in the process" is invaluable, and the already-mentioned support by the plugin for generating 3D algorithms significantly simplify the process itself. Figure 9 shows us a partial reconstruction of the digitized object.

Regarding digitization as such, it is necessary to point out that all achievements of modern CAD modelling apply and work in the VR environment. Using constraints, capturing points, and working with surfaces are part of the functions that are fully available in this environment [18].

4   Conclusion

The overview article informatively describes the current state of software solutions and the possibilities of implementing elements of reverse engineering in a virtual environment. An illustrative example describes the procedure and possibilities for solving the problem of digitizing the laboratory room and points out other possibilities of such a digitized room as part of the educational process. Figure 10 represents the resulting model of a digitized room, which is the result of the reconstruction of digital objects in a virtual environment.

The article describes the process of digitizing models using photogrammetry and subsequent data processing in its entirety. It thus informs about the possibilities of working with this kind of hardware and software equipment, its advantages and disadvantages, and the subsequent possibilities of using this procedure also in the distance form of education.

Fig. 10. The resulting model after complete reconstruction

Considering the number of actions that accompanied the demonstration and were implemented in the VR, in the end, it is possible to draw several strong arguments that in the future can significantly influence the use of these technologies to improve specific parts of education. The first of them is the possibility of reconstruction of digitized objects in VR. It can have e.g. a great advantage with the Building Information Modeling (BIM) method. Placing the design implementer directly in the designed laboratory, robotic workplace, etc. can significantly affect the entire design. The second is the fact that, after the situations of previous years, the distance form of education has become an inseparable part in many aspects. Also, it is necessary to pay increased attention to this area and try to improve the quality of this form of education.

The third and not the last advantage is the use of the platform for connecting more users, schematically the principle of operation of this connection can be seen in Fig. 11. The creation of such a digital space within education and the use of available VR devices can contribute to a significant streamlining of the entire educational process. It is known from the preparation process that all objects placed in VR are fully interactive with all users. In the case of e.g., training in the field of machining processes thus provides an opportunity for detailed display and interaction with digital copies of machining centres without endangering the health or disrupting production processes.

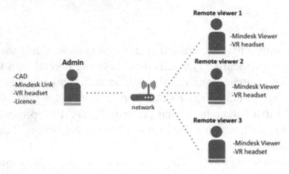

Fig. 11. Schematic display of interaction between multiple users [16]

Acknowledgements. This work was supported by the projects VEGA 1/0268/22, KEGA 004TUKE-4/2022 granted by the Ministry of Education, Science, Research and Sport of the Slovak Republic.

References

1. Li, Q., Huang, H., Yu, W., Jiang, S.: Optimized views photogrammetry: precision analysis and a large-scale case study in Qingdao. IEEE J. Select. Top. Appl. Earth Observations Remote Sens. **16**, 1144–1159 (2023)
2. Top 8 Best Photogrammetry Software. https://manufactur3dmag.com/top-8-best-photogram metry-software-free-paid/. Accessed 28 Feb 2021
3. Qureshi, A.H., et al.: Evaluation of photogrammetry tools following progress detection of rebar towards sustainable construction processes. Sustainability **15**(1), 21 (2023)
4. Franas, E., Kočiško, M., Kaščak, J., Hlavatá, S., Vodilka, A.: Virtual reality and its possible integration into the process of distance learning focused on technically oriented subjects. In: IOP Conference Series: Materials Science and Engineering, vol. 1199, no. 1, p. 012028. IOP Publishing (2021)
5. Jasińska, A., Pyka, K., Pastucha, E., Midtiby, H.S.: A simple way to reduce 3D model deformation in smartphone photogrammetry. Sensors **23**(2), 728 (2023)
6. Buń, P., Trojanowska, J., Rewers, P.: VR and AR in lean manufacturing classes. In: Trojanowska, J., Ciszak, O., Machado, J.M., Pavlenko, I. (eds.) MANUFACTURING 2019. LNME, pp. 342–351. Springer, Cham (2019). https://doi.org/10.1007/978-3-030-18715-6_29
7. Costa, R., Neves, J., Novais, P., Machado, J., Lima, L., Alberto, C.: Intelligent mixed reality for the creation of ambient assisted living. In: Neves, J., Santos, M.F., Machado, J.M. (eds.) EPIA 2007. LNCS (LNAI), vol. 4874, pp. 323–331. Springer, Heidelberg (2007). https://doi.org/10.1007/978-3-540-77002-2_27
8. Knapčíková, L., Husár, J., Behúnová, A., Hrehová, S.: Augmented reality as a tool of increasing of competitiveness of enterprise. In: Perakovic, D., Knapcikova, L. (eds.) FABULOUS 2021. LNICSSITE, vol. 382, pp. 337–349. Springer, Cham (2021). https://doi.org/10.1007/978-3-030-78459-1_25
9. Esteves, M., Miranda, F., Machado, J., Abelha, A.: Mobile collaborative augmented reality and business intelligence: a system to support elderly people's self-care. In: Rocha, Á., Adeli, H., Reis, L.P., Costanzo, S. (eds.) WorldCIST'18 2018. AISC, vol. 747, pp. 195–204. Springer, Cham (2018). https://doi.org/10.1007/978-3-319-77700-9_20

10. Kaufmann, H.: Collaborative augmented reality in education. Inst. Softw. Technol. Interact. Syst. Vienna University of Technology, 2–4 (2003)
11. Lazár, I., Husár., J.: Validation of the serviceability of the manufacturing system using simulation. J. Effi. Responsib. Educ. Sci. 5(4), 252–261 (2012)
12. Mota, J.M., Ruiz-Rube, I., Dodero, J.M., Molina, D.: Learning augmented reality in the classroom. In: ICERI2017 Proceedings, pp. 8579–8582 (2017)
13. Yusuf, Y.A.M., Ismail, I., Hamzah, W.M.A.F.W., Amin, M.A.M., M. Arsad, M.A.: A literature review on mobile augmented reality in education. In: Alareeni, B., Hamdan, A. (eds.) Innovation of Businesses, and Digitalization during Covid-19 Pandemic. ICBT 2021. Lecture Notes in Networks and Systems, vol. 488, pp. 875–888. Springer, Cham (2023). https://doi.org/10.1007/978-3-031-08090-6_56
14. Schramm, L.T., Hariharan, A., Götz, T., Fegert, J., Schmidt, A.P.: Facilitating mixed reality public participation for modern construction projects: guiding project planners with a configurator. In: Wölfel, M., Bernhardt, J., Thiel, S. (eds.) ArtsIT, Interactivity and Game Creation. ArtsIT 2021. Lecture Notes of the Institute for Computer Sciences, Social Informatics and Telecommunications Engineering, vol. 422, pp. 275–291. Springer, Cham (2021). https://doi.org/10.1007/978-3-030-95531-1_19
15. Ivanov, V., Pavlenko, I., Trojanowska, J., Zuban, Y., Samokhvalov, D., Bun, P.: Using the augmented reality for training engineering students. In: 4th International Conference of the Virtual and Augmented Reality in Education, VARE 2018, pp. 57–64 (2018)
16. Husár, J., Knapčíková, L., Hrehová, S.: Augmented reality as a tool of increasing the efficiency of RFID technology. In: Perakovic, D., Knapcikova, L. (eds.) FABULOUS 2021. LNICSSITE, vol. 382, pp. 401–414. Springer, Cham (2021). https://doi.org/10.1007/978-3-030-78459-1_30
17. Trojanowska, J., Kolinski, A., Galusik, D., Varela, M.L.R., Machado, J.: A methodology of improvement of manufacturing productivity through increasing operational efficiency of the production process. In: Hamrol, A., Ciszak, O., Legutko, S., Jurczyk, M. (eds.) Advances in Manufacturing. LNME, pp. 23–32. Springer, Cham (2018). https://doi.org/10.1007/978-3-319-68619-6_3
18. Bower, M., Howe, C., McCredie, N., Robinson, A., Grover, D.: Augmented reality in education–cases, places and potentials. Educ. Media Int. 51(1), 1–15 (2014)

Enhancing Circular Economy Using Expert Systems

Lucia Knapčíková[1]([✉]) [iD], Annamária Behúnová[2] [iD], Jozef Husár[1] [iD],
Rebeka Tauberová[1], and Matúš Martiček[1]

[1] Faculty of Manufacturing Technologies with a Seat in Prešov, Department of Industrial
Engineering and Informatics, The Technical University of Košice, Bayerova 1, 080 01 Prešov,
Slovak Republic
{lucia.knapcikova,jozef.husar,rebeka.tauberova}@tuke.sk,
matus.marticek@student.tuke.sk
[2] Faculty of Mining, Ecology, Process Control and Geotechnologies, Institute of Earth
Resources, Technical University of Kosice, Letna 9, 04200 Kosice, Slovak Republic
annamaria.behunova@tuke.sk

Abstract. An important measure of the success of the expert system's implementation is its users' acceptance. An expert system doesn't have to provide very good conclusions when its use is very complex and time-consuming both in learning and in use. From the user's point of view, it is important that working with the system is easy and easy to understand. It is appropriate for the system to be able to correct the most common user errors. It is necessary to note that expert systems can also be used for training new experts when workers are familiarized with evaluating input data and the possible conclusions that may result from them with the help of the explanatory mechanism of the system. We cannot get complete information to solve most problems. It remains only to fill in the information data gaps while considering the possibility of error. During processing, the effects of stored knowledge and probabilities are combined. In the post, the main problem was the determined amount of tyres provided to each driver for the race. The work deals with t collecting and processing data on the climate, the type of circuit and the subsequent use of this data in motorsport to reduce the number of tyres provided for the benefit of expert systems.

Keywords: Monitoring · Industry · Expert Systems · IoT · Tyres

1 Introduction

The tyre is a critical component of the automobile. Understanding and predicting its behaviour is one of the main keys to performance [1]. A motorsport tyre is designed to absorb and transmit energy in large quantities. The tire is light, strong, and, like every car component, works at the performance limits [2]. The modern tyre generates side loads in corners higher than at any other stage in the sport's history [1, 2].

D. Perakovic and L. Knapcikova (Eds.): FABULOUS 2023, LNICST 542, pp. 74–84, 2024.
https://doi.org/10.1007/978-3-031-50051-0_6

It carries enormous traction and braking loads and absorbs an extreme amount of radiant heat from carbon/carbon brake material systems. As part of the design, the tire generally has an operating duty cycle of 120–150 km. A motorsport tire has a relatively complicated structure, ensuring it can withstand a very high load in operation. The technologies used in its design and production are very advanced [3]. Each tire, including those used in motorsports, has its specific construction. The bottom part is called the bead, the reinforcing part of the tire that rests on the steel rim [3]. It is used for anchoring and ensures safe seating of the tyre on edge. Its core is formed by the heel cable, which is located in the heel. Its main function is strengthening and also ensures the tightness of the connection to the rim and the transmission of longitudinal forces [4]. The entire inner side of the tire is made up of a rubber layer, the main task of which is to prevent air from escaping from the inside of the tire, or in tubeless tyres it fulfils the role of the inner tube, as in the case of motorsport tyres. It is made mainly of butyl rubber compounds, which prevent the pressure from leaking from the tyres and ensure its optimal level [4, 5]. The sidewall is an integral part of every tire. It is the transitional part between the frame and the tread. The role of the bumper is to stabilize the track and increase the tyre's impact resistance. There are at least three buffer layers in each tire. Nowadays, they are mostly made of steel or other solid material. At the very top of the tire is the tread [6]. This part of the tire is in contact with the track all the time, which means that the secret of success and failure is hidden in this part of the tire. The tread compound varies with each type, but the properties of each compound determine how quickly the tire heats up and wears. The thickness also varies according to the type of hardness, but in general, a worn tire is about half a centimeter [7, 8].

1.1 The Circular Economy of Selected Materials in the Motorsport

The key property of tyres is grip - adhesion. It is the ability of two, mostly different materials to adhere to each other [8]. In the case of tyres and asphalt on the road, we can talk about dispersion adhesion, otherwise known as Van der Waals force, which works on the intermolecular attraction at the contact surfaces in the pores of the materials. On one side, there is a partially positive charge, and on the other, partially negative [4, 8]. During operation, the F1 tyre continuously absorbs and transfers kinetic, radiant and mechanical energy through the tire sidewall to the tread platform and vice versa. The tire is constantly heating, cooling, expanding and contracting [9]. When analyzing an F1 tire from a structural point of view, it is important to recognize that the structure is a composite matrix of different materials, the structural fibres and the binders that hold them together. The softest tyres from the SOFT series are among the fastest tyres in the world [10]. They are created for quick starts or, since they are the smallest compound, they can develop the best tap at the beginning. However, it is not due to adhesion. In this case, it is the temperature that is decisive. The softest tyres warm up the fastest, often after three or five laps, depending on where the race is held and the air and road temperatures, but they warm up on every circuit by the tenth lap. The tire has its ideal performance when it is heated to 90 °C−110 °C A driver can last a maximum of 30 laps on these tyres, but in most cases, the pit stop usually takes place between the 20th and 25th lap. Tyres have ideal performance between the tenth and fifteenth lap. If the tire overheats or is overloaded, of course, it loses its long-term properties, and with soft tyres it can be up to two seconds of power loss per lap, as they are adapted for a short period. So the maximum time is only 35–35 min.

Tyres one degree harder, but still relatively soft [11]. As Formula 1 requires one change of tyres during each race, MEDIUM tyres are often used as a second (or first) complementary compound to a harder or softer compound. The advantage is that they still heat up to the ideal operating temperature, 105 °C–135 °C. They can do it by the fifteenth round at the most. Opo wear sometimes occurs around 30–35 laps on warmer circuits, even earlier, but the tyres can last 40 laps. Again, the tread, the surface of the tire that is in contact with the road, constantly rubs and rubs, but MEDIUM tyres resist wear visibly better than SOFT tyres, which are visible even to the naked eye of the viewer on some circuits. The composition of this compound is adapted to suit most laps. Tyres last 55–65 min [11, 12]. The hardest and most consistent mixture can last even 70 min without any major problems (HARD). Of course, the performance is not always the same this time either. The tire is difficult to heat up. It often reaches its ideal temperature window, 110 °C–140 °C, only in the twentieth lap. At first glance, it may look like a big complication, but the tyres last almost 50 laps, so if the team chooses the right strategy, all the other teams will gradually change the tyres, and the Formula with these tyres can get a few rungs progressively ahead. The wear-in occurs around the fortieth lap, so the tire is in ideal performance for at least twenty laps [13, 14]. But what can be a problem if it is used at the wrong time or on the bad lap, during the warm-up, the competitor can lose a lot of time and positions that are difficult to catch up. Also, during the introduction, the rider must be careful when cornering and braking, as the tyres tend to slide.

Intermediates are a very interesting type of tyre. We do not know more species or types divided according to hardness or other properties. One single species with amazing properties. Their use is in moments when it is drizzling, light rain is falling on the track, or it is after rain, and the way is not yet dry, or even if there are only wet areas on it. SLICK tyres do not handle driving on water, aquaplaning occurs immediately after entering a wet place, and the car slides uncontrollably since there are no grooves on the tyres [8, 15]. Therefore, Intermediate tyres are used for these situations, with symmetrical grooves adapted to drain water. One tire can drain 30 L of water in 1 s at a speed of 300 km/h. The wear of the tyres is manifested primarily by the fact that the grooved part of the tread changes almost to a SLICK tyre. That is, if the track is completely dry after rain and the tyres already have grooves, they can function on a dry track as SLICK tyres for several laps. However, it is not advantageous in the long run, as they are slower than them.

Interestingly, the pit stop rule does not apply to these tyres [6, 16]. It means that if it rains during the entire race or if the race is shortened, for this reason, it is not necessary to replace the tyres, and they can be stripped down to the canvas, which is located under the tread. Tyres for heavy rain, as the name implies (FULL WET) [15, 17]. The deep asymmetric grooves of each tyre ensure that one tyre can drain up to 85 L of water in 1 s at a speed of 300 km/h. It may seem like an unimaginable amount, but in reality, it looks like a huge spray of water is created behind the Formula, which makes it impossible for the following rider to see. It is where the real riding prowess and anticipation of each rider's situation will be shown. It's really dangerous, so these tyres are rarely used, except when it starts raining during the race and looks like a short rain.

If it rains before the start, there is a high probability that the start will be postponed, the race will be cancelled completely, or several laps will be driven behind the Safety Car [17]. In general, the greatest risk of tire wear arises from so-called over braking. It is mostly the driver's fault, paid for by the loss of positions. The problem occurs during right-angled and sharp-angled turns and overtaking manoeuvres [12, 15]. The driver tries to brake as late as possible before the corner and to add gas as soon as possible. Still, if the driver attempts to overtake, does not estimate the distance and force, and starts braking too hard, a place is created on the tire where the materials under the tread are often visible. It's called a flat spot, and for the driver who made this mistake, it means that if it's on a large surface or deep, he has to head to the pits and change the tyres. It's not always necessary, but the tire will still lose a significant portion of its performance [17].

2 Definition of Expert Systems

They are systems that contain certain knowledge or issue a recommendation for a decision based on the entered data [14, 19]. They are artificial intelligence systems with a knowledge base for solving problems. They are called expert systems because they simulate the work of an expert. It is known from the history and origins of artificial intelligence that knowledge is the most important for expert systems [17, 18]. To this day, the information required by expert systems is still entered into computers manually. Although there are known machine learning methods, they cannot exactly imitate the process of human learning and thinking. Despite this, expert systems are already used in common practice today [20]. Figure 1 presents the basic structure of the expert system.

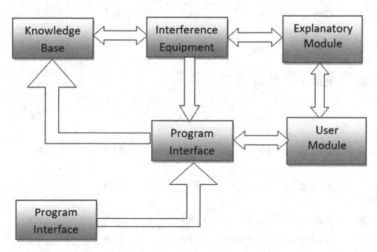

Fig. 1. Expert systems [Authors own processing]

3 Results and Discussion

For the two known types of laps, city and racing, the work focuses on conditions such as the probability of rain and the average temperature when races are held on the given lap [17]. The data needed to create the graphs are collected from statistical data from the past years and the race schedule for 2022. All these data are processed in the following table (Table 1).

Table 1. Climate data on individual circuits [Authors own processing, 2]

State/City	Lap type	Month	Average air temperature [°C]	Average humidity [%]	Rain forecast [%]
Bahrain, Sakhir	Racing	March	22	46,1	0
Saudi Arabia, Jeddah	City	March	26,2	46,7	0
Australia, Melbourne	City	April	22,7	61,4	14
Italy, Imola	Racing	April	14,2	61,6	12
USA, Miami	City	May	26,6	60,5	19
Spain, Barcelona	Racing	May	17,9	63	9
Monaco, Monaco	City	May	18,2	64,2	18
Azerbaijan, Baku	City	June	24,8	60,3	5
Canada, Montreal	City	June	19,2	57,5	28
Great Britain, Silverstone	Racing	July	13,5	65,2	4
Austria, Spielberg	Racing	July	21,6	60	34
France, Le Castellet	Racing	July	24,4	53,9	0
Hungary, Mogyoród	Racing	July	23,1	47,6	2
Belgium, Spa	Racing	August	16,1	69,1	26
Netherland, Zandvoort	Racing	September	14,8	75,8	27
Italy, Monza	Racing	September	19,3	58,4	7

(*continued*)

Table 1. (*continued*)

State/City	Lap type	Month	Average air temperature [°C]	Average humidity [%]	Rain forecast [%]
Russia, Sochi	Racing	September	21	66,5	14
Singapur, Marina Bay	City	October	28,5	72,6	11
Japan, Suzuka	Racing	October	17,6	68,5	23
USA, Austin	Racing	October	21,8	51,8	13
Mexico, Mexico city	Racing	October	16,6	54,1	13
Brazil, Sao paulo,	Racing	November	22,4	62,1	0
United Arab Emirates, Abu Dhabi	Racing	November	26,2	48	1

These data are analyzed together with data on the condition of the asphalt on the circuits, and then the Pirelli team selects the compounds most suitable for each circuit. However, the condition of the asphalt changes every year, or some laps are not used every year, so statistically we cannot determine the nature of the asphalt in advance before carrying out tests before the start of the season [2, 18, 20]. After choosing these three compounds, each team will determine its tire strategy.

The teams also consider other criteria, such as the effect of weather and climate, namely the length of the circuit, the number of laps and the effect of the asphalt on the tyres. Subsequently, the teams determine a strategy, most often chosen from three options. Data on circuits and strategies are processed in the following table (Table 2), where we also see the possible start on tyres in the last column. The table contains statistical data from previous years.

The strategies are repeated during the circuits, so all strategy options are listed in the table (Table 3), from which it is subsequently possible to create rules for strategy selection.

Table 2. Circuit parameters and possible tyre strategies [Authors own processing, 2]

State/City	Lap's length [km]	No. Round	Strategy a	Strategy b	Strategy c	Starting tyres
Bahrain, Sakhir	5,412	49	soft-hard-medium	soft-medium-hard	soft-medium-soft	SOFT
Saudi Arabia, Jeddah	6,174	50	medium-hard	medium-hard-medium	soft-hard	MEDIUM
Australia, Melbourne	5,303	58	soft-soft-medium	medium-soft	soft-hard	SOFT
Italy, Imola	4,909	63	medium-soft	soft-hard	medium-hard	MEDIUM
Spain, Barcelona	4,675	66	soft-medium	soft-medium-soft	soft-hard	SOFT
Monaco, Monaco	3,337	78	soft-medium	soft-hard	medium-soft	SOFT
Azerbaijan, Baku	6,003	51	soft-hard	medium-hard	soft-hard-soft	SOFT
Canada, Montreal	4,361	70	medium-hard	soft-hard	soft-medium-medium	SOFT
Great Britain, Silverstone	5,891	52	medium-hard	soft-medium-medium	soft-hard	SOFT
Austria, Spielberg	4,318	71	medium-hard-hard	medium-hard	hard-medium	MEDIUM
France, Le Castellet	5,842	53	medium-hard	hard-medium	hard-soft	HARD
Hungary, Mogyoród	4,381	70	medium-hard	soft-hard-medium	soft-hard	SOFT
Belgium, Spa	7,004	44	medium-hard	soft-hard	soft-medium	SOFT
Netherland, Zandvoort	4,259	72	soft-hard	medium-hard	soft-medium-soft	SOFT
Italy, Monza	5,793	53	medium-soft	soft-medium	medium-hard	MEDIUM
Russia, Sochi	5,848	54	medium-hard	hard-medium	medium-hard-medium	MEDIUM
Singapur, Marina Bay	5,063	61	soft-medium	medium-hard	soft-hard	SOFT
Japan, Suzuka	5,807	53	soft-medium	medium-soft	soft-soft-medium	SOFT
USA, Austin	5,513	56	medium-hard-hard	soft-hard-hard	medium-hard-medium	MEDIUM
Mexico, Mexico city	4,304	71	medium-hard	medium-hard-medium	medium-hard-hard	MEDIUM
Brazil, Sao Paulo,	4,309	71	medium-hard	medium-hard-soft	soft-hard	MEDIUM
United Arab Emirates, Abu Dhabi	5,281	58	medium-hard	soft-hard-medium	medium-hard-medium	MEDIUM

Table 3. Unification and designation of strategies [Authors own processing, 2]

Start probability/tyres	Description	Label
SOFT	soft - hard -medium	S1
	soft - medium	S2
	soft-hard	S3
	soft-medium-soft	S4
	soft-soft-medium	S5
	soft-hard-hard	S6
	soft-medium-hard	S7
	soft-hard-soft	S8
	soft-medium-medium	S9
MEDIUM	medium-soft	M1
	medium-hard-hard	M2
	medium-hard	M3
	medium-hard-medium	M4
	medium-hard-soft	M5
HARD	hard-medium	H1
	hard-soft	H2

3.1 Utilization of Acquired Data Using Expert Systems

By using filtering based on some of the columns in the above tables, it is possible to create a system that can be used to determine the choice of strategy [15, 19]. The parameters are circuit type, season, likely start on tyres, probability of rain and location and are marked as follows:

- Lap type: C – City, R – racing
- Season: SPRING (March, April, May), SUMMER (June, July, August), FALL (September, October, November), WINTER (December, January, February)
- Probable start on tyres: SOFT, MEDIUM, HARD
- Chance of rain: LOW (< = 10%), MEDIUM (11–18%), HIGH (>19%)
- Race venue

From these five criteria, a general notation is created, for example, as follows:
If C and SPRING and SOFT and LOW and PLACE ◊STRATEGY
In this way, it is possible to choose a strategy for each lap, e.g.:
R and SPRING and SOFT and LOW and BAHRAIN ◊S1 or S7 or S4
Subsequently, the team chooses the one that best suits the current situation on the circuit from these three strategies. All three strategies suitable for the race in Bahrain, where the track is 5.4 km long and runs 49 laps, take into account two pit stops because the circuit in Bahrain is treated with anti-sand substances on the track during the competition weekend. However, there is still some sand on the track.

Another criterion for choosing two pit stops is the difficulty of the track. Rather, it belongs to the technical, not very fast tracks, where tire wear in the turns is medium to high [2,22].

The S1 strategy, i.e. SOFT – HARD – MEDIUM, will be used in case the team wants to use and gain as much as possible at the start. Subsequently, sometimes by the 10th lap, they switch to HARD tyres, on which the rider can consistently last until approximately 35–40. Wheels and change to MEDIUM tyres in the second pit stop. In this case, it can be seen that the times driven on the tyres are short, also because the average air temperature in Bahrain is 22 °C and the road has an even higher temperature, so there is no problem with a long warm-up of the tyres. The S7 strategy, SOFT – MEDIUM – HARD, is different only in the order of the tyres. The S4, SOFT – MEDIUM – SOFT strategy may look unreliable at first glance, and it may seem that these sets will not be able to ride the entire race. Still, suppose the rider is in a position not to engage in aggressive battles and overtaking manoeuvres on the track. In that case, this strategy can ensure a safe and quickly arrive at the destination and get valuable points [2].

Another example can be the circuit in Brazil.

R and AUTUMN and MEDIUM and LOW and BRAZIL ◊C3 or C5 or S3

The Interlagos lap in Sao Paulo is known for its many challenging corners, elevation changes, rough surfaces and minimal room for error. These errors also include changing tyres at the wrong time.

The C3 strategy, MEDIUM–HARD, is effective as it is very consistent, and the track surface requires tyres that do not wear much and quickly. The C5 strategy, MEDIUM–HARD–SOFT, allows the driver to drive a fast lap on soft tyres at the end of the race or make a few more overtaking manoeuvres. The S3 strategy, SOFT–HARD, is probably the most effective, as the rider can secure a quick start and can drive most of the laps on HARD tyres if he can handle these tyres sensibly.

This tyre selection system can be used especially when choosing strategies for new circuits. In 2021, it raced in the Netherlands, in the city of Zandvoort, after several years, which means that strategy had to be chosen again, as the circuit was modified, new asphalt was laid, etc.

In 2022, a lap in the USA, Miami, was added to the calendar. Data that are known about the circuit are listed in the table (Table 4). We can see that the air temperature is quite high, and so is the probability of rain and the average humidity.

Table 4. Characteristics of the lap in the USA – Miami [Auhtors own processing, 2]

Country/City	Lap's type	Month	Lap's lenght [km]	Lap's No	Average air temperature [°C]	Average humidity [%]	Rain forecast [%]
USAMIAMI	City	May	5,41	57	26,6	60,5	19

It is possible to assume that the likely start will be on MEDIUM tyres, as asphalt temperatures can reach over 40 °C, which is disadvantageous for SOFT tyres at the beginning of the race. In some cases, the HARD compound can also be used for the start, but it will not be preferred due to the slow start and the driver may lose valuable positions in the first laps.

4   Conclusion

If it were possible, based on statistics, observation and expert systems, to determine possible tire strategies used on certain circuits, such quantities of tyres would not have to be offered for each driver or team. It would reduce the number of tyres that are absolutely destroyed after every competition weekend. An example can be the circuit in Saudi Arabia, where the probability of rain is 0%, so it is possible to consider light rain and heavy rain tyres unnecessary for this weekend. Of course, nature is unpredictable, so to be sure, it is advisable to leave one set of both types for both riders. Despite this, it is possible to save up to ten sets of tyres, which in total cost 25,200€, which we can save in just one competition weekend [9, 20]. Expert systems have one more important feature. It is an explanatory mechanism that, at any stage of task processing, can provide the user with information about what has already been inferred, what is the current goal of the inference (i.e., an explanation of "why the user was asked for this particular information") and how any of the conclusions of the expert system. The explanation mechanism is used very rarely during the operation of the expert system, but the feeling of its existence usually greatly increases the users' confidence in the system. It has an irreplaceable role in the system's design, modification, control and debugging.

Acknowledgement. This work was supported by the projects VEGA 1/0268/22, KEGA 038TUKE-4/2022 granted by the Ministry of Education, Science, Research and Sport of the Slovak Republic.

References

1. Peña Miñano, S., et al.: A review of digital wayfinding technologies in the transportation industry. In: Advances in Transdisciplinary Engineering. IOS Press BV, pp. 207–212 (2017)
2. Rusnakova, L.: A study of selected properties of tyres used in motor sport with regard to the economic and environmental impact on society, FVT TUKE (2022)
3. Nagyova, A., Pacaiova, H., Markulik, S., et al.: Design of a model for risk re-duction in project management in small and medium-sized enterprises. Symetry-Basel **13** (5), 763 (2021). https://doi.org/10.3390/sym13050763
4. Periša, M., Cvitić, I., Peraković, D., Husnjak, S.: Beacon technology for real-time in forming the traffic network users about the environment. Transport **34**, 373–382 (2019). https://doi.org/10.3846/transport.2019.10402
5. Mesaros, P., et al.: The impact of information and communication technology on cost reducing in the execution phase of construction projects. TEM J. **9**(1), 78–87 (2020)
6. Tran, H.Y., Hu, J.: Privacy-persevering big data analytics a comprehensive survey. Parallel distrib. Comput. **134**, 207–218 (2019)
7. Straka, M., Khouri, S., et al.: Utilization of computer simulation for waste separation design as a logistics system. Int. J. Simul. Model. **17**(4), 83–596 (2018). https://doi.org/10.2507/IJSIMM17(4)444

8. Walker, N.L., Williams, A.P., Styles, D.: Key performance indicators to explain energy and economic efficiency across water utilities and identifying suitable proxies. J. Environ. Manage. **169**, 1–10 (2020)

9. Meinig, M., Sukmana, M.I., Torkura, K.A., Meinel, C.J.P.C.S.: Holistic strategy-based threat model for organizations. Proc Comput Sci **151**, 100–107 (2019)

10. Gou, Z., Yamaguchi, S., et al.: Analysis of various security issues and challenges in cloud computing environment: a survey. In: Identity Theft: Breakthroughs in Research and Practice, pp. 221–247. IGI global (2017)

11. Periša, M., Kuljanić, T.M., Cvitić, I., Kolarovszki, P.: Conceptual model for informing user with innovative smart wearable device in industry 4.0. Wireless Netw. **27**(3), 1615–1626 (2019). https://doi.org/10.1007/s11276-019-02057-9

12. Rosová, A., et al.: Case study: the simulation modeling to improve the efficiency and performance of production process. Wirel. Netw. J. Mob. Commun. Comput. Inf. 1-10 (2020)

13. Olakanmi, O.O., Dada, A.: An efficient privacy-preserving approach for secure verifiable outsourced computing on untrusted platforms. Int. J. Cloud Appl. Comput. (IJCAC) **9**(2), 79–98 (2019)

14. Islam, M.A., Vrbsky, S.V.: Transaction management with tree-based consistency in cloud databases. Int. J. Cloud Comput. **6**(1), 58–78 (2017)

15. Singh, R., Davim, J.P.: Additive Manufacturing: Applications and Innovations, 1st ed.; CRC Press: Boca Raton, FL, USA, p. 280 (2018)

16. Song, D., Shi, E., Fischer I., Shankar, U.: Cloud data protection for the masses. Computer **45**(1), 39–45 (2012)

17. Hugos, M.H., Hulitzky, D.: Business in the Cloud: What Every Business Needs to Know About Cloud Computing. John Wiley & Sons, p. 139 (2010)

18. Prandi, C., Nunes, N., Ribeiro, M., Nisi, V.: Enhancing sustainable mobility awareness by exploiting multi-sourced data: the case study of the Madeira Islands. In: Sustainable Internet and ICT for Sustainability (SustainIT), Funchal, pp. 1–5 (2017)

19. Fiebig, S., Sellschopp, J., Manz, H., Vietor, T., Axmann, K., Schumacher, A.: Future challenges for topology optimization for the usage in automotive lightweight design technologies. In: Proceedings of the 11th World Congress on Structural and Multidisciplinary Optimization, Sydney, Australia, 7–12 June 2015; vol. 42, pp. 1–8 (2015)

20. Kotliar, A., et al.: Ensuring the economic efficiency of enterprises by multi-criteria selection of the optimal manufacturing process. Manag. Product. Eng. Rev. **11**(1), 52–61 (2020). https://doi.org/10.24425/mper.2020.132943

Digital Twin Ecosystem Built with PLM Software for Smart Factory

Jozef Husár[1]([⊠]) [iD], Stella Hrehova[1] [iD], Lucia Knapčíková[1] [iD], Jakub Kaščak[2] [iD], and Justyna Trojanowska[3] [iD]

[1] Faculty of Manufacturing Technologies with a Seat in Prešov, Department of Industrial Engineering and Informatics, Technical University of Košice, Bayerova 1, 080 01 Prešov, Slovak Republic
{jozef.husar,stella.hrehova,lucia.knapcikova}@tuke.sk
[2] Faculty of Manufacturing Technologies with a Seat in Prešov, Department of Computer Aided Manufacturing Technologies, Technical University of Košice, Štúrova 31, 080 01 Prešov, Slovak Republic
jakub.kascak@tuke.sk
[3] Faculty of Mechanical Engineering, Department of Production Engineering, Poznan University of Technology, Piotrowo Street 3, 61-138 Poznan, Poland
justyna.trojanowska@put.poznan.pl

Abstract. The article points to a new trend in the digital twins creation. It is the use of Product Lifecycle Management (PLM) software to create online twins, which are supported by simulation. Some definitions state that a digital twin is a virtual copy of a real object, but the digital twin ecosystem presented by us combines a virtual twin, simulation, Programmable Logic Controller (PLC), Industrial Internet of Thing (IIoT) and sensors. In the article, we gradually offer an overview of the digital twins development with the proposal of the Digital Twin Ecosystem, which we presented on a practical example in a case study. We describe the step-by-step process from component selection, gradual construction, assembly to final inspection and packaging. This entire technological procedure is transferred to the simulation tool Tecnomatix Plant Simulation and the steps for connecting the simulation with the digital twin created according to the experimental workplace are described step by step. The hardware and software requirements for the design of a complex interactive ecosystem are described in detail in the individual steps. In the conclusion, the benefits of the digital twin are highlighted and potential issues that need attention are outlined. In the article, we wanted to show the process of creating the Digital Twin Ecosystem and that it is becoming a promising tool for optimizing testing in smart companies

Keywords: Digital Twin · PLM software · IIoT gateway · ecosystem

1 Introduction

The term digital twin was first mentioned in the mid-90s of the 20th century. More than 30 years have passed since then, and the digital twin is once again remembered as a pioneer in the engineering-focused manufacturing industry [1]. At the beginning,

D. Perakovic and L. Knapcikova (Eds.): FABULOUS 2023, LNICST 542, pp. 85–98, 2024.
https://doi.org/10.1007/978-3-031-50051-0_7

the digital twin was aimed at creating a virtual twin of the production product and the production system, then the digital twin was applied to create a physical twin of the entire production line, and last but not least, entire production twins of complete production halls are created. However, the spectrum of use of the digital twin has not yet reached an end, and therefore another goal of the application of the digital twin is its application in the design of production and logistics systems [2]. The emergence of the digital pairs concept was related to the growth of production processes digitization, during which physical or analogue sources were replaced by informational or digital ones. Organizations follow the latest trends and try to identify how digital solutions can help them gain operational and strategic advantages. Until the second half of 2010, due to technical limitations, it was not possible to create computer systems that would replicate the properties of physical objects in almost real time [3]. And only a significant breakthrough in the digital technologies development, which made it possible to increase computing power and reduce the price of their use, allowed leading companies to combine information technology with operational processes and create digital duplicates of enterprises [4].

1.1 Literature Review

By some definitions, a digital twin is an integrated product model that is intended to reflect any manufacturing defects and it is constantly updated to include wear and tear over the life of its use [5]. Other definitions describe a digital twin as a sensor-based digital model of a physical object that simulates the object in an active setting. The digital twin is based on massive, cumulative measurement data in real time, in the real world, and across a range of dimensions. These measurements can create an evolving process or object profile of an in the digital world that can provide important insights into system performance, leading to actions in the physical world, such as changing the product design or manufacturing process [6]. As mentioned at the beginning of this article, the digital twin was created in the mid-1990s. But the evolution of the digital twin continued and gradually went through digital simulation, the Internet of Things, and today it is influenced by mixed reality and artificial intelligence, as you can see in Fig. 1 [7].

The digital twin will form an integral part of the production process in the future companies. In Fig. 2 we can see how production enterprises should change in terms of production enterprises time and strategies [8].

Manufacturing companies can be divided into four strategies types. In the past, the production company operated on a reactive strategy [9]. This strategy dealt with different types of problems only after something happened. The second type of strategy followed, namely the real-time strategy, which was able to solve problems in real-time production. The future of manufacturing companies is a predictive strategy, which is influenced by the Digital Twin and Big Data [10]. In addition to the digital twin, artificial intelligence has already been mentioned in the proactive strategy.

→ Production operations, new services, models			
→ R & D and engineering			
Mirror model of information	Digital simulation, 3D printing	Internet of Things services	Mixed reality and artificial intelligence
Digital twin as a concept R & D and engineering Dedicated workstations and servers	Collaboration, simulation and workflow in a global enterprise Browser and web access	Unification of data between the physical and virtual worlds IoT, Big Data, Cloud	Holography, virtual and augmented reality Artificial intelligence
1985 -2002 (18 years)	2003-2014 (12 years)	2014 – 2016 (3 years)	2017 - presentness
Powerful 3D modeling and analysis Programming of CNC machines and robots	Digital design, virtual assembly and simulation before physical deployment 3D printing	Fast feedback in design, production and operation products Expanded with digital services	Accompanying Interactions mixed human-machine collaboration Autonomy and self-healing

Fig. 1. The digital twin evolution

→ Time			
Past	Presence	Future	
First level	Second level	Third level	Fourth level
Reactive strategy	Real-time strategy	Predictive strategy	Proactive strategy
	Internet of things	Digital Twin Big Data	Artificial intelligence
			Digital Twin
			....
→ Difficulty and uncertainty			

Fig. 2. Development of management of the production company

The basic tasks of digital twin implementing include:

- Creation of 2D or 3D objects of the production product, system or production hall,
- Collecting real data from real production operations,
- Implementation of collected data into simulation software,
- Starting a simulation with continuous data evaluation,
- Verification of results and their implementation in a real production environment

When processing the first step of the digital twin implementation itself, we have to create 3D objects of the real operation in CAD software (AutoCAD, Process Designer, CEIT Table, etc.). The method of 3D the production operation scanning can also be used for an extensive type of objects [11]. After creating a physical twin in CAD software, we need to collect data from real production. At the beginning of the data processing cycle, the first step is the selection of the real part from which we want to create a digital twin. The following is data collection, which we can implement using various types of sensors, detectors and intelligent production systems. Intelligent production systems include e.g. RTLS system, which serves as monitoring of the movement of objects in a defined space in real time [12]. Wireless technologies are used for information transfer, be it Bluetooth, Wi-fi, Ultra-Wide-Band, Lora, Sigfox, etc. methods. The collected data are stored on a server (Cloud), which all production company employees have access to, where they can view and edit the data [13]. All data located in the Cloud is referred to as Big Data. These Big Data are finally transformed into simulation software, where they are then connected to physical objects that were created in 3D software. After the input data implementation, the simulation of the production process can be started, which will evaluate the required information about the production process state. The goal of the digital twin is actually to constantly evaluate the collected data, which are interconnected by simulation software and optimize them, so that they could then be converted back into the production process of real operation. This is a system for implementing a digital twin in a manufacturing enterprise [14].

2 Methodology

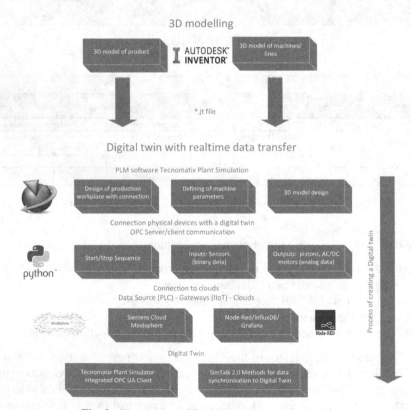

Fig. 3. The process of Digital twin ecosystem creating

The digital twin was initially created as a concept of creating a physical twin of a production product and a production system. In our article, we focused on the individual stages of creating a digital twin. The proposal consists of a model solution that we can apply to any smart enterprise. In the following figure, we have described the process of creating a digital twin in the PLM program Tecnomatix Plant Simulation [15] (Fig. 3).

2.1 Case Study

When we want to start creating an ecosystem, it is necessary to choose the object of our interest. The first step in creating a digital twin was the selection of an automated workplace and a product. We chose a cam switch as a product. It is intended for multiple switching in the main and auxiliary circuits. As motor switches, they are intended for direct on-line switching on and off of single-phase and three-phase motors. They can also be used as star-delta switches, reverse switches, motor switch pole switching, switches in auxiliary and measuring circuits. The advantages of cam switches are: good ability to switch on and off, electrical and mechanical endurance, small dimensions. Specifically, it is a cam switch S 16 16A/3P. It is a simple part consisting of 42 parts, of which 23 components are different [16] (Fig. 4).

Fig. 4. Cam switch S 16 16A/3P 0–1 level

After the product is defined, the next step is to define the automated workplace. In our case, it is a conveyor system with production equipment and an assembly workplace. This system is located on the grounds of the Technical University in Košice, Faculty of Production Technologies with headquarters in Prešov, and is a SmartTechLab laboratory for Industry 4.0 [17] (Fig. 5).

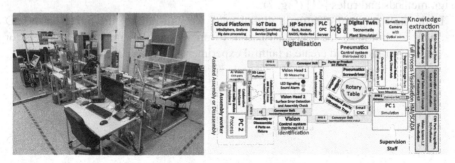

Fig. 5. Experimental automated workplace SmarTechLab for Industry 4.0

It is a partially automated line with integrated control systems. It is equipped with a robotic workplace and an assembly workplace with a collaborative robot. A partially automated assembly line is cost-effective and can later be integrated into a fully auto-mated line. The next step is to build a model of the given workplace and product. The cam switch can be seen in Fig. 6 on the left and on the right is a 3D model of the line constructed in Autodesk Inventor Professional version 2021 [18].

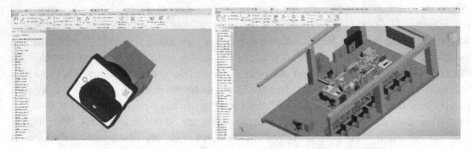

Fig. 6. 3D component model and experimental workplace

We will then transfer the 3D models to PLM (Product Lifecycle Management) soft-ware, which is used to manage and control the product life cycle. It is an integrated system that includes various functions such as product design, development, manufac-turing, delivery and maintenance. PLM software enables organizations to streamline and automate their product processes and improve their results in terms of quality, avail-ability and efficiency. PLM software can be used in conjunction with digital twins to improve product design and manufacturing. Digital twins can be integrated into PLM software and used to simulate and optimize product design and manufacturing processes. In this way, organizations can get a better idea of how the product will work in a real environment and what its features and performance will be [19]. The Tecnomatix Plant Simulation application (developed by Siemens PLM Software) will be used for our digital twin design. It is a simulation tool for a wide range of systems and processes [20]. First, we propose an informative model. Subsequently, we define the machines and equipment layout, we define the technological sequence of operations and times and assign methods and rules [21] (Fig. 7).

In the next stage of creating a digital twin, we will modify the model in the 2D interface, according to the real distribution of operations. We import 3D models for individual operations and create a faithful experimental workplace copy. See Fig. 8.

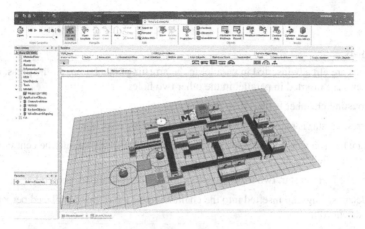

Fig. 7. Informative model in PLM tool

Fig. 8. 2D and 3D display of a digital twin

Following the creation of the model, the simulation will be set up and the individual steps necessary for the assembly of the cam switch will be defined. For easier assembly at the experimental workplace, we divided the individual activities into stages [22]. The first is the preparation of components from the incoming warehouse. An empty handling pallet arrives at the entrance, then it is fitted with a preparation in which all the plastic components necessary for assembly are placed. Next, the pallet with the preparation moves along the conveyor system and goes through the inspection process under the camera system [23]. It identifies the presence of individual components. After the inspection, the fitted pallet is moved to the assembly workplace. Manual assembly will take place here according to the Table 1.

Table 1. Cam switch assembly procedure

№	Procedure
1	Two nuts are already inserted in parallel in the arresting chamber under the press, and two set screws are inserted in parallel in the other two holes
2	The arresting chamber is placed on the rear attachment
3	The arresting star is placed in the centre of the arresting chamber
4	A square rod (on which there is already a locking ring) is inserted into the centre of the chamber through the arresting star
5	Next to the locking star, two locking rollers are inserted parallel to each other
6	Two detent springs are inserted into the chamber and each of them is placed perpendicular to the detent rollers
7	A stop plate is placed on top
8	Two stops and a washer are placed in the middle
9	The switching chamber is placed
10	Two cams are placed one on top of the other on the shaft
11	Two left and two right terminals are inserted in the corners of the switching chamber
12	The connector is inserted into the guide and the contact spring is placed in the centre of the connector
13	The lead with the connector and the contact spring is placed in the upper part of the switching chamber between the right and left terminals
14	The connector is inserted into the guide and the contact spring is placed in the centre of the connector
15	A lead with a connector and a contact spring is placed in the lower part of the switching chamber between the right and left terminals
16	The switching chamber is placed
17	Two cams are placed one on top of the other on the shaft
18	The right and left terminals are inserted into the upper part of the switching chamber
19	Two insulating tubes are placed on the set screws (through the holes in the switching chamber)
20	The connector is inserted into the guide and the contact spring is placed in the centre of the connector
21	A guide with a connector and a contact spring is inserted between the terminals
22	The switching chamber is closed by the plastic lid of the cam switch
23	Nut washers and two nuts are inserted
24	Nuts are screwed in
25	A type label is affixed to the arrester chamber
26	The contacts are tight

This entire assembly process takes about 4 min. By using assisted assembly using the ABB YUMI collaborative robot, we can shorten this process to 3 min. After the final assembly, the transfer of the cam switch to the pallet for output inspection is ensured. After the functionality is tested, the product is moved to the packaging and to the output warehouse [24] (Fig. 9).

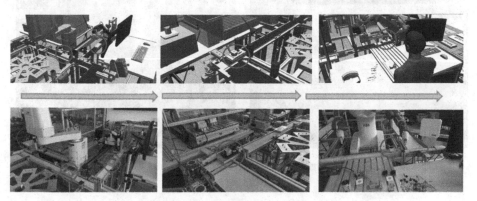

Fig. 9. Digital and physical model

3   Results

An improvement of the proposed approach is online optimization within the digital twin and synchronization with the real system. In the setup, the Python OPC UA server is responsible for transferring data from the digital twin to the PLC system. Thus, we can synchronize the simulation with the experimental workplace control system with online data recording (Fig. 10).

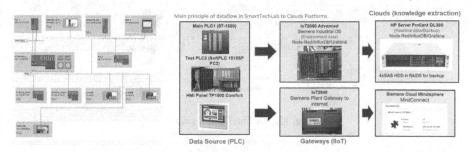

Fig. 10. TIA portal Software with OPC Server and Communication scheme of Data Storage

Data transfer to the cloud is ensured using IIoT gateways Siemens 2040 and 2050s with OPC server network interfaces. We use 2 communication gateways sending data to 2 clouds. One connection is freely available and works on the principle of connecting Node-Red/InfluxDb/Grafana with its own cloud storage on its own server storage. The second connection uses the cloud as service (CaaS) cloud platform through the MindConnect Mindsphere network unit. Any sensors can be connected to the proposed ecosystem if they are compatible with digital and analogue inputs/outputs from PLC/IIoT.

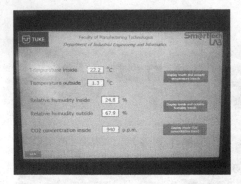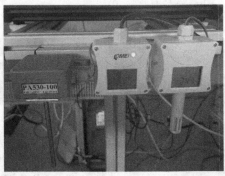

Fig. 11. Measured data and sensors

An example of measured data can be seen in Fig. 11. The OPC server must secure three communications: the first with the digital twin model, the second with cloud platforms and the third with the PLC system. For this reason, a customized OPC server written in the Python programming language was designed and implemented. To transfer data to the PLM system, we use:

- Tecnomatix Plant Simulator integrated OPC UA Client,
- SimTalk 2.0 Methods for data synchronisation to Digital Twin.

We set up a connection to the server and display the monitored data in a simulation environment (Fig. 12).

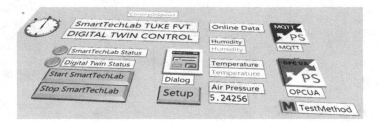

Fig. 12. Online Digital twin

This interface provides us data monitoring in the simulation tool. In our design, we observe:

- Start/Stop Sequence synchronization,
- Digital Twin Status,
- Inputs: sensors (Binary data, humidity, temperature, air pressure),
- Outputs: pneumatics pistons (Binary data), AC/DC motors (Analog data),

- 2D image/3D model data transfer: in development.

All these data are presented in online 3D models and also on cloud platforms. See Fig. 13.

Fig. 13. Measured data v prostredí Siemens MindSphere a Grafana SmartTechLab

The number of monitored data is unlimited depending only on the number of sensors connected to the experimental ecosystem. The presented article provides an insight into the complex system.

4 Conclusion

The proposed digital twin experimental system will serve for further research and also for educational purposes. The use of advanced technologies based on the concept of Industry 4.0/5.0 can help the development of new Smart enterprises. The designed and tested digital twin ecosystem using a PLM program with full data digitization provides a universal digital model that can be used as a template for real production of small and medium enterprises. In general, our proposal brings several benefits for the smart industry:

- Improvement of efficiency: Digital twins make it possible to simulate and analyze the operation of equipment and processes and find out where savings and efficiency improvements are possible.
- Cost reduction: Digital twins can help organizations reduce the cost of manufacturing and operating equipment, for example by helping to identify and eliminate unnecessary or inefficient processes.
- Quality improvement: Digital twins can help organizations improve the quality of their products and services by allowing them to simulate and test different scenarios to see how they will affect quality
- Improving security: Digital twins can help organizations improve the security of their devices and processes by allowing them to simulate and test different scenarios to see how they will affect security.
- Environmental improvement: Digital twins can help organizations improve their environmental impact by allowing them to simulate and test different scenarios to see what their environmental impact will be.

The implementation of digital twins in production is a necessary condition of product life cycle management (PLM) to ensure sustainable production. There are several trends in digital twins that could improve in the future:

- Integration with artificial intelligence: Digital twins can be integrated with artificial intelligence and machine learning, which would enable them to better predict and solve problems
- Uses in various industries: Digital twins can be used in various industries such as manufacturing, transportation, energy and healthcare, helping to improve efficiency and reduce costs.
- Greater integration with IoT: Digital twins can integrate with IoT devices, allowing them to better collect and process data about the devices and processes operation.
- Real-time use: Digital twins can be used for real-time monitoring and control of equipment and processes, helping to improve their efficiency and reduce costs
- Greater availability: Digital twins are becoming more accessible and affordable for smaller organizations, enabling them to improve their processes and reduce costs.

Our ecosystem was created in the Tecnomatix Plant Simulation environment and we applied it to the experimental workplace. It brings a lot of knowledge from IIoT issues, digitization and simulation. In the future, we want to focus on the emerging trend of industry 5.0 and connect our proposed ecosystem with collaborative robotics, artificial intelligence and product sustainability.

Acknowledgements. This work was supported by the Slovak Research and Development Agency under the contract No. APVV-19–0590, by the projects VEGA 1/0268/22, KEGA 038TUKE-4/2022 granted by the Ministry of Education, Science, Research and Sport of the Slovak Republic.
Paper is the result of the Project implementation: Development of excellent research capacities in the field of additive technologies for the Industry of the 21st century, ITMS: 313011BWN5, supported by the Operational Program Integrated Infrastructure funded by the ERDF."

References

1. Wagg, D.J., Worden, K., Barthorpe, R.J., Gardner, P.: Digital twins: state-of-the-art and future directions for modeling and simulation in engineering dynamics applications. ASCE-ASME J. Risk Uncertainty Eng. Syst. Part B-Mech. Eng. **6**(3), 030901 (2020). https://doi.org/10.1115/1.4046739
2. Saniuk, S., Saniuk, A., Cagáňová, D.: Cyber industry networks as an environment of the industry 4.0 implementation. Wireless Netw **27**, 1649–1655 (2021). https://doi.org/10.1007/s11276-019-02079-3
3. Pacaiova, H., Sinay, J., Markulik, S., et al.: Measuring the qualitative actors on copper wire surface. Measurement **109**, 359–365 (2017). https://doi.org/10.1016/j.measurement.2017.06.002
4. Kaščak, J., Husár, J., Knapčíková, L., Trojanowska, J., Ivanov, V.: Conceptual use of augmented reality in the maintenance of manufacturing facilities. In: Trojanowska, J., Kujawińska, A., Machado, J., Pavlenko, I. (eds.) MANUFACTURING 2022. LNME, pp. 241–252. Springer, Cham (2022). https://doi.org/10.1007/978-3-030-99310-8_19
5. Araújo, A.F., Varela, M.L.R., Gomes, M.S., Barreto, R.C.C., Trojanowska, J.: Development of an intelligent and automated system for lean industrial production, adding maximum productivity and efficiency in the production process. In: Hamrol, A., Ciszak, O., Legutko, S., Jurczyk, M. (eds.) Advances in Manufacturing. LNME, pp. 131–140. Springer, Cham (2018). https://doi.org/10.1007/978-3-319-68619-6_13

6. Knapčíková, L., Martiček, M., Husár, J., Kaščak, J.: Intelligent monitoring of loading and unloading process in enterprise transport system. In: Perakovic, D., Knapcikova, L. (eds.) Future Access Enablers for Ubiquitous and Intelligent Infrastructures. FABULOUS 2022. Lecture Notes of the Institute for Computer Sciences, Social Informatics and Telecommunications Engineering, vol. 445. Springer, Cham, (2022). https://doi.org/10.1007/978-3-031-15101-9_14

7. Tao, F., Zhang, H., Liu, A., Nee, A.Y.C.: Digital twin in industry: state-of-the-Art. IEEE Trans. Ind. Inform. **15**(4), 2405–2415 (2019). https://doi.org/10.1109/TII.2018.2873186

8. Arrais-Castro, A., Varela, M.L.R., Putnik, G.D., Ribeiro, R.A., Machado, J., Ferreira, L.: Collaborative framework for virtual organisation synthesis based on a dynamic multi-criteria decision model. Int. J. Comput. Integr. Manuf. **31**(9), 857–868 (2018). https://doi.org/10.1080/0951192X.2018.1447146

9. Lazar, I., Husar, J.: Validation of the serviceability of the manufacturing system using simulation. J. Effi. Responsib. Educ. Sci. **5**(4), 252–261 (2012). https://doi.org/10.7160/eriesj.2012.050407

10. Trojanowska, J., Pająk, E.: Using the theory of constraints to production processes improvement. In: Proceedings of the 7th International Conference of DAAAM Baltic Industrial Engineering, Kyttner R. [Ed.], Tallin, Estonia, vol. 1, pp. 322–327 (2010)

11. Behúnová, A., Husár, J., Behún, M., Knapčíková, L.: Manufacturing processes simulation of mass customization used by education of technical and economical subjects, In: 15th International Conference on Emerging eLearning Technologies and Applications (ICETA), Stary Smokovec, Slovakia, pp. 1–6, (2017). https://doi.org/10.1109/ICETA.2017.8102467

12. Varela, M.L., et al.: Collaborative paradigm for single-machine scheduling under just-in-time principles: total holding-tardiness cost problem. Manag. Product. Eng. Rev. **9**(1), 90–103 (2018). https://doi.org/10.24425/119404

13. Möller, J., Pörtner, R.: Digital twins for tissue culture techniques—concepts, expectations, and state of the art. Processes **9**, 447 (2021). https://doi.org/10.3390/pr9030447

14. Kaiblinger, A., Woschank, M.: State of the art and future directions of digital twins for production logistics: a systematic literature review. Appl. Sci. **12**, 669 (2022). https://doi.org/10.3390/app12020669

15. Pekarcikova, M., Trebuna, P., Kliment, M., Dic, M.: Solution of bottlenecks in the logistics flow by applying the kanban module in the tecnomatix plant simulation software. Sustainability **13**, 7989 (2021). https://doi.org/10.3390/su13147989

16. Kovbasiuk, K., Balog, M., Žídek, K.: Designing an automated assembly workplace in a simulation environment. In: Trojanowska, J., Kujawińska, A., Machado, J., Pavlenko, I. (eds.) MANUFACTURING 2022. LNME, pp. 35–49. Springer, Cham (2022). https://doi.org/10.1007/978-3-030-99310-8_4

17. Žídek, K., Piteľ, J., Adámek, M., Lazorík, P., Hošovský, A.: Digital twin of experimental smart manufacturing assembly system for industry 4.0 concept. Sustainability **12**, 3658 (2020). https://doi.org/10.3390/su12093658

18. Mascenik, J., Coranic, T.: Experimental determination of the coefficient of friction on a screw joint. Appl. Sci. **12**, 11987 (2022). https://doi.org/10.3390/app122311987

19. Antosz, K., Pasko, L., Gola, A.: The use of artificial intelligence methods to assess the effectiveness of lean maintenance concept implementation in manufacturing enterprises. Appl. Sci. **10**, 7922 (2020). https://doi.org/10.3390/app10217922

20. Straka, M., Hricko, M.: Software system design for solution of effective material layout for the needs of production and logistics. Wireless Netw. **28**, 873–882 (2022). https://doi.org/10.1007/s11276-020-02267-6

21. Husar, J., Knapcikova, L., Balog, M.: Implementation of material flow simulation as a learning tool. In: Ivanov, V., Rong, Y., Trojanowska, J., Venus, J., Liaposhchenko, O., Zajac, J.,

Pavlenko, I., Edl, M., Perakovic, D. (eds.) DSMIE 2018. LNME, pp. 33–41. Springer, Cham (2019). https://doi.org/10.1007/978-3-319-93587-4_4

22. Kujawińska, A., Diering, M.: The impact of the organization of the visual inspection process on its effectiveness. Int. J. Adv. Manuf. Technol. **112**, 1295–1306 (2021). https://doi.org/10.1007/s00170-020-06543-9

23. Kluz, R., Antosz, K.: Simulation of flexible manufacturing systems as an element of education towards industry 4.0. In: Trojanowska, J., Ciszak, O., Machado, J.M., Pavlenko, I. (eds.) MANUFACTURING 2019. LNME, pp. 332–341. Springer, Cham (2019). https://doi.org/10.1007/978-3-030-18715-6_28

24. Straka, M.: Design of a computer-aided location expert system based on a mathematical approach. Mathematics **9**, 1052 (2021). https://doi.org/10.3390/math9091052

Empirical Evaluations of Machine Learning Effectiveness in Detecting Web Application Attacks

Muhusina Ismail[1], Saed Alrabaee[1(✉)], Saad Harous[2],
and Kim-Kwang Raymond Choo[3]

[1] Department of Information Systems and Security, CIT, United Arab Emirates
University, Al Ain, UAE
{201990139,salrabaee}@uaeu.ac.ae
[2] Department of Computer Science, College of Computing and Informatics,
University of Sharjah, Sharjah, UAE
harous@sharjah.ac.ae
[3] Department of Information Systems and Cyber Security, University of Texas at
San Antonio, San Antonio, USA
raymond.choo@fulbrightmail.org

Abstract. Web applications remain a significant attack vector for cybercriminals seeking to exploit application vulnerabilities and gain unauthorized access to privileged data. In this research, we evaluate the efficacy
of eight supervised machine learning algorithms - Naive Bayes, Decision
Tree, AdaBoost, Random Forest, Logistic Regression, K-Nearest Neighbor (KNN), Support Vector Machine (SVM), and Artificial Neural Network (ANN) - in detecting and countering web application attacks. Our
results indicate that KNN and Random Forest classifiers achieve an accuracy rate of 89% and an area under the curve of 94% on the CSIC
HTTP dataset, a commonly used benchmark in the field. Meanwhile, the
Naive Bayes classifier proves the most efficient, taking the least computational time when differentiating between malicious and benign HTTP
requests. These findings may help direct future efforts towards more efficient, machine learning-driven defenses against web application attacks.

Keywords: Web Vulnerabilities · Web Attacks · Machine Learning

1 Introduction

Web applications (or apps) are pervasive in our current society, ranging from e-
commerce to e-government, and so on. These applications enable organizations
to collect, analyze, and store confidential user information such as credit card
numbers and social security records. These applications interact with online
databases, presenting data to users dynamically via a web server application.
However, web applications with sensitive data can be targeted by cybercriminals,
for example by exploiting vulnerabilities to directly manipulate data on various

D. Perakovic and L. Knapcikova (Eds.): FABULOUS 2023, LNICST 542, pp. 99–116, 2024.
https://doi.org/10.1007/978-3-031-50051-0_8

websites [1]. High-risk web applications include those handling large volumes of user data. Attack methods, such as SQL injection and cross-site scripting (XSS), identified by OWASP as particularly dangerous, can lead to users being directed to phishing pages. Despite existing efforts to secure web applications [2–10], this topic remains a research challenge; hence, the focus of this paper.

Specifically, we introduce a comparative framework for detecting SQL injection and XSS attacks, using eight supervised machine learning algorithms (i.e., Naive Bayes, Decision Tree, AdaBoost, Random Forest, Logistic Regression, K-Nearest Neighbor (KNN), Support Vector Machine (SVM), and Artificial Neural Network (ANN)). We employ seven performance metrics to evaluate these eight algorithms, namely: accuracy, precision, recall, F1-score, ROC, AUC, and computation time. Our model parses HTTP requests to extract features, generates a hashmap key, and establishes a whitelist of standard HTTP queries during learning. Request parameters are encoded as a feature vector, following the technique explained by Kozik et al. [11], and transformed into constant-length histograms to train a classifier. In doing so, we seek to gain a better understanding of the accuracy of existing machine learning approaches in attack detection, and identifying effective algorithm(s) in detection.

In the next section, we'll discuss related work, followed by a brief overview of the essential background materials.

2   Related Work

Signature-based methods such as SCALP, PHP-IDS, and Snort are commonly used to detect web application attacks because they can process vast volumes of data [12,13]. These techniques can quickly match text patterns using specific algorithms, typically PCRE standard phrases [14]. However, they require expertise to define attack patterns and struggle with concealed SQL injection attacks using URL encoding. Kozik et al. proposed using data from client-to-web-server HTTP requests to detect web attacks [15]. Their approach employs a machine learning model with two stages: learning and assessment. The learning phase uses labeled data to model normal machine operation. In the assessment phase, HTTP requests are encoded into vectors providing full request details. This method has been applied to HTTP request data, like those in the Apache Connection Log, from traffic generated by e-commerce web applications, identifying various web application cyberattacks.

S.Sharma et al. used machine learning for intrusion detection, and found the J48 decision tree algorithm to be most effective in terms of True Positive Rate, Precision, and Recall [16]. Oumaima, Chakir, et al. evaluated the efficiency of certain machine learning algorithms for intrusion detection [17]. Offutt et al. demonstrated the effectiveness of Bypass Testing to validate application inputs [18]. Sun et al. showed the feasibility of using system conversion and machine learning to detect in-process cyber-attacks on web applications running on a Java Virtual Machine [19]. M. Cova et al. proposed a strategy to detect and study JavaScript code abuses that lead to drive-by-download threats. They combined malicious JavaScript code for anomaly detection and auto-identification, and used a HTML unit browser to serve web pages [20]. They developed a method that utilized standard JavaScript code to introduce features using various feature and machine learning techniques.

XSnare, an XSS solution extension for Firefox, uses prior knowledge of web application HTML content to thwart XSS attacks [21]. It incorporates a database with exploit descriptions informed by past CVEs. XSSDS is another system that passively identifies successful XSS attacks through HTTP traffic monitoring [22]. DeepXSS, a deep learning-based system for XSS detection, extracts XSS features' payload using word2vec, mapping each payload to a feature vector [23]. It then employs Long Short-Term Memory (LSTM) recurrent neural networks for training and testing the detection model. Such research informs further efforts to detect and mitigate XSS threats using artificial intelligence methods [24]. G. Kaur et al. proposed a blind XSS detection method using machine learning, notably the Linear Support Vector Machine (LSVM) classifier, to identify potential threats and distinguish between cached and blind XSS [25].

SQLIDS is a real-time SQL injection detection system that monitors Java-based applications [26]. Zhang et al. proposed an adaptive random testing aimed at triggering SQL injections within limited attempts [27] SEPTIC and SPHERES are systems designed for preventing DBMS attacks and analyzing web traffic respectively, with the latter applying specific filtering rules to requests, website structures, and user sessions [28, 29]. Zhuo et al. and Li et al. introduced systems that use long short-term memory and deep forest-based methods to detect SQL Injection Attacks [30, 31]. DIAVA is a traffic-based system for detecting SQL injection attacks and analyzing vulnerabilities [32]. Batista et al. proposed a fuzzy rules set for constructing expert systems in cybernetic data attacks, specifically SQL Injection attacks [33]. WOVSQLI and DeepSQLi are systems utilizing word vectors of SQL tokens, long short-term memory neural networks, and deep natural language processing to identify SQL injection attacks and create test cases for detection [34, 35]. Chen et al. recently introduced an SQL injection detection system utilizing a natural language processing model and deep learning framework, which does not rely on previous rules [36]. A comparison of these studies using the HTTP CSIC 2010 dataset is provided in Table 1.

Table 1. Comparison of some related work

Study	Technique	Dataset	Problem Domain	Evaluation Metrics
[37]	Generic-Feature-Selection (GeFS)	CSIC 2010 HTTP Dataset	Web Applications Attack	Accuracy
[15]	Naive Bayes, AdaBoost, Part and J48	CSIC 2010 HTTP Dataset	Web Applications Attack	False Positive Rate
[38]	Naïve Bayes, Bayes network, decision stump RBF Network	ECML-PKDD 2007 HTTP, CSIC HTTP 2010	Web Applications Attack	False Positive Rate
[16]	J48, Naïve Bayes, OneR, Decision table	CSIC 2010 HTTP Dataset	Web Applications Attack	Precision, Recall, Accuracy, and F-measure metrics
[17]	KNN, Decision Tree, Multinomial, and Bernoulli Naive Bayes, SVM Linear, Sigmoid, and RBF	CSIC 2010 HTTP Dataset	Web Applications Attack	Accuracy, Recall, Precision, F-value, FPR, and FNR

3 Background

3.1 XSS: Cross-Site Scripting

Cross-site scripting (XSS) is a common hacking technique where malicious code, often JavaScript, is injected into web applications, affecting user's browsers [39, 40]. This can spread via legitimate pages, with XSS attacks categorized as non-persistent or persistent.

Non-Persistent XSS Attack. In a non-persistent XSS attack, users click a malicious link created by hackers, triggering the execution of the attacker's vulnerable code in their browser. Listing 1 demonstrates a typical attack.

```
1   <?php
    $name = $_GET['name'];
3   echo "Hello Welcome $name <br>";
    echo "<a href="http://xssattackdemo.com/">Click to Download
        </a>";
5   ?>
    index.php? name = guest<script>alert ('Hacked') </script>
```

Listing 1.1. Script for non-persistent XSS attack

Persistent XSS Attack. In this type of attack, the attacker injects a malicious script into a repository. The malicious string originates from the website's database. This can be done by having the victim's browser parse the following HTML code:

```
    <script>
2   window.location='http://attacker/?cookie='+document.cookie
    </script>
```

Listing 1.2. Script for a persistent XSS attack

In this form of XSS attack, a script redirects the user's browser to a URL that sends the victim's cookies to the attacker's server. The attacker can then impersonate the victim using these cookies, launching further attacks. This persistent type of XSS attack, aimed at exploiting a website's vulnerability to steal cookies, is generally more damaging than non-persistent ones.

3.2 SQL Injection Attack

In SQL injection attacks, an attacker uses a web page input to introduce harmful SQL commands into an SQL statement, compromising the web system's security. These malicious commands can modify an SQL statement, leading to unauthorized access or other adverse effects. The attack might involve inserting malicious code directly into user input variables or storing it within certain database tables, which is later compiled and added to a dynamic SQL command [41]as displayed in Listing 3.

```
1 EmployeeDetails = Request. Form ("EmployeeDetails ");
  var sql = "select * from OrdersTable where EmployeeDetails =
     '" + EmployeeDetails + "'";
```

Listing 1.3. Script for a basic SQL Injection Attack

The following describes an example of an SQL injection attack. First, the user is asked to write down the name of an employee. When a user enters Steve as the employee name, the query will be a collected script as shown in Listing 4.

```
Select * FROM OrdersTable WHERE EmployeeDetails = 'Steve'
```

Listing 1.4. Query for retrieving details from table

The script merges hardcoded and user-inserted strings to generate an SQL query, retrieving specific employee details. SQL injections typically target URL styles like $http : /www.targetdb.com/index.php?id = 2$. Attackers use certain inputs, like single or double quotes or Boolean expressions, to provoke an SQL Injection attack. For example, a MySQL-backed webpage susceptible to SQL injection might display a data error message like $mysql_num_rows()$ or $mysql_fetch_array()$ on the webpage, indicating vulnerability to such attacks.

4 System Methodology

4.1 Design Choice

This study proposes a method for detecting web-based application attacks using supervised machine learning algorithms, given the availability of labeled data. The approach is applicable to various real-world scenarios like facial recognition, healthcare, Siri, weather forecasting, spam filtering, and fraud detection. The methodology utilizes eight different supervised classification machine learning algorithms to predict attacks. The workflow of the proposed method and details about the utilized algorithms will be elaborated further.

This study implements eight machine learning classification algorithms: Naive Bayes, Decision Tree, AdaBoost, Random Forest, Logistic Regression, K-Nearest Neighbor (KNN), Support Vector Machine (SVM), and Artificial Neural Network (ANN). These fall under three categories: Probabilistic, Tree, and Miscellaneous. The probabilistic category includes Naive Bayes and Logistic Regression, both leveraging the principle of probability. Naive Bayes, a powerful classifier, is based on Bayes' Theorem and assumes feature independence within classes [42]. Logistic Regression, a predictive mathematical model, estimates binary reliability parameters. It predicts the probability of target variable belonging to a particular category, thus effectively used for various analytical problems such as disease detection and malicious attack detection [43]. Despite its simplicity, it has a broad range of applications including spam detection, injection attack detection, XSS attacks detection, etc.

The study also employs tree-based machine learning algorithms: Decision Tree, Random Forest, and AdaBoost. AdaBoost, or Adaptive Boosting, is a popular machine learning technique that collaboratively develops a model, learning from previous errors, and works particularly well with Decision Trees [44,45]. The Decision Tree is a supervised algorithm that can be used for both classification and regression tasks. It employs a tree-like model of decisions, where each node represents a feature, each branch signifies a decision rule, and each leaf node represents an outcome [46]. Decision Trees are often favored for their ease of interpretation and decision-making process representation. In this study, the Decision Tree Classifier model is utilized due to its predictive capability and its ability to evaluate potential outcomes effectively.

The Random Forest (RF) classifier is a supervised machine learning algorithm used in this study to detect web application attacks [47,48]. This ensemble method creates a robust forest by averaging results from multiple decision trees, effectively preventing over-fitting and providing faster results. Other machine learning algorithms employed include the K Nearest Neighbor (k-NN), Support Vector Machine (SVM), and Artificial Neural Network (ANN) [49]. The k-NN algorithm, a non-parametric method used for classification and regression, predicts class membership based on the closest instances in the feature space. The performance of this method depends on whether it is used for isolation or regression.

The K-Nearest Neighbor (k-NN) algorithm is a model-based, or lazy learning method, used mainly for prediction of categorical values. This non-parametric algorithm assigns an item to the class of its most frequent nearest neighbor, with the item's value being the output of the k-NN regression, the value of the closest neighbor. It uses all available data for training and makes no assumptions about the underlying data, and it was used in this study to detect XSS and SQL injection attacks in web applications [50]. The Support Vector Machine (SVM) is a robust supervised machine learning model, introduced in the 1960s and further refined in the 1990s [51,52]. This algorithm, effective for both classification and regression, separates classes in multidimensional space via a hyperplane, iteratively refined to reduce errors and avoid overfitting. SVM uses kernels (linear, sigmoid, and polynomial in this study) to transform input data into the desired form, its main goal being the identification of the maximum marginal hyperplane that divides the dataset into classes.

Lastly, the Artificial Neural Network (ANN) [42,53,54], also called a neural network, is a group with a perceptron/neuron in each layer. It is a computational model made up of three layers, generally consisting of an input layer, an output layer, and a hidden layer (which is between the input and output layers). Inputs from the dataset are given to the input layers, which then go through the hidden layers for further processing. The output layer will then generate the results. This network is capable of learning nonlinear functions with the help of an activation function. This can be the ANN's powerhouse. In our study, we used the backpropagation neural network, which works by internally adjusting the weights with a non-linear connection between the input and output. To process the information and to produce consequential results, it has a substantial processing unit that is connected and works together.

4.2   System Work Flow

The workflow of our methodology encompasses three phases: Phase A: Data Collection, Phase B: Pre-Processing, and Phase C: Building a Model.

Step 1: Data Collection. The first step in the workflow involves collecting the dataset. We conduct an experimental analysis in this study using the CSIC 2010 HTTP dataset. This dataset is used in state-of-the-art existing works. This dataset contains real-life data developed in the Spanish Research National council in 2010 and is a publicly available dataset [55]. Specifically, it encompasses 1,000 HTTP (Hyper Text Transfer Protocol) requests. HTTP is the cornerstone for exchanging information over the World Wide Web. A very large quantity of data regularly flows over this protocol, and attacks towards this protocol are rapidly increasing. In this phase, HTTP traffic is analyzed and detected from within the CSIC 2010 HTTP dataset. Previously, classification of the CSIC 2010 HTTP dataset was used mainly with the purpose of instance and feature selection analysis. This dataset consists of 223,585 instances and 18 attributes. Moreover, it incorporates traffic maliciously targeting e-commerce web applications. The dataset is split into a collective set of normal and anomalous traffic requests. There are approximately 25, 000 anomalous requests and 36, 000 normal requests. We extracted the Cross-site Scripting (XSS) and SQL Injection (SQLI) attacks for our analysis from this dataset, since these two attacks fall under dynamic attacks that could harm users by stealing their confidential information. From the CSIC HTTP 2010 dataset, we eliminate unintentionally illegal requests, static attacks, and some dynamic attacks like buffer overflows and CRLF injection. As such, a total of 3096 instances are contained in our subset dataset, of which 1548 are anomalous (XSS+SQL) requests and 1548 are normal requests.

Despite its age, this dataset continues to be one of the most comprehensive and widely used in our field. There are many recent studies used this dataset for their experimental evaluations [56–62]. It contains a wide array of HTTP requests, both legitimate and malicious, making it ideal for testing and evaluating web application attack detection methods. Moreover, it enables the comparison of our results with those of past researches, contributing to a coherent body of knowledge. However, we understand the need for incorporating more recent datasets and will consider this in future studies to stay updated with the evolving web attack patterns.

Step 2: Pre-Processing. Following the collection of the dataset, the preprocesing step involves training the model. This step is completed using the normalization technique. Data normalization is a procedure by which all attributes are taken under the standard scale to pre-process the data. It is a preliminary processing which renders data compatible for analysis. Data processing is widely recognized as an important part of anomaly detection [63]. Pre-processing includes all of the tasks performed prior to structured data processing, such as data cleaning, normalization, conversion, extraction, and selection of features [45]. Based on both resources and time, the pre-processing stage necessitates a significant amount of work, so it is necessary to pay attention to this step. Generally, about half the effort of an entire project is used to prepare the data [64]. This preparation step not only influences the efficacy of storing data, but also the effectiveness of the adoption process [63].

Step 3: Build a Model. The normalized data was divided into 80% for training and 20% for testing. The eight supervised machine learning classification algorithms used the training set to create models that could predict web application attacks. Each model's performance was assessed and compared using various evaluation metrics. The entire experiment was performed 50 times, with results averaged for accuracy. K-fold cross-validation also confirmed similar results. The aim was to identify the algorithm that most accurately classified normal and anomalous traffic requests. Results and detailed comparisons are provided in the experimental section.

5   Experimental Results

The experimental results and their evaluation are discussed in this section. Here we use seven performance metrics to determine the best algorithm. While evaluating the machine learning (ML) models, it is imperative to choose precise performance metrics [65]. Different performance criteria are proposed for evaluating ML models in diverse applications. The metrics that we chose to compare the algorithms are classification metrics such as accuracy, precision, recall (sensitivity), F_1-score, and Receiver Operating Characteristic (ROC) curve. Other popular metrics, such as time and Area Under the Curve (AUC), are also evaluated.

Accuracy: This is explained as the proportion of records correctly categorized over the total number of records. $Accuracy = (TP+TN)/(TP+TN+FP+FN)$. An accuracy value of 0.75 means that 75 of every 100 HTTP protocol requests is predicted correctly. Our system works to detect web application attacks based on the CSIC http 2010 dataset, which has a target class of 2 anomalous and normal web requests. According to our proposed definition of accuracy, it is the proportion of correctly identified anomalous and normal requests to the total number in our subset dataset.

Precision (P): This is defined as the proportion of true positive (TP) records divided by the total of true positive (TP) and false positive (FP) records classified. $P = TP/(TP + FP)$. Our intended definition of precision is that it is the ratio of precisely detected anomalous requests to the overall number of positive predictions. A precision value of 0.77 means that 77 out of 100 HTTP protocol requests were precisely predicted.

Recall (R): This is known as the mean value of actual true positive records divided by the number of classified records of true positives and false negatives. It is also known as sensitivity, or the True Positive Rate. $TPR = Sensitivity = Recall = TP/(TP + FN)$. A recall value of 0.70 means that 30 of every 100 HTTP protocol requests to the web application are missed by the proposed detection system, and 70 are correctly predicted.

F_1 **score (F):** Also known as the F_1 Score and $F-$Measure, this score is defined as the harmonic mean of precision and recall and represents a balance between them. $F = 2 * P * R/(P + R)$.

Specificity: $TrueNegativeRate = TN/(TN + FP)$, where time is the amount of time intervals utilized by the metric system. A specificity value of 60% means that 40 out of every 100 HTTP protocol requests to the web application are mislabeled as anomalous requests and 60 are correctly labeled as normal requests. In our study, we did not use specificity as a performance metric.

ROC Curve: The Receiver Operating Characteristics Curve is a probability curve. It is basically illustrating, for different threshold values, the true positive rate (TPR) against the false positive rate (FPR) on the Y and X axis, respectively. $FPR = 1 - specificity$.

AUC: This is the Area Under the Curve. A higher AUC means that the model is predicting positives as positives and negatives as negatives. In our system, a higher AUC means the model can easily distinguish web requests as anomalous or normal. An AUC of 0.80 means the model can classify between anomalous and normal requests. On the contrary, an AUC of 0.50 means the model is not good at distinguishing web requests.

Time: This refers to computational time, which is the time taken by the system to predict the results.

The given input dataset is split into an 80:20 ratio, which means (80%) for training and (20%) for testing. Labels were assigned to anomalous (1) and normal (0) requests. We empirically evaluated the system by repeating the experiment 50 times on the subset dataset containing XSS and SQL injection anomalous HTTP requests, including balanced normal HTTP requests from the CSIC 2010 HTTP dataset. In the proposed system, the feature of input data is given to several classifier models to build the model and evaluate the performance of each classifier shown in Table 10. As mentioned earlier, we use eight different machine learning models. Table 10 illustrates the eight different supervised machine learning classifier algorithms that are used to classify the 2 target categorical values of anomalous (bad request) and normal (good request) labels from the input data to predict the results.

Tables 2 through 9 show the results obtained from the experimental evaluations. Each individual table shows the result of different machine learning classifier models with different parameters used to predict web attacks based on web requests. As previously mentioned, we have two types of requests: bad and good, i.e., anomalous and normal, respectively. The classifiers are trained and tested accordingly so that we may obtain the corresponding values of the evaluation metrics. We can thus compare and analyze each model and reach a final conclusion for the classifier that outperforms the others in terms of accuracy, computational complexity, and so on.

Table 2. Naive Bayes Classifier Results. Prec: Precision; Acc: Accuracy

Model	Time(s)	Acc.	Prec	Recall	F-1	AUC
Naive Bayes	0.027	0.75	0.77	0.75	0.75	0.80

Table 2 provides the results obtained using the Naive Bayes classifier. This classifier yields a classification result with an accuracy of 0.75, a precision of 0.77, a recall of 0.75, an F_1 score of 0.75, and an AUC of 0.80. The time taken by the classifier for the prediction was 0.027. In terms of computational time, the Naive Bayes classifier outperforms the other classification models as it is much quicker, as depicted in Table 10.

Table 3. AdaBoost Classifier Results. Prec: Precision; Acc: Accuracy; Estim: Estimators

No. Estim	Time(s)	Acc.	Prec	Recall	F-1	AUC
50	1.98	0.75	0.77	0.75	0.75	0.80
60	2.55	0.75	0.77	0.75	0.75	0.80

The results obtained using the meta-learning method AdaBoost are shown in Table 3. The classification results of this model are evaluated by setting three parameters: the base estimator, the number of estimators, and the learning rate. In this experiment, we set the learning rate as 1 and the base estimator as tree or by default. This method will use the decision tree as the learner model. However, we try to find the different classification results by changing the number of estimators, which is the number of learners to be trained iteratively. We found that as the number of estimators change, there is no variation in accuracy, precision, recall, F1 score, or AUC, but there is a variation in time. As there is a slight difference found in the computational time, we are considering the best result obtained when the number of estimators = 50 at its initial stage, which yields a value of 0.77 precision, and a value of 0.75 in accuracy, recall, and F1 score, a value of 0.80 for the area under the curve, and a computational time of 1.98s, as depicted in Table 10.

Table 4 summarizes the results acquired using the random forest classifier, yet another ensemble learning method for both classification as well as regression. We evaluated the random forest classifier model with a different number of trees. We found that as the number of trees increases, there is no significant variation in performance metrics, but there are some variations in overall classification time. The best classification result was obtained with a number of trees equal to 5, which yielded a value of 0.77 precision, and a value of 0.75 for accuracy, recall, and F_1 score, a value of 0.80 for the AUC, and a time of 0.366 (see Table 10).

Table 4. Random Forest Classifier Results. Prec: Precision; Acc: Accuracy

No. Trees	Time(s)	Acc.	Prec	Recall	F-1	AUC
5	0.366	0.75	0.77	0.75	0.75	0.80
10	0.47	0.75	0.77	0.75	0.75	0.80
20	0.577	0.75	0.77	0.75	0.75	0.80

The decision tree classifier results are depicted in Table 5. The decision tree can also be used for both classification and regression problems; however, this method mainly focuses on classification. Here we used the decision tree classifier with different parameters. We used tree depth set at 100, a condition that does not split the subset smaller than 5, and, for the minimum number of instances in leaves, we used different values ranging from 2 to 15. Throughout the experiment, we understood that even if we change the number of instances in leaves, there is no dissimilarity in the classification results of the evaluation metrics and there are negligible changes in the computational time. The estimated results of the classifier model when the number of instances = 4 and time = 0.40s provides an accuracy of 0.73, a precision of 0.75, a recall and F_1 score of 0.73, and an AUC of 0.80, as shown in Table 10.

Table 5. Decision Tree Classifier Results. Prec: Precision; Acc: Accuracy; Inst: Instances

No. Inst	Time(s)	Acc.	Prec	Recall	F-1	AUC
2	0.45	0.73	0.75	0.73	0.73	0.80
4	0.40	0.73	0.75	0.73	0.73	0.80

In the logistic regression classifier, the results from Table 6 indicate that the regularization parameter 'C' does not have a significant impact on performance metrics. Weak and strong values of 'C' show only slight variations in computational time. The accuracy, recall, and F_1 score have values of 0.75, while precision is 0.77, and the AUC is 0.80. The appropriate selection of the regularization parameter allows the classifier to provide a good fit without underfitting or overfitting, depending on the dataset.

Table 6. Logistic Regression Classifier Results. Prec: Precision; Acc: Accuracy

C-value	Time(s)	Acc.	Prec	Recall	F-1	AUC
1000	0.324	0.75	0.77	0.75	0.75	0.80
7	0.319	0.75	0.77	0.75	0.75	0.80
9	0.33	0.75	0.77	0.75	0.75	0.80
10	0.321	0.75	0.77	0.75	0.75	0.80
0.001	0.315	0.73	0.73	0.72	0.72	0.80

Table 7 represents the results obtained when using an Artificial Neural Network (ANN) with different hidden layers. In this study, we used an Artificial Neural Network (ANN) with various hidden layers and the Adam optimization algorithm. Different hidden layers didn't notably affect system classification performance, except for a rise in computational time with increasing layers. Performance metrics showed consistent results across different configurations, with accuracy, precision, recall, and F_1 score all equal to 0.75, and an AUC of 0.80. Hence, using different hidden layers in the ANN had little impact on system performance except for computation time.

The K-Nearest Neighbor (k-NN) classifier, a supervised machine learning algorithm for classification and regression, was used in the experiment. Different integer values of k - the number of nearest data points - were selected. Distance metrics (Euclidean, Manhattan, and Chebyshev) were used to calculate the distance between the testing and each row of training data. The performance evaluation metrics showed minor differences for the k-NN classifier with different k values and distance metrics, with slight impact on system performance. The best results were found with the Manhattan distance metric and showed insignificant impact across different k values. When $k = 7$ or 9, the accuracy, precision, and recall were 0.72 and 0.73 respectively, with an F_1 score of 0.72 and an AUC of 0.78. Some slight but significant changes were noted in computational time across all k values and distance metrics.

In our study, the Support Vector Machine (SVM), a supervised machine learning algorithm for classification and regression, was employed with varying kernels (Linear, Sigmoid, and Polynomial) and C values. For the Linear kernel, we observed a significant change in performance metrics with different C values, but found no such impact for the Sigmoid and Polynomial kernels. The time for model predictions varied slightly. The best results were obtained with a Linear kernel and $C = 0.01$, producing an accuracy of 0.58, precision of 0.60, recall of

Table 7. ANN Classifier Result. Prec: Precision; Acc: Accuracy; Hidd. L: Hidden Layers

Hidd. L	Time(s)	Acc.	Prec	Recall	F-1	AUC
50	0.502	0.75	0.77	0.75	0.75	0.80
80	0.542	0.75	0.77	0.75	0.75	0.80
100	0.563	0.75	0.76	0.75	0.75	0.80

0.58, F_1 score of 0.57, AUC of 0.368, and a time of 1.028s. However, the SVM did not perform well for classifying anomalous and normal HTTP requests in our subset dataset.

Table 8. K-Nearest Neighbor Classifier Results. Prec: Precision; Acc: Accuracy; Hidd. L: Hidden Layers. K: K-value

K	Metric	Time	Acc	Prec	Recall	F-1	AUC
5	Euclidean	4.035	0.71	0.72	0.71	0.71	0.76
	Manhattan	4.143	0.71	0.72	0.71	0.71	0.76
	Chebyshev	3.217	0.71	0.71	0.71	0.71	0.77
7	Euclidean	3.7	0.71	0.72	0.71	0.71	0.77
	Manhattan	4.244	0.72	0.72	0.71	0.71	0.77
	Chebyshev	3.19	0.72	0.72	0.72	0.72	0.78
9	Euclidean	3.71	0.73	0.73	0.73	0.72	0.78
	Manhattan	4.326	0.73	0.73	0.73	0.72	0.78
	Chebyshev	3.542	0.73	0.73	0.73	0.72	0.78

Table 9. SVM Classifier Results. Prec: Precision; Acc: Accuracy. C: C-value

C	Kernel	Time	Acc	Prec	Recall	F-1	AUC
0.1	Linear	0.76	0.57	0.57	0.57	0.57	0.49
	Sigmod	1.028	0.58	0.60	0.58	0.57	0.368
	Polynomial	.836	0.58	0.61	0.57	0.54	0.487
0.5	Linear	0.829	0.55	0.56	0.55	0.52	0.47
	Sigmod	0.986	0.58	0.60	0.58	0.56	0.36
	Polynomial	0.840	0.56	0.61	0.57	0.53	0.52

Table 10 shows the overall best result obtained using different classifiers after comparing their different parameters. The table also includes the confusion matrix of each classifier, which demonstrates the number of requests out of the 3096 instances in the total subset dataset that were correctly predicted as anomalous or normal requests.

Table 10. Experimental results of proposed work.

Different Classifier Comparison

Classifier	Confusion Matrix			AUC	Classification Accuracy	Precision	Recall	F score
	Class	anom (1)	norm (0)	0.80	0.75	0.77	0.75	0.75
Logistic Regression	anom (1)	9855	5645					
	norm (0)	1986	13514					
k-NN	anom (1)	10227	5273	0.78	0.73	0.73	0.73	0.72
	norm (0)	3237	12263					
AdaBoost	anom (1)	9855	5645	0.80	0.75	0.77	0.75	0.75
	norm (0)	2016	13484					
Random Forest	anom (1)	9887	5613	0.80	0.75	0.77	0.75	0.75
	norm (0)	2048	13452					
SVM	anom (1)	12318	3182	0.49	0.58	0.61	0.57	0.54
	norm (0)	9695	5805					
Neural Network	anom (1)	9855	5645	0.80	0.75	0.77	0.75	0.75
	norm (0)	2001	13499					
Naive Bayes	anom (1)	9855	5645	0.80	0.75	0.77	0.75	0.75
	norm (0)	2010	13490					
Decision Tree	anom (1)	10227	5275	0.80	0.73	0.75	0.73	0.73
	norm (0)	3235	12263					

6   Conclusion

Eight (8) supervised machine learning classification algorithms were tested on a subset of the CSIC 2010 HTTP dataset to determine their effectiveness in detecting web application attacks, focusing on XSS and SQLI dynamic attacks. Experimental results showed that Random Forest, Neural Networks, Naive Bayes, Logistic Regression and AdaBoost classifiers performed best based on metrics like accuracy, precision, recall, F1 Score, AUC, ROC, and time [42–44, 48]. SVM and KNN appeared to achieve lower accuracy and performance. Naive Bayes, Logistic Regression and Decision Tree algorithms were quickest, with SVM only faster when using a linear kernel. These results offer satisfactory solutions for detecting web application attacks.

In summary, our findings show KNN and Random Forest classifiers achieve 89% accuracy and 94% AUC on the CSIC dataset, while the Naive Bayes classifier excels in computational efficiency when distinguishing between malicious and benign HTTP requests.

Future work could involve unsupervised machine learning, deep learning algorithms, or new publicly available datasets.

Acknowledgment. This work was supported by grant number 12R170.

References

1. Mikheeva, O.I., Gatchin Yuri, A., Savkov, S.V., Khammatova, R.M., et al.: Search methods for abnormal activities of web applications. J. Sci. Tech. Inf. Technol. Mech. Optics **126**(2), 233–242 (2020)
2. Holz, T., Marechal, S., Raynal, F.: New threats and attacks on the world wide web. IEEE Secur. Priv. **4**(2), 72–75 (2006)
3. Moshchuk, A., Bragin, T., Deville, D., Gribble, S.D., Levy, H.M.: SpyProxy: Execution-based detection of malicious web content. In: USENIX Security Symposium, pp. 1–16 (2007)
4. Tekerek, A.: A novel architecture for web-based attack detection using convolutional neural network. Comput. Secur. **100**, 102096 (2021)
5. Huang, Y., Li, T., Zhang, L., Li, B., Liu, X.: JSContana: malicious javascript detection using adaptable context analysis and key feature extraction. Comput. Secur. **104**, 102218 (2021)
6. Phung, N.M., Mimura, M.: Detection of malicious javascript on an imbalanced dataset. Internet of Things **13**, 100357 (2021)
7. Nithya, V., Pandian, S.L., Malarvizhi, C.: A survey on detection and prevention of cross-site scripting attack. Int. J. Secur. Its Appl. **9**(3), 139–152 (2015)
8. Tariq, I., Sindhu, M.A., Abbasi, R.A., Khattak, A.S., Maqbool, O., Siddiqui, G.F.: Resolving cross-site scripting attacks through genetic algorithm and reinforcement learning. Expert Syst. Appl. **168**, 114386 (2021)
9. Jeitner, P., Shulman, H.: Injection attacks reloaded: tunnelling malicious payloads over DNS. In: 30th {USENIX} Security Symposium ({USENIX} Security 21), pp. 3165–3182 (2021)
10. Kc, G.S., Keromytis, A.D., Prevelakis, V.: Countering code-injection attacks with instruction-set randomization. In: Proceedings of the 10th ACM conference on Computer and communications security, pp. 272–280 (2003)
11. Hazel, P.: Perl compatible regular expressions, The University of Cambridge, p. 114 (2012)
12. Erlacher, F., Dressler, F.: On high-speed flow-based intrusion detection using snort-compatible signatures. IEEE Trans. Dependable Secur. Comput
13. Fredj, O.B., Cheikhrouhou, O., Krichen, M., Hamam, H., Derhab, A.: An OWASP top ten driven survey on web application protection methods. In: Garcia-Alfaro, J., Leneutre, J., Cuppens, N., Yaich, R. (eds.) CRiSIS 2020. LNCS, vol. 12528, pp. 235–252. Springer, Cham (2021). https://doi.org/10.1007/978-3-030-68887-5_14
14. Perl-compatible regular expressions (PCRE), http://www.pcre.org (2021)
15. Kozik, R., Choraś, M., Renk, R., Hołubowicz, W.: A proposal of algorithm for web applications cyber attack detection. In: Saeed, K., Snášel, V. (eds.) CISIM 2014. LNCS, vol. 8838, pp. 680–687. Springer, Heidelberg (2014). https://doi.org/10.1007/978-3-662-45237-0_61
16. Sharma, S., Zavarsky, P., Butakov, S.: Machine learning based intrusion detection system for web-based attacks. In: 2020 IEEE 6th Intl Conference on Big Data Security on Cloud (BigDataSecurity), IEEE Intl Conference on High Performance and Smart Computing, (HPSC) and IEEE Intl Conference on Intelligent Data and Security (IDS), IEEE, pp. 227–230 (2020)
17. Oumaima, C., Abdeslam, R., Yassine, S., Abderrazek, F.: Experimental study on the effectiveness of machine learning methods in web intrusion detection. In: Maleh, Y., Alazab, M., Gherabi, N., Tawalbeh, L., Abd El-Latif, A.A. (eds.) ICI2C 2021. LNNS, vol. 357, pp. 486–494. Springer, Cham (2022). https://doi.org/10.1007/978-3-030-91738-8_44

18. J. Offutt, Y. Wu, X. Du, H. Huang, Bypass testing of web applications. In: 15th International Symposium on Software Reliability Engineering, IEEE, pp. 187–197 (2004)
19. Sun, F., Zhang, P., White, J., Schmidt, D., Staples, J., Krause, L.: A feasibility study of autonomically detecting in-process cyber-attacks. In: 2017 3rd IEEE International Conference on Cybernetics (CYBCONF), IEEE, pp. 1–8 (2017)
20. Cova, M., Kruegel, C., Vigna, G.: Detection and analysis of drive-by-download attacks and malicious JavaScript code. In: Proceedings of the 19th international conference on World wide web, pp. 281–290 (2010)
21. Pazos, J.C., Légaré, J.-S., Beschastnikh, I.: XSnare: application-specific client-side cross-site scripting protection. In: 2021 IEEE International Conference on Software Analysis, Evolution and Reengineering (SANER), IEEE, pp. 154–165 (2021)
22. Johns, M., Engelmann, B., Posegga, J., Xssds: Server-side detection of cross-site scripting attacks. In: Annual Computer Security Applications Conference (ACSAC). IEEE, vol. 2008, pp. 335–344 (2008)
23. Fang, Y., Li, Y., Liu, L., Huang, C.: DeepXSS: cross site scripting detection based on deep learning. In: Proceedings of the 2018 International Conference on Computing and Artificial Intelligence, pp. 47–51 (2018)
24. Rodríguez, G.E., Torres, J.G., Flores, P., Benavides, D.E.: Cross-site scripting (XSS) attacks and mitigation: a survey. Comput. Netw. **166**, 106960 (2020)
25. Kaur, G., Malik, Y., Samuel, H., Jaafar, F.: Detecting blind cross-site scripting attacks using machine learning. In: Proceedings of the 2018 International Conference on Signal Processing and Machine Learning, pp. 22–25 (2018)
26. Kemalis, K., Tzouramanis, T.: SQL-IDS: a specification-based approach for SQL-injection detection. In: Proceedings of the 2008 ACM symposium on Applied computing, pp. 2153–2158 (2008)
27. Zhang, L., Zhang, D., Wang, C., Zhao, J., Zhang, Z.: ART4SQLI: the art of SQL injection vulnerability discovery. IEEE Trans. Reliab. **68**(4), 1470–1489 (2019)
28. Medeiros, I., Beatriz, M., Neves, N., Correia, M.: SEPTIC: detecting injection attacks and vulnerabilities inside the DBMS. IEEE Trans. Reliab. **68**(3), 1168–1188 (2019)
29. Fredj, O.B.: SPHERES: an efficient server-side web application protection system. Int. J. Inf. Comput. Secur. **11**(1), 33–60 (2019)
30. Zhuo, Z., Cai, T., Zhang, X., Lv, F.: Long short-term memory on abstract syntax tree for SQL injection detection. IET Softw. **15**(2), 188–197 (2021)
31. Li, Q., Li, W., Wang, J., Cheng, M.: A SQL injection detection method based on adaptive deep forest. IEEE Access **7**, 145385–145394 (2019)
32. Gu, H., et al.: DIAVA: a traffic-based framework for detection of SQL injection attacks and vulnerability analysis of leaked data. IEEE Trans. Reliab. **69**(1), 188–202 (2019)
33. Batista, L.O.: Fuzzy neural networks to create an expert system for detecting attacks by SQL injection, arXiv preprint arXiv:1901.02868
34. Fang, Y., Peng, J., Liu, L., Huang, C.: WOVSQLI: detection of SQL injection behaviors using word vector and LSTM. In: Proceedings of the 2nd International Conference on Cryptography, Security and Privacy, pp. 170–174 (2018)
35. Liu, M., Li, K., Chen, T.: DeepSQLi: deep semantic learning for testing SQL injection. In: Proceedings of the 29th ACM SIGSOFT International Symposium on Software Testing and Analysis, pp. 286–297 (2020)
36. D. Chen, Q. Yan, C. Wu, J. Zhao, Sql injection attack detection and prevention techniques using deep learning. J. Phys. Conf. Series **1757**, 012055 IOP Publishing (2021)

37. Nguyen, H.T., Torrano-Gimenez, C., Alvarez, G., Petrović, S., Franke, K.: Application of the generic feature selection measure in detection of web attacks. In: Herrero, Á., Corchado, E. (eds.) CISIS 2011. LNCS, vol. 6694, pp. 25–32. Springer, Heidelberg (2011). https://doi.org/10.1007/978-3-642-21323-6_4

38. Yavanoglu, O., Aydos, M.: A review on cyber security datasets for machine learning algorithms. In: IEEE International Conference on Big Data (big data). IEEE, vol. 2017, pp. 2186–2193 (2017)

39. Kascheev, S., Olenchikova, T.: The detecting cross-site scripting (XSS) using machine learning methods. In: Global Smart Industry Conference (GloSIC). IEEE, vol. 2020, pp. 265–270 (2020)

40. Mereani, F.A., Howe, J.M.: Detecting cross-site scripting attacks using machine learning. In: Hassanien, A.E., Tolba, M.F., Elhoseny, M., Mostafa, M. (eds.) AMLTA 2018. AISC, vol. 723, pp. 200–210. Springer, Cham (2018). https://doi.org/10.1007/978-3-319-74690-6_20

41. Halfond, W.G., Viegas, J., Orso, A., et al.: A classification of SQL-injection attacks and countermeasures. In: Proceedings of the IEEE International Symposium on Secure Software Engineering, IEEE, vol. 1, pp. 13–15 (2006)

42. Saritas, M.M., Yasar, A.: Performance analysis of ANN and naive Bayes classification algorithm for data classification. Int. J. Intell. Syst. Appl. Eng. 7(2), 88–91 (2019)

43. Garg, A., Roth, D.: Understanding probabilistic classifiers. In: De Raedt, L., Flach, P. (eds.) ECML 2001. LNCS (LNAI), vol. 2167, pp. 179–191. Springer, Heidelberg (2001). https://doi.org/10.1007/3-540-44795-4_16

44. Kulkarni, C.C., Kulkarni, S.: Human agent knowledge transfer applied to web security. In: 2013 Fourth International Conference on Computing, Communications and Networking Technologies (ICCCNT), IEEE, pp. 1–4 (2013)

45. Zhang, H.: The optimality of naive Bayes. Aa 1(2), 3 (2004)

46. Myles, A.J., Feudale, R.N., Liu, Y., Woody, N.A., Brown, S.D.: An introduction to decision tree modeling. A J. Chemom. Soc. 18(6), 275–285 (2004)

47. Liaw, A., Wiener, M., et al.: Classification and regression by randomforest. R News 2(3), 18–22 (2002)

48. Howe, J., Mereani, F.: Detecting cross-site scripting attacks using machine learning. In: Advances in Intelligent Systems and Computing 723

49. Zhang, Z.: Introduction to machine learning: k-nearest neighbors. Anna. Transl. Med. 4(11)

50. Bhor, R., Khanuja, H.: Analysis of web application security mechanism and attack detection using vulnerability injection technique. In: 2016 International Conference on Computing Communication Control and automation (ICCUBEA), IEEE, pp. 1–6 (2016)

51. Jakkula, V.: Tutorial on support vector machine (SVM), School of EECS, Washington State University 37

52. Rawat, R., Shrivastav, S.K.: SQL injection attack detection using SVM. Int. J. Comput. Appl. 42(13), 1–4 (2012)

53. Braspenning, P.J., Thuijsman, F., Weijters, A.J.M.M. (eds.): Neural Network School 1999. LNCS, vol. 931. Springer, Heidelberg (1995). https://doi.org/10.1007/BFb0027019

54. Manzoor, I., Kumar, N., et al.: A feature reduced intrusion detection system using ANN classifier. Expert Syst. Appl. 88, 249–257 (2017)

55. CSIC 2010 Dataset, https://petescully.co.uk/research/csic-2010-http-dataset-in-csv-format-for-weka-analysis/ (2021)

56. Bhatnagar, M., Rozinaj, G., Yadav, P.K.: Web intrusion classification system using machine learning approaches. In: International Symposium ELMAR. IEEE, vol. 2022, pp. 57–60 (2022)

57. Ramos Júnior, L.S., Macêdo, D., Oliveira, A.L.I., Zanchettin, C.: Detecting Malicious HTTP Requests Without Log Parser Using RequestBERT-BiLSTM. In: Xavier-Junior, J.C., Rios, R.A. (eds) Intelligent Systems. BRACIS 2022. LNCS(), vol 13654 . Springer, Cham (2022). https://doi.org/10.1007/978-3-031-21689-3_24

58. Ghazal, S.F., Mjlae, S.A.: Cybersecurity in deep learning techniques: Detecting network attacks. Int. J. Adv. Comput. Sci. Appl. **13**(11)

59. Li, W., Zhang, X.Y.: GBLNet: Detecting Intrusion Traffic with Multi-granularity BiLSTM. In: Groen, D., de Mulatier, C., Paszynski, M., Krzhizhanovskaya, V.V., Dongarra, J.J., Sloot, P.M.A. (eds) Computational Science – ICCS 2022. ICCS 2022. LNCS, vol 13353. Springer, Cham (2022). https://doi.org/10.1007/978-3-031-08760-8_32

60. Tan, S., Sun, R., Liang, Z.: Detection of malicious web requests using neural networks with multi granularity features. In: Proceedings of the 5th International Conference on Big Data Technologies, pp. 83–89 (2022)

61. Shaheed, A., Kurdy, M.: Web application firewall using machine learning and features engineering, Secur. Commun. Netw. (2022)

62. Toprak, S., Yavuz, A.G.: Web application firewall based on anomaly detection using deep learning. Acta Infologica **6**(2), 219–244 (2022)

63. J. J. Davis, A. J. Clark, Data preprocessing for anomaly based network intrusion detection: a review. Comput. Secur. **30**(6–7), 353–375 (2011)

64. Kotsiantis, S.B., Kanellopoulos, D., Pintelas, P.E.: Data preprocessing for supervised leaning. Int. J. Comput. Sci. **1**(2), 111–117 (2006)

65. Performance metrics, https://towardsdatascience.com/20-popular-machine-learning-metrics-part-1-classification-regression-evaluation-metrics1ca3e282a2ce (2021)

Parameters of Sustainability in the Context of Decarbonization and Circular Construction Sector

Peter Mésároš[1] , Mária Grazianová[1] , Jana Smetanková[2,3]([✉]) ,
Katarína Krajníková[1] , and Annamária Behúnová[4]

[1] Faculty of Civil Engineering, Institute of Construction Technology, Technical University of Kosice, Economics and Management Vysokoskolska 4, 042 00 Kosice, Slovakia
[2] Faculty of Civil Engineering, Experts Institute in Construction, Technical University of Kosice, Vysokoskolska 4, 042 00 Kosice, Slovakia
jana.smetankova@tuke.sk
[3] National Infrastructure for Technology Transfer Support in Slovakia II – NITT SK II, Lamačská cesta 8/A, 840 05 Bratislava, Slovakia
[4] Faculty of Mining, Ecology, Process Control and Geotechnologies, Institute of Earth Resources, Technical University of Košice, Letna 9, 042 00 Košice, Slovakia

Abstract. Climate change is a 21st century phenomenon and is becoming one of the major challenges of environmental policy. While the manifestations of climate change are diverse across the world and across regions, its negative consequences on socio-economic and natural systems are increasingly significant and require active resolution. To this end, many organizations, associations, and governments are approaching the introduction of new measures that will help eliminate the negative effects of human activity on the environment. To this end, for example, green (energy) taxes are introduced, the amount of waste produced is monitored more and the rate of recycling and reuse of materials is supported, thus meeting the fundamental aspects of the circular economy. The contribution provides an overview and thus comparisons of selected European countries in the field of parameters supporting sustainable development, such as green, energy taxes and revenues from their collection, waste management and waste recycling rate in the construction sector. The result of the research will be the creation of a ranking of countries, based on the punctual assessment, in income from energy tax collection and in the area of waste generation, waste recycling and waste recovery rate from construction and demolition. The declared results will subsequently constitute the basis for the development of a strategic crisis plan, which can be implemented within the individual economies of European countries.

Keywords: Sustainability · Parameter · Decarbonization · Circular construction sector

D. Perakovic and L. Knapcikova (Eds.): FABULOUS 2023, LNICST 542, pp. 117–132, 2024.
https://doi.org/10.1007/978-3-031-50051-0_9

1 Introduction

Climate change in the world is already affecting people's health and interfering with individual aspects of our lives. Climate change, global warming and the excessive opt-out of our planet are affecting all of us. For example, many people's awareness of climate change is relatively low.

Environmental changes and problems are a natural part of every planet's life. Although climate change is a natural process, it is gaining faster and more vigorous fallout due to human activity. The visible impacts of environmental change have been observed since the second half of the twentieth century. These include the threat of the use of nuclear weapons, the weakening of the ozone layer and the inevitable climate change.

Environmental problems such as loss of biological diversity, pollution of water, air and soil, depletion of natural resources and overexploitation of land are increasingly threatening the earth's livelihood systems [1]. Social expectations are not being met, for example, due to high unemployment, poor working conditions, social vulnerability, poverty, intergenerational inequality, and growing inequality [2]. Financial problems such as resource risk, problematic ownership structures, unregulated markets and dysfunctional stimulus structures are increasingly causing financial and economic instability for individual firms and entire economies [3]. To address these and other sustainable development issues, the concept of the circular economy has recently been reflected in national policy agendas [4]. This can be seen, for example, in the European Circular Economy Package.

Environmental change and the availability of resources are forcing large infrastructure companies to seek greater flexibility and efficiency in organizing, improving, and transporting large projects around the world. One of the flexible approaches is the concept of a circular economic model. The construction and engineering industry is the largest buyer of natural materials in the world. It accounts for half of the world's steel production and burns more than 3 billion large amounts of natural substances. Current resources are now being burned twice as fast as they are provided. By 2050, this could be several times higher. Competition for resources and supply disruptions now increase unpredictable material costs, making vulnerability temporary and increasing overall costs. For the construction and engineering sectors, an effective solution to prevent this disaster is to adapt the approach from both sides [5].

Efficient use of resources enables more efficient use of infrastructure, vehicles, and space in the built environment. In a built-up environment, resource owners can rent or share unused space, building and development materials, and equipment. Shared and customizable workspaces are gradually making their way into densely populated urban areas. With less space consumption and reduced resource downtime, fewer resources are expected to provide the same energy or management and therefore generate less waste. This includes welcoming more people to a more ground-level atmosphere, making continuous use of workplaces and workspaces, and sharing vehicles and offices [5].

2 Literature Review

2.1 Sustainability and Its Aspects

The concept of sustainability is increasingly resonating in individual segments of society. The generally accepted definition dates to 1987 and is found in the so-called Brundtland Report – entitled "Our Common Future" – which focuses attention on the principles of intergenerational and intragenerational justice. For the first time, the report identifies sustainability as a condition for development capable of "ensuring that the needs of the present generation are met without jeopardizing the ability of future generations to fulfill their own" [6].

Compared to the first versions of sustainability, the Treccani encyclopedia emphasizes that sustainability is a profound evolution that is based on a vision focused primarily on ecological aspects and arrives at a more global significance that, in addition to the environmental dimension, also considers the economic and social aspect. However, these three aspects were considered in a synergistic and systemic relationship and were used to varying degrees to arrive at a definition of progress and well-being that somehow goes beyond traditional GDP-based rates of wealth and economic growth. Ultimately, sustainability means constant and, as far as possible, growing (environmental, social, economic) well-being and the prospect of leaving future generations behind, with a quality of life no inferior to the current one [6].

When talking about sustainable development, we refer to the relationship we have with the natural environment on which we depend in terms of water, energy, raw materials, and food. Added to this is also the relationship we have with the global economic system in terms of the acquisition of raw materials, production, and trade of products. Sustainability refers to our interrelationships, the values of the society we live in compared to other societies. Protecting and nurturing the natural environment by maintaining clean air, clean water, fertile soil and thriving biological systems are criteria for an environmentalist's judgment. On the other hand, the business point of view can also agree, but considers the economic health of a company or a country as the last resort. Even the simplest concept of sustainability has three dimensions: environmental, social, and economical. Western democracies have experienced strong economic development based on urbanization and technological innovation, using energy and natural environmental resources to produce goods and improve health, transportation, financial and other systems. While recognizing that natural resources are limited, advocates point out that technological advances have more than offset resource depletion and there is no reason to believe that this will not be the case in the future. The economic history of developed countries shows a natural progression from early agricultural societies through industrialization and post-industrial economies, where wealth increased more rapidly than population, allowing for constant economic growth. In this way, less developed countries should emulate the Western model and seek to open their countries to Western values and global trade in resources, goods, and services. However, the concept of sustainability challenges this vision. Today, the view of nature as a resource to meet human needs ignores the needs of other life forms and future human generations [7].

The 2008 banking crisis, the failure of democracy and the rapid spread of the coronavirus in 2020 call into question the ideals of the Western free market economy. The

Earth's atmosphere is unable to absorb emissions, the natural water cycle is unable to provide the fresh water needed, and the current international competition to ensure the availability of minerals means that these too are under pressure. All human activities affect the environment in which we live. The environment has a certain capacity to cope with this and can absorb some of it without causing permanent damage [7].

In this context, the World Business Council for Sustainable Development (WBCSD), which includes 165 of the world's largest companies, has stated that it 'shares a commitment to sustainability through three pillars: economic growth, ecological balance and social development' [7]. The concept of sustainability consists of three pillars: environmental, social, and economic. The 2030 Agenda for Sustainable Development combines the ecological, economic, and social dimensions into one:

- The most discussed is environmental protection. Address reducing carbon footprint, water consumption, non-degradable packaging, and wasteful processes as part of the supply chain. The technical description of environmental sustainability comes from The Natural Step, an international non-profit organization dedicated to innovation through sustainability, which focuses on four types of reductions: reducing the extraction of natural substances from the earth's crust (metals, fossil fuels, etc.); reduce the production of chemicals and compounds (plastics, dioxins, etc.); reduce the physical degradation of nature and natural processes (marine, forest habitats, etc.); reduce barriers that prevent people from meeting basic human needs (working conditions, health, etc.). These are powerful concepts that go beyond the idea of environmental sustainability linked only to recycling, reuse and biodegradability, and lead us further to the more general idea of reducing and remodulating consumption, which the market has been supporting for decades through the creation of excess needs and still new ones.
- Social development is about treating employees fairly and ensuring responsible, ethical, and sustainable treatment of employees, stakeholders, and the community in which the company operates. It is a state that preserves the cohesion of society and its ability to support its members in working together to achieve common goals, while meeting individual needs for health and well-being, adequate nutrition and shelter, expression, and cultural identity. And political commitment.
- Economic development is probably the simplest form of sustainable development. For a business to be profitable, it needs to generate sufficient revenue to continue in the future. The challenge of this form of sustainability is to find a balance. Instead of making money at any cost, companies should strive for profit in line with other elements of sustainability [8].

The 2030 Agenda challenges complexity: since the three dimensions of development (economic, environmental, and social) are closely related, each objective cannot be considered separately, but must be pursued based on a systemic approach that considers the interrelationships and does not have a negative impact on other spheres of development. Only the integrated growth of all three components will make it possible to achieve sustainable development [9].

2.2 Sustainability of Buildings

The construction industry is one of the largest industries. As a key player in society, the construction sector is responsible for leading the way in implementing sustainable practices and limiting their impact on the environment. Green buildings will continue to grow and become the new normal, and the aim will be to do more for the long-term impact of our resources [10].

A green building refers to philosophies and processes to achieve the creation and use of a built environment that is as environmentally friendly as possible. From the design stage through construction to the operation of the finished structure, green buildings aim to reduce negative impacts on the planet and ultimately deliver positive returns. All constructions have an inevitable impact on the environment. As sustainability becomes increasingly important around the world, when constructing a new building, we want to minimize our environmental impact and ensure that the building remains sustainable in the years to come. Green buildings are the answer to this challenge and a rapidly growing aspect of the sector. Below are some of the new processes and innovations that are part of the green building movement [10].

There are countless approaches to greener building, from innovative designs that maximize the use of natural resources to the use of alternative energy sources and recycled materials, but the focus is pollution, waste generation, water saving, energy and resource efficiency [11].

The construction of green buildings requires the integration of sustainable construction methods at all stages of the project life cycle (from planning and design to operation and maintenance) to meet the necessary standards. Close cooperation between key stakeholders is essential for this. The use of environmentally friendly technologies and materials can have a high upfront cost, but in the long run it can pay off in terms of factors such as lower energy consumption costs that make the investment worthwhile [11].

Planning and design play a key role in integrating sustainable construction and green technologies into construction. From the materials used in the design itself, there are many factors that can influence the overall sustainability of construction and maintenance that need to be considered during these early stages of a construction project [11].

Materials are often the first thing that comes to mind when you're thinking about building an environmentally sustainable building. The use of organic or recycled materials is becoming increasingly popular due to their low environmental impact. In addition, some standard building materials, such as wood, require less energy to produce and are considered more sustainable than materials such as concrete and steel. When it comes to choosing green materials for work, anything from adhesives and paints to insulation and flooring can be considered. However, it is not only the type of material used that is important, but also its quality [11].

Another important aspect of sustainable architectural design is to harness the power of natural elements. For tall buildings such as skyscrapers, wind energy can also be used to power a building with natural energy. Installing solar panels that absorb sunlight is also a popular source of sustainable energy.

The power of the sun's rays is also transmitted through heat-absorbing surfaces and strategically located windows that provide additional sources of natural heat and reduce dependence on gas or electricity. The design of a passive house, which is considered one of the most advanced forms of sustainable living, is strongly based on this concept [11].

Alternative energy technologies are not the only innovations used in green buildings. The implementation of smart home technologies, energy-efficient appliances and water-saving devices will allow for a more efficient use of energy in the operation of the building, thereby significantly reducing waste and costs in the long term. Cool, reflective roofs and water-saving technologies such as rainwater collection, double pipes and grey water recycling also help reduce energy consumption [11].

In general, a large amount of waste is generated on construction sites. Using materials that are organic, biodegradable, or reusable on-site can reduce waste during the construction process. The construction site emits a lot of CO_2 and other emissions during the construction process. You cannot completely avoid this, but it can be reduced by efficiency on the spot. Overall, by incorporating processes that help ensure a smoother and faster running of construction projects, you will spend less time on site and reduce the environmental impact of the project. Ensuring the efficient use of manpower and machinery can have a similar effect. Another way to reduce construction time and thus reduce waste and emissions is to invest in prefabrication in a controlled environment that produces less waste and consumes less energy than standard on-site construction [11].

Whether a construction project is small or large, we can incorporate sustainable construction and green technologies into all phases of your project. The application of these ecological changes in the construction process, from waste reduction on site to the design of buildings, will become increasingly important in the coming years, as the number of customers interested in the design of green buildings continues to grow and profitability increases [11].

2.3 Decarbonization and Its Impact on Industry

The construction sector is an energy-intensive sector, which is directly reflected and does not contribute to the promotion of environmental sustainability. As a direct consequence of this, the construction sector is gradually implementing a few practices in the process of promoting sustainability in the construction sector, despite many conflicting objectives and complex challenges. According to a recent global survey, the construction sector has made great strides in promoting sustainability and eliminating negative environmental impacts. Industry leaders in engineering and construction have made the most progress towards sustainability, especially in the design phase, stating that sustainability is their most important or primary concern. Increased regulation is forcing engineering and construction companies to look for more circular and sustainable solutions [12].

Climate change and environmental degradation are an existential crisis for Europe and the world. To tackle these challenges, Delivering will transform the European Green Deal into a modern, resource-efficient, and competitive economy. Climate change is the biggest challenge in our deal and presents an opportunity to build a new economic model. 'Delivering the European Green Deal' sets out a roadmap for this transformation: All 27 EU Member States committed to make the EU the first climate neutral continent by 2050. The main goal of the deal is to reduce emissions by at least 55% below 1990 levels by 2030. This will create new opportunities, investments, and jobs (promoting career development), reduce emissions, tackle energy poverty, reduce dependence on foreign energy and improve our health and well-being [13].

Alongside the Green Deal, the European Agreement also highlighted several organizations and associations that promote and develop sustainability in the construction sector. One of these organizations is the World Green Building Council (World GBC). World GBC is an organization whose main objective is to build a sustainable and decarbonized environment. It works with businesses, organizations, and governments to achieve the Paris Agreement and the UN Sustainable Development Goals, and its main goal is to achieve a decarbonized and sustainable construction sector by 2030, where systemic change drives market change and promotes good practice [14].

'Decarbonization' refers to the process of reducing 'carbon intensity', usually by reducing greenhouse gas emissions from the combustion of fossil fuels. Typically, this reduces the amount of carbon dioxide produced per unit of electricity generated. Reducing the amount of carbon dioxide produced by transportation and power generation is essential to meet the global temperature standards set by the Paris Agreement and the UK Government [8].

Decarbonization means increasing the importance of low-carbon energy production and consequently reducing the use of fossil fuels. This includes the use of renewable energy sources such as wind, solar and biomass. In addition to 'cleaner' technologies, the widespread use of electric vehicles can also reduce the use of coal-based electricity. By reducing the carbon intensity of the energy and transport sectors, net zero emission targets can be achieved sooner and in line with government standards [8].

Decarbonization efforts are underway in many countries, with more than 150 governments presenting plans to reduce carbon emissions by 2030. Paris has committed to ban diesel vehicles by 2040, while London has committed to electric buses and hybrid, electric and black taxis. Renewable energy sources, which now produce a third of the world's total energy capacity, are also being used more. Greenhouse gas emissions from fossil fuel power plants can be limited using carbon capture and storage (CCS) technologies. Around 20 large-scale CCS plants are currently in operation worldwide, with many more under construction [8].

More energy efficient and less carbon-intensive energy sources are part of an important pathway to decarbonization. The global transportation system runs primarily on carbon-based fuels such as diesel and oil, but the widespread use of electric vehicles will increase the contribution of the transport sector to reducing carbon emissions [8].

The UK's independent Commission on Climate Change (CCC) has stated that energy sector CO2 emissions could reach 98.3 million tons by 2050, up from 3 million tons in 2018. Carbon neutrality through decarbonization processes [8].

2.4 Circular Construction

The circular economy is a closed economic system in which raw materials, components and products lose as little value as possible when using renewable energy sources [15].

More than 100 different definitions of circular economy are used in scientific literature and in specialized journals. So many different definitions are used because the term is used by a diverse group of researchers and practitioners [16]. Academics emphasize different aspects of this concept than financial analysts. Due to the variety of definitions, it is also difficult to measure circularity. Definitions often focus on the use of raw materials or systemic changes.

Definitions that focus on resource use often follow the 3Rs approach:

• reduce - reduce (minimum use of raw materials),
• reuse - reuse (maximum reuse of products and components),
• recycle – recycling (reuse of high-quality raw materials) [15, 16].

In a circular economy, material loops are closed throughout the ecosystem. There is no waste, since all the remaining material can be used to make a new product. Toxic substances are eliminated, and residual flows are divided into biological and technical cycles. After use, manufacturers take their products back and repair them to a new life cycle [18]. Therefore, it is important in this system not only that the materials are properly recycled, but also that the products, components, and raw materials in these cycles retain high quality [17].

As with raw materials and products, energy in a circular economy will last as long as possible. The circular economy system draws its strength from renewable energy sources. Since energy is not recyclable, we are not talking about energy cycles, but about "continuous energy flows" [17]. An example is CHP.

The construction industry produces about 20% of total anthropogenic greenhouse gases worldwide [19] and uses many natural resources. For example, sand and gravel are the most mined group of materials [20] and their subsequent extraction has a very strong impact on biodiversity [21].

The construction industry is also responsible for around 50% of the waste generated in the European Union and 25% of the solid waste generated worldwide. The subsequent use of this waste has a very negative impact on our environment [22]. This waste contains approximately 75% of natural land or rock [23].

3   Research Methodology and Data

3.1   Research Aim

The research methodology consisted of analyzing and comparing selected parameters within the field of green (environmental) taxes and the generation and/or management of waste within selected European countries. As part of this research, the following parameters were analyzed and subsequently compared:

• energy taxes,
• environmental (green) tax revenues,
• energy taxes in construction sector,
• waste generation,
• municipal waste recycling rates in Europe,
• waste generation in the construction industry,
• recovery rate of construction and demolition waste.

3.2 Data Collection and Research Sample

The main obstacle to research was the availability of data. Every year, the European Union publishes, within the framework of the European Happiness System (Eurostat database), selected statistical dates for EU needs, which are statistically harmonized in all Member States. Data update and availability is slower due to the large volume of data and the complexity of evaluation. Within that database, therefore, the data available for 2020 were the most readily available. Based on the above, the analysis and evaluation of selected parameters within the European countries for the year 2020 was the subject of research.

3.3 Research Step and Methodology

To achieve the main objective of the contribution, the following procedural steps were taken:

- research of issues in the field of auctionability and its aspects - defining the concepts of sustainability, sustainable development, the concept of auctionability and basic pillars,
- addressing the issue of building sustainability – deification of the concept of green buildings, the principles of construction and use, and green buildings,
- research on decarbonization issues and its impact on industry – definition of the concept of decarbonization, overview of initiatives supporting sustainable industry,
- research on issues in the field of circular construction,
- an overview of the current state of play in the field of green and energy taxes within selected European countries,
- an overview of the current state of play in the field of waste generation, recycling of municipal waste, generation of waste in construction and the rate of recovery of construction and demolition waste. Individual countries were assigned position/ranking followed by the number of points,
- data analysis – defining evaluation criteria, compiling rankings, defining conclusions and future recommendations.

4 Results and Discussion

4.1 Green Taxes, Energy Taxes

Climate change is the greatest environmental threat that we, as humanity, wish for. For this purpose, many innovative tools and techniques are being introduced that contribute to sustainable development. Such a tool also includes green taxes. Green taxes are taxes designed to "tax behavior that is harmful to the health of the planet." The principle of taxes is based on the principle: "Those who pollute pay" [26].

According to a statistical framework developed jointly in 1997 by Eurostat, the European Commission, the Organization for Economic Co-operation and Development (OECD) and the International Energy Agency (IEA), an environmental/green tax is defined as 'a tax base composed of units of materials (or similar) that have a specific and demonstrated negative impact on the environment' [26].

Green taxes are based on the simple principle that polluters pay for pollution. Green taxes are essential to stop climate change. Climate change is the greatest environmental threat we face as humans. That is why we need to reduce greenhouse gas emissions globally, and international bodies such as the International Monetary Fund, environmental organizations and many economists have agreed that environmental taxation is a key tool in the fight against climate change [26].

The IMF has proposed to introduce a carbon tax for the countries that emit the most greenhouse gases. According to the organization, this rate should be \$75/€68 per tons by 2030. From an industrial point of view, energy is the most affected by environmental taxes. According to Eurostat, energy taxes in the European Union (EU) accounted for more than three quarters of total environmental tax revenues in 2020 (77.2% in total), compared to transport taxes (19.1%) and environmental taxes and withholdings, which were significantly exceeded. (3,7%) [26].

The benefits of introducing green taxes, which demonstrably confirm the need for them and directly help to promote sustainable development, include the following aspects:

- internalization of negative externality,
- promoting energy savings and the use of renewable resources,
- discouraging anti-ecological behavior,
- motivation to implement sustainability innovations,
- generating revenue for governments (direct impact on the reduction of other taxes or the implementation of environmental projects
- protection of the environment [26].

Each country has its own design regarding green taxes. Green taxes focus primarily on the following aspects:

- emissions of nitric oxide-NO and nitric oxide-NO2, which are mainly produced by combustion vehicles,
- emissions of Sulphur dioxide – SO2, which is the main cause of acid rain (arising from the combustion of petroleum products and the combustion of coal),
- carbon dioxide emissions - CO2,
- waste management,
- noise caused by take-off and landing of aircraft,
- sources of water pollution (pesticides, fertilizers, acids, and others)
- energy products - gasoline, diesel, natural gas, coal, fuel, and electricity production - their combustion causes the creation of SO2 emissions,
- handling and extraction of soil and use of natural resources,
- ozone-depleting products,
- transport – registration, use, import and sale of polluting vehicles [26].

In 2020, revenues from energy taxes within the European Union (27 countries) amounted to EUR 231 552.11 million [27].

In that year, within the European Union (27 countries), revenues from environmental (green) taxes were also tracked, which was at the level of 5.57%, revenues from energy taxes in the construction sector were at EUR 6 737.23 million, which represented a share of about 2.91% of total energy taxes [28–30].

Based on the available information, a ranking of selected European countries was created, considering the results in the field of energy taxes, revenues from environmental (green) taxes and energy taxes in the construction sector. A position/ranking has been assigned to each country. Within the individual sections, parameters, the number, the ranking was assigned to the country with the most favorable result within that section, that is, the country that had the highest value of energy taxes, revenues from environmental (green) taxes and energy taxes in the construction sector (income in millions of euros and percentage of the total number of energetic taxes). Based on the above ranking, points were subsequently awarded to individual countries, where position number 1 was rated more favorably, i.e., 30 points.

Based on the points earned, the following ranking was created. The leader in energy, green taxes in 2020 was the Netherlands with 95 points. Denmark is in second position with 92 points, and Italy closes the top three, with 89 points. The next ranking was as follows, with Finland in fourth place (84 points), Norway in fifth place (80 points), Belgium in sixth place (78 points), Sweden in seventh place (77 points), Germany in eighth place (76 points), France in ninth place (72 points) and Bulgaria in the top 10 with 71 points. More detailed results are shown on Fig. 1. Ranking of countries in the field of green (environmental) taxes [27–30].

Data for year 2020														
	Energy taxes			Environmental (green) tax revenues			Energy taxes in construction sector			Energy taxes by paying sector - construction			Total score - points	Total score - ranking
County	Million EUR	Ranking (explanations: 1- high value, 30- low value)	Points (30 - best, 1 - worst)	Percent - %	Ranking (explanations: 1- high value, 30- low value)	Points (30 - best, 1 - worst)	Million EUR	Ranking (explanations: 1- high value, 30- low value)	Points (30 - best, 1 - worst)	Percent - %	Ranking (explanations: 1- high value, 30- low value)	Points (30 - best, 1 - worst)		
Belgium	7961,1	7	24	5,82	20	11	298,67	8	23	3,75	11	20	78	6
Bulgaria	1642,08	21	10	9,89	1	30	58,97	18	13	3,59	13	18	71	10
Czechia	3880,7	15	16	5,35	22	9	193,65	12	19	4,03	8	25	69	13
Denmark	5165,8	10	21	6,76	4	27	251,44	11	20	4,87	7	24	92	2
Germany	47642,29	1	30	4,27	29	2	1480,3	1	30	3,11	17	14	76	8
Estonia	601,64	26	5	7,2	9	22	30,96	23	8	5,15	5	26	61	18
Ireland	2767,86	18	13	6,04	18	13	42,94	20	11	1,55	25	6	43	24
Greece	4826	11	20	9,99	3	28	7,25	28	3	0,15	29	7	53	22
Spain	16020	4	27	4,74	27	4	417,9	5	26	2,61	20	11	68	14
France	41272	2	29	4,78	26	5	844,92	3	28	2,05	21	10	72	9
Croatia	1262,72	22	9	8,85	4	27	43,45	19	12	3,44	16	15	63	17
Italy	40281	3	28	7,11	12	19	1122,07	2	29	2,79	18	13	89	3
Cyprus	410,4	27	4	7,15	10	21	19,76	25	6	4,81	8	23	54	21
Latvia	791,67	25	6	9,82	2	29	28,39	24	7	3,59	14	17	59	20
Lithuania	859,37	23	8	6,26	17	14	13,88	26	5	1,52	26	5	32	29
Luxembourg	810,58	24	7	3,62	30	1	36,69	21	10	4,53	9	22	40	26
Hungary	2279,36	19	12	6,01	19	12	178,66	13	18	7,84	2	29	71	11
Malta	143,33	28	3	7,66	7	24	2,76	29	2	1,92	23	8	37	27
Netherland	14318	5	26	7,97	5	26	583	4	27	3,51	15	16	95	1
Austria	4599,4	13	18	5	24	7	125,54	26	5	2,73	19	12	42	25
Poland	11711,97	6	25	7,12	11	20	135,58	16	15	1,16	27	4	64	16
Portugal	3398,51	17	14	6,76	15	16	129,4	15	16	3,6	12	19	65	15
Romania	3878,69	16	15	7,3	8	23	75,44	17	14	1,95	22	9	61	19
Slovenia	114,46	29	2	7,84	6	25	10,46	27	4	0,94	28	3	34	28
Slovakia	1965,13	20	11	6,81	13	18	32,69	22	9	1,66	24	7	45	23
Finland	4605,14	12	19	6,52	16	15	177,3	9	22	6,02	3	28	84	4
Sweden	7142,91	8	23	4,73	28	3	375,97	7	24	5,26	4	27	77	7
Iceland	UD	UD	UD	5,56	21	10	UD	UD	UD	UD	UD	UD	UD	UD
Norway	4256,44	14	17	5,25	23	8	383,85	6	25	9,02	1	30	80	5
Switzerland	6278,79	9	22	4,96	25	6	263,8	10	21	4,2	10	21	70	12
Explanations: UD - unavailable data														

Fig. 1. Ranking of countries in the field of green (environmental) taxes [27–30]

In 2021, revenues from taxes and social contributions in the EU increased by €520 billion to €6,058 billion compared to 2020. This is a change compared to 2020, when there was a decrease [31].

4.2 Waste and Recycling

Environmentally friendly waste management and the use of secondary materials they contain are key pillars of the European Union's environmental policy. The main objective of EU waste policy is to contribute to the circular economy, by reusing high-quality resources from waste. The European Green Deal aims to boost growth by moving towards a modern, resource-efficient, and competitive economy. As part of this transition, several pieces of EU waste legislation will be reviewed. The Waste Framework Directive is the EU's legal framework for waste management and management in the EU. It introduces a ranking of waste management preference called the 'waste hierarchy'. Certain categories of waste require specific approaches. The EU therefore has many laws to address different types of waste in addition to an overarching legal framework [32].

The Waste Framework Directive sets out basic concepts and definitions related to waste management, including definitions of waste, recycling, and recovery. Between the basic principles of waste management include the following aspects:

- waste management without endangering human health and harming the environment,
- dealing with waste without risk to water, air, soil, plants, or animals,
- chuckling with waste without being bothered by noise or smell,
- dealing with waste without adversely affecting the landscape or places of special interest [33].

The ratio of the total amount of waste generated, excluding major mineral wastes, to the amount loaded through the recycling process remains below the total waste production for the period when data are available. In 2020, total recycling was reported at 46%. The progress made in three key waste streams (packaging, municipal waste, electrical and electronic waste) has been highlighted as progress in total recycling. This reflects the importance of strong European Union policies, including recycling targets, in supporting the improvement of waste management. However, their recycling rate is still below half of the waste generated, except for packaging, which reached 64% in 2020 [34].

Most countries in Europe have significantly increased the recycling rate of municipal waste, which clearly indicates an improvement in waste management. However, the difference in municipal waste recycling performance between the countries with the highest and lowest recycling rates is significant. In the Member States of the European Union, rates ranged from 70% (Germany) to 11% (Malta), with Kosovo, for example, registering no recycling rate. Germany, Austria, Slovenia, the Netherlands, Switzerland, Luxembourg, Belgium, and Italy performed best, achieving recycling rates of more than 50%. As many as seven countries have recycled less than 20% of municipal waste, helping to slow down improvements in waste management [34].

In 2020, the total waste generated in the EU by all economic activities and households was 2 151 million tons or 4 808 kg per capita. In terms of economic activities and households, the construction sector accounted for the largest share of waste generation and production (37.1% of the total), followed by mining and quarrying (23.4%), manufacturing (10.9%, waste and water services (10.7%) and households (9.5%); the remaining 8.4% were wastes from other economic activities, in particular services (4.5%) and energy (2.3%) [35].

Based on the available information, a ranking of selected European countries has been created, considering the results in the field of waste generation, recycling of municipal waste, generation of waste in construction and recovery rates of construction and demolition waste. Each country was assigned the position/ranking followed by the number of points. The order and number of points was assigned within each section as follows:

- In waste generation – position number 1 was assigned to the country with the lowest waste generation value, at the same time the country in position 1 received the highest number of points within that section,
- in the field of municipal waste recycling – position number 1 was assigned to the country with the highest municipal waste recycling value, at the same time the country in position 1 received the highest number of points within that section,
- in the field of waste generation in construction – position number 1 was assigned to the country with the lowest waste generation rate in construction, at the same time the country in position 1 received the highest number of points within that section,
- In recovery rate of construction and demolition waste – position number 1 was assigned to the country with the highest value of the recovery rate of construction and demolition waste, at the same time the country in position 1 received the highest number of points within that section.

Based on the points obtained, a ranking of selected European countries in the field of waste generation and management was established. Slovenia took first place with 98 points, followed by Lithuania (97 points) and Latvia closes the top 3 with 94 points. Greece (4th place - 86 points), Slovakia (5th place - 83 points), Italy (6th place - 81 points), Portugal (7th place - 79 points), Hungary (8th place - 78 points), Belgium (9th place - 76 points) and the Czech Republic closes the top 10 with 74 points. More detailed results are shown on Fig. 2. *Ranking of countries in the field of waste generation and recycling* [36–39].

County	Waste generation (kg per capita)			Municipal waste recycling rates in Europe by country			Waste generation in the construction industry			Recovery rate of construction and demolition waste			Total points	Total score - ranking
	Kg per capita	Ranking (explanations: 1- low value, 30- high value)	Points (30 - best, 1 - worst)	Percent - %	Ranking (explanations: 1- high value, 30- low value)	Points (30 - best, 1 - worst)	Percent share of total waste - %	Ranking (explanations: 1- low value, 30- high value)	Points (30 - best, 1 - worst)	Percent -%	Ranking (explanations: 1- high value, 30- low value)	Points (30 - best, 1 - worst)		
Belgium	5899	21	10	52,3	7	24	30,5	18	13	99	2	29	76	9
Bulgaria	16785	28	3	34,6	21	10	1,6	3	28	96	5	26	67	17
Czechia	3598	15	16	45,4	9	22	42,9	21	10	96	5	26	74	10
Denmark	3453	13	18	45	11	20	54,8	23	8	97	4	27	73	12
Germany	4824	19	12	69,6	1	30	56,3	24	7	94	7	24	73	13
Estonia	12171	25	6	28,9	24	7	9,8	10	21	93	8	23	57	23
Ireland	2874	11	20	40,4	16	15	13,6	14	17	UD	UD	UD	UD	UD
Greece	2295	6	25	21	28	5	1,1	2	29	97	4	27	86	4
Spain	2236	5	26	36,4	20	11	30,7	19	12	85	12	19	68	16
France	4657	18	13	42,7	13	18	67,6	26	5	74	15	16	52	25
Croatia	1483	1	30	29,5	23	8	23,8	16	15	89	10	21	74	11
Italy	2942	12	19	51,4	8	23	37,8	20	11	98	3	28	81	6
Cyprus	2488	9	22	16,6	27	4	20,5	15	16	79	14	17	59	22
Latvia	1501	2	29	39,7	17	14	9,7	9	22	99	2	29	94	3
Lithuania	2396	8	23	45,3	10	21	8,3	6	25	98	3	28	97	2
Luxembourg	14618	26	5	52,8	5	26	82,1	28	3	99	2	29	63	19
Hungary	1648	4	27	32	22	9	27,1	17	14	98	3	28	78	8
Malta	5823	20	11	10,5	29	2	82,7	29	2	100	1	30	45	27
Netherland	7145	22	9	56,9	4	27	65,4	25	6	100	1	30	72	14
Austria	7728	24	7	62,3	2	29	76,5	27	4	91	9	22	62	20
Poland	4492	17	14	38,7	18	23	13	13	18	74	15	16	71	15
Portugal	1612	3	28	26,5	25	6	10,7	11	20	95	6	25	79	7
Romania	7338	23	8	13,7	28	3	0,9	1	30	88	11	20	61	21
Slovenia	3576	14	17	59,3	3	28	6,3	5	26	97	4	27	98	1
Slovakia	2341	7	24	42,2	14	17	9	7	24	81	13	18	83	5
Finland	20993	29	2	41,6	15	16	11,8	12	19	63	17	14	51	26
Sweden	14664	27	4	38,3	19	12	9,3	8	23	74	15	16	55	24
Iceland	3667	16	15	UD	UD	UD	3,9	4	27	UD	UD	UD	UD	UD
Norway	2610	10	21	45	12	19	44,2	22	9	64	16	15	64	18
Switzerland	UD	UD	UD	52,8	6	25	UD	UD	UD	UD	UD	UD	UD	UD

Explanations: UD - unavailable data

Fig. 2. Ranking of countries in the field of waste generation and recycling [36–39]

5 Conclusion

The concept of sustainability represents a broad political concept in public discourse and is often understood in terms of three fundamental pillars, namely the environmental, economic, and social aspects. These fundamental pillars of sustainability are increasingly reflected in individual processes and principles across all aspects of society. The company's goal is to build a sustainable society. Based on the above, many organizations, governments and associations are approaching the introduction of various mechanisms and principles that help to build a sustainable society. Within the European Union, the SDGs are agreed at the highest political level. The EU institutions and Member States, including regional and local authorities, work more closely together to ensure better coordination and monitoring of progress in the process of implementing the milestones to be met under the 2030 Agenda. Based on the mentioned aspects, aspects such as the amount of waste produced, the recycling rate of municipal waste, the quantity and rate of recovery of waste produced within individual industrial sectors, and the level of revenues from energy and green taxes within the countries of Europe are gradually being monitored within the European Union.

The research analyses the 2020 results in countries in the field of green taxes and the generation and/or management of waste. Based on the available data, their thorough analysis and considering the established criteria, the Netherlands is among the leaders in the field of energy/green taxes, followed by Denmark and Italy. Lithuania ranked last in the above ranking. In terms of waste generation, recycling of municipal waste, generation of waste in construction and recovery rates of construction and demolition waste, Slovenia ranked first in our assessment, followed by Lithuania and Latvia. It was very interesting to find that, although Lithuania was one of the worst rated countries in terms of green taxes, it was among the top 3 in terms of waste generation and packaging. Malta ranked last in the ranking (creation and feeding of waste), losing 53 points to the leader in that ranking. These results show significant differences in the priorities that each government sets itself to promote sustainability. Therefore, the initiatives of individual organizations are welcome and will greatly help to develop a strategic crisis plan, the result of which will be the elimination of the adverse effects of industry on the environment and the health of the population.

Acknowledgments. The paper presents partial research results of project APVV-17–0549 "Research of knowledge-based and virtual technologies for intelligent designing and realization of building projects with emphasis on economic efficiency and sustainability" and and APVV-22–0576 "Research of digital technologies and building information modeling tools for designing and evaluating the sustainability parameters of building structures in the context of decarbonization and circular construction". This article was created thanks to support under the Operational Program Integrated Infrastructure for the project: National infrastructure for supporting technology transfer in Slovakia II – NITT SK II, co-financed by the European Regional Development Fund.

References

1. Rockstrom, J., et al.: Planetary boundaries: exploring the safe operating space for humanity. Ecol. Soc. **14** (2), 32 (2009). http://www.ecologyandsociety.org/vol14/iss2/art32/. Accessed 02 Jan 2023

2. Banerjee, A., Duflo, E.: Poor Economics: a Radikal Rethinking of the Way to Fight Global Poverty, PublicAffairs, 320f. (2011). ISBN 978–1610390934
3. Sachs, J.: The Age of Sustainable Development. New York: Columbia University Press, 543 (2015). ISBN: 978–0–231–17315–5
4. Brennan, G., Tennant, M., Blomsma, F.: Business and production solutions. In: Kopnina, H., Shoreman-Ouimet, E. (Eds.), Sustainability: Key Issues. EarthScan. Routledge, pp. 219–239 (2015)
5. Civil Bites. Is it any environment benefits of the circular economy for civil engineering? (2022). https://www.civilsbites.com/2021/11/12/is-it-any-environment-benefit-of-the-circular-economy-for-civil-engineering/. Accessed 22 Dec 2022
6. Treccani Sostenibilitá (2022). https://www.treccani.it/enciclopedia/sostenibilita. Accessed 22 Dec 2022
7. Ashby, M.F.: Materials and sustainable development. Chapter 2- What is a Sustainable Development (2016). https://www.sciencedirect.com/science/article/pii/B9780081001769000025. Accessed 22 Dec 2022
8. TWI Global. What is sustainability and why is it so important? (2023). https://www.twi-global.com/technical-knowledge/faqs/faq-what-is-sustainability. Accessed 02 Jan 2023
9. Network DIGITAL 360- ESG360. CEO e sostenibilitá: focus sulla creazone di nuovo valore nel tempo a sulla resilienza (2022). https://www.esg360.it/. Accessed 22 Dec 2022
10. Arnholz, J.: Build Your Future: What is Green Construction? (2021). https://byf.org/what-is-green-construction/. Accessed 20 Dec 2022
11. THINK PROJECT. Everything to know about green construction (2022). https://thinkproject.com/blog/everything-to-know-about-green-construction/. Accessed 18 Dec 2022
12. Magyar, J.: Forbes: The Construction Industry Is Getting Greener: Why, how, And What´s Changing? (2021). https://www.forbes.com/sites/sap/2021/08/25/the-construction-industry-is-getting-greener why-how-and-whats-changing/?sh=5d9ed49952bc. Accessed 18 Dec 2022
13. European Commission. Delivering the European Green Deal (2021). https://ec.europa.eu/info/strategy/priorities-2019-2024/european-green-deal/delivering-european-green-deal_en. Accessed 18 Dec 2022
14. World Green Building Council. Who we are (2022). https://worldgbc.org/. Accessed 18 Dec 2022
15. Kenniskaarten. What is the definition of a circular economy? (2022). https://kenniskaarten.hetgroenebrein.nl/en/knowledge-map-circular-economy/what-is-the-definition-a-circular-economy/. Accessed 15 Dec 2022
16. Kirchherr, J., Reike, D., Hekkert, M.: Conceptualizing the circular economy: an analysis of 114 definitons. In: Resources, Conservation and Recycling, vol. 127, pp. 221–232 (2017). https://doi.org/10.1016/j.resconrec.2017.09.005. Accessed 15 Dec 2022
17. Ellen Macarthur Foundation. Towards a circular economy: Business rationale for an accelerated transition (2015). https://kidv.nl/media/rapportages/towards_a_circular_economy.pdf? 1.2.1. Accessed 15 Dec 2022
18. Korhonen, J., Nuur, C., Feldmann, A., Birkie, S.: Circular economy as an essentially contested concept. J. Cleaner Product. 175, 544–522 (2018). https://www.sciencedirect.com/science/article/pii/S0959652617330706. Accessed 15 Dec 2022
19. Edenhofer, O., et al.: The IPCC at a crossroads: Opportunities for reform (2015). https://archive.ipcc.ch/pdf/assessment-report/ar5/wg3/ipcc_wg3_ar5_summary-for-policymakers.pdf. Accessed 15 Dec 2022
20. Bendixen, M., Best, J., Hackney, C., Lønsmann Iversen, L.: Times is running out for sand. Natures 571, 29–31 (2019). https://doi.org/10.1038/d41586-019-02042-4. Accessed 15 Dec 2022

21. Park, E., et al.: Dramatic decrease of flood frequency in the Mekong Delta due to river-bed mining and dyke cosntruction. Sci. Total Environ. **723**, 138066 (2020). https://doi.org/10. 1016/j.scitotenv.2020.138066. Accessed 15 Dec 2022

22. Benachio, G.L.F., do Carmo Duarte Freitas, M., Tavares, S.F.: Circular economy in the construction industry: a systematic literature review. J. Clenaer Product. **260**, 121046 (2020). https://doi.org/10.1016/j.jclepro.2020.121046. Accessed 15 Dec 2022

23. Eras, C., José, J., Gutiérrez, A.S., Capote, D.H., Hens, L., Vandecasteele, C.: Improving the environmental performance of an earthwork project using cleaner production strategies. J. Cleaner Product. **47**, 368–376 (2013). https://doi.org/10.1016/j.jclepro.2012.11.026. Accessed 15 Dec 2022

24. Hamard, E., Cazacliu, B., Razakamanantsoa, A., Morel, J-C.: Cob, a vernaculart earth construction processs in the context of modern sustainable building. Build. Environ. **106**, 103–119 (2016). https://doi.org/10.1016/j.buildenv.2016.06.009. Accessed 15 Dec 2022

25. Sauvage, M.: Debuts de l'architecture de terre au Proche-Orient. In: Achenza, M.M., Correia, H (eds.). Guillaud Mediterra 2009, 1st Mediterranean Conference on Earth Architecture , pp. 189–198. Cagliari, Italy: Edicom Editions (2009)

26. IBERDOLA: Environmental taxes make way to protect the environment. (2022). https://www. iberdrola.com/sustainability/green-and-environmental-taxes. Accessed 15 Dec 2022

27. Eurostat. Energy taxes (2023). https://ec.europa.eu/eurostat/databrowser/view/ten00139/def ault/table?lang=en. Accessed 02 Jan 2022

28. Eurostat. Environmental tax revenues (2023). https://ec.europa.eu/eurostat/databrowser/view/ ten00141/default/table?lang=en. Accessed 02 Jan 2022

29. Eurostat. Environmental taxe by economic activity (NACE Rev.2) (2023). https://ec.eur opa.eu/eurostat/databrowser/view/ENV_AC_TAXIND2__custom_4492777/default/table? lang=en. Acccessed 02 Jan 2022

30. Eurostat. Energy taxes by paying sector(2023). https://ec.europa.eu/eurostat/databrowser/ view/ENV_AC_TAXENER__custom_4493334/default/table?lang=en. Accessed 02 Jan 2022

31. Eurostat. Environmental tax statistics (2023). https://ec.europa.eu/eurostat/statistics-exp lained/index.php?title=Environmental_tax_statistics#Environmental_taxes_in_the_EU. Accessed 03 Jan 2023

32. European Commission. Waste and recycling (2023). https://environment.ec.europa.eu/topics/ waste-and-recycling_en. Accessed 03 Jan 2022

33. European Commission. Waste Framework Directive (2023). https://environment.ec.europa. eu/topics/waste-and-recycling/waste-framework-directive_en. Accessed 03 Jan 2022

34. European Environment Agency. Waste recycling in Europe (2023). https://www.eea.europa. eu/ims/waste-recycling-in-europe. Accessed 03 Jan 2022

35. Eurostat. Waste statistics (2023). https://ec.europa.eu/eurostat/statistics-explained/index. php?title=Waste_statistics#Waste_generation_excluding_major_mineral_waste. Accessed 04 Jan 2022

36. Eurostat. Total waste generation (2023). https://ec.europa.eu/eurostat/statistics-explained/ index.php?title=Waste_statistics#Total_waste_generation. Accessed 04 Jan 2022

37. European Environment Agency. Chart- Municipal wast recycling rates in Europe by country (2023). https://www.eea.europa.eu/data-and-maps/daviz/municipal-waste-recycled-and-com posted-6#tab-chart_7. Accessed 05 Jan 2022

38. Eurostat. File: Waste gerenation by economic activities and households, 2020 (% share of total waste) (2023). https://ec.europa.eu/eurostat/statistics-explained/index.php?title=File: Waste_generation_by_economic_activities_and_households,_2020_(%25_share_of_total_ waste_).png. Accessed 05 Jan 2022

39. Eurostat. Recovery rate of construction and demoliton waste (2023). https://ec.europa.eu/eur ostat/databrowser/view/cei_wm040/default/table. Accessed 05 Jan 2022

Smart Environment Applications/Scenarios

Online Monitoring and Control FDM Devices: Study

Rebeka Tauberová(✉) ⓘ, Peter Lazorík ⓘ, Lucia Knapčíková ⓘ, and Jozef Husár ⓘ

Faculty of Manufacturing Technologies with a Seat in Presov, Department of Industrial Engineering and Informatics, Technical University of Košice, Bayerova 1, 08001 Prešov, Slovakia

{rebeka.tauberova,peter.lazorik,lucia.knapcikova, jozef.husar}@tuke.sk

Abstract. Digitization is the key word of the term Industrial Revolution of fourth generation. Digitization in industrial enterprises makes it possible to examine various influences on production processes without the necessary entry into real production. Thanks to technologies, that are part of the digitization of manufacturing enterprises such as, augmented reality, virtual reality, additive manufacturing, digital twin, and artificial intelligence, we can monitor selected parameters without interfering with the production process. The funds spent, ensuring the transformation of a traditional enterprise into a digital enterprise, ultimately save production costs. The concept of digitization within industrial enterprises has taken on much greater dimension and importance in connection with events such as COVID 19, which has affected everyday life all over the Earth. At that moment, many companies realized, what a great advantage digitalization of the entire production is. The pressure of events and economic influences led to the accelerated adoption of digitization and intelligent automation. Introduction of digital technologies ultimately makes it possible to use resources, which are entering the production process, more efficiently and intensively. The advantage of digitization of production is increasing material productivity, and the optimization of input production costs. The implementation of artificial intelligence tools in production enables remote control of production in additive manufacturing. Advancing digitalization is big change in many fields such as aviation, medicine, engineering, and automotive industry. Main and necessary pillar are the employees with their skills, knowledge, and years of experiences. Additive manufacturing is field with great potential for the future. There is a big space for new innovations, process improvement and also for quality monitoring. This study is reporting about the online monitoring and control for Fused Deposition Model devices.

Keywords: Additive manufacturing · Fused Deposition Modeling · Online monitoring · Octoprint

D. Perakovic and L. Knapcikova (Eds.): FABULOUS 2023, LNICST 542, pp. 135–146, 2024.
https://doi.org/10.1007/978-3-031-50051-0_10

1 Introduction

The basic elements of additive manufacturing were commercially developed and researched since the end of 1980s. Additive manufacturing (AM) is a process of creation physical objects from 3D models layering and application of material. It is advanced manufacturing technology, which is creating 3D objects from based on drawings created in CAD system. Technology of additive manufacturing is well known and widespread throughout the engineering industry. But also, in specific areas such as custom – made products, also in a medical purposes and automotive industry as well. 3D printing can be defined as the opposite of traditional manufacturing such as turning or milling. Advantage od additive manufacturing is not only that it is cheaper and more accessible, but also AM is more environmentally friendly. Compared to traditional production additive manufacturing produce at least almost no material waste, which represents a more sustainable way of technology, which saves and reduces the amount of material entering the production process. Advantage of AM is the possibility to connect the 3D printer with the external devices such as virtual glasses, sensors or with programmable logic controller. In general, there are several methods of additive manufacturing on the market. Most often used methods are FDM (Fused Deposition Modeling), DMD (Direct Metal Deposition), SLS (Selective Laser Sintering), IJM (Inject Modeling) and SLA (Stereo Lithography).

This study is focused primarily on the FDM method in 3D printing and online monitoring and control of specific device. Huge benefit in additive manufacturing is the possibility to control the particular 3D printer remotely. It is possible through the Octoprint, which is free open-source applications, that allows a remote-control 3D printer remotely. Octoprint can be connected to the smartphone, which can control the start of the printing anytime. Before successful remote control, 3D printer must be connected through (USB) Universal Serial Bus with the single board computer Raspberry Pi on which Octoprint is running. Single board computer (Raspberry Pi) has to be connected to the network, where Octoprint is running as a supplementary application. For remote control of 3D printer, it is necessary to be connected on a local network, where the IP address is assigned. If the IP address is not public Octoprint has to be linked with the cloud platform through the authentication data. Cloud application will allow us to connect remotely with the Octoprint, anywhere with the available internet connection. If the mentioned steps are followed correctly, it is possible to communicate with the 3D printer. Most frequently used cloud applications are for instance Karmen and Octoprint Everywhere.

2 Fused Deposition Modeling Method

The FDM (Fused Deposition Modeling) method is the most widespread among the others mentioned, mainly due to its simple operation and relatively low price. Before printing starts it is necessary to create or download 3D model in STL format. STL format must be converted to the GCODE language, which can communicate with the specific printer. Then the created file is connected via Universal Serial Bus (USB) to the 3D printer. Basic principle of FDM method starts with the advancement of thermoplastic filament from large spool. Filaments is captured by the extruder gear and pushed down towards the hot end. Subsequently the nozzle is heated to melt the filament and moved in the x,y and z directions according to a pre-determined design. Due to the rapid hardening of the material, the model is created immediately after the filament is extruded from the nozzle by layering the material. If we want to achieve the desired fiber connection effect, it is necessary to control the printing parameters, such as the printing temperature and the material application speed. The printing temperature is often closely related to the selected filament. If the mentioned procedure is followed, it is possible to achieve the required quality of product printing. Following figure shows FDM 3D printer. (Fig. 1).

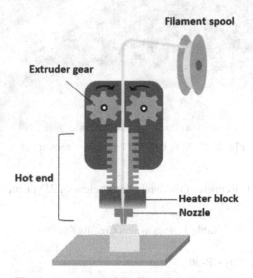

Fig. 1. Fused Deposition Modeling 3D Printer

Specific printer which is connected to the Octoprint is Creality CR-30. This 3D printer uses technology FDM for printing. Specific property of Creality CR-30 is infinity Z axis printing zone, which allows users to print unlimited. Another advantage of this printer is built in rolling conveyor belt. This type of printer is suitable to be placed on conveyor belt in production as it is shown in the next Fig. 2.

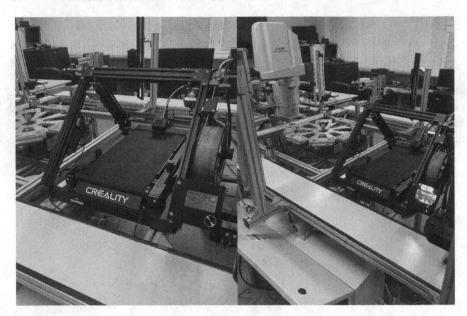

Fig. 2. Creality CR-30 placed on conveyor belt

Following Table 1. Represent the basic parameters of 3D printer Creality CR-30.

Table 1. Parameters Creality CR-30

Product Parameters Creality CR-30	
Print tech: FDM	Nozzle Qty: 1
Print Size: 200 * 170 * ∞ mm	Hot Bed Temperature: ≤ 00 °C
Product Size: 535* 656 * 410 mm	Nozzle Temperature: ≤240 °C
Package Size: 685 * 565 * 302 mm	Layer Height: 0,1 mm-0,4 mm
Product Net Weight: 16,5 kg	Maximum Power Consumption: 350W
Package Gross Weight: 20,5 kg	Power Requirement: AC 100–200/200–240, DC 24V
Slicing Software: Crealitybelt	Supported Materials: PLA/TPU/PETG
Printing Precision: ± 0,1 mm	Filament Diameter: 1,75 mm
Nozzle Diameter: 0,4 mm	

2.1 OctoPrint and Software

Octoprint can be connected to the smartphone, which can control the start of the printing anytime. Before successful remote control, 3D printer must be connected through (USB) Universal Serial Bus with the single board computer Raspberry Pi on which Octoprint is running. Single board computer (Raspberry Pi) has to be connected to the network, where Octoprint is running as a supplementary application. For remote control of 3D printer, it is necessary to be connected on a local network, where the IP address is assigned. If the IP address is not public Octoprint has to be linked with the cloud platform through the authentication data. Cloud application will allow us to connect remotely with the Octoprint, anywhere with the available internet connection. If the mentioned steps are followed correctly, it is possible to communicate with the 3D printer. Most frequently used cloud applications are for instance Karmen and Octoprint Everywhere. Following block diagram on the Fig. 3 represents software and hardware system.

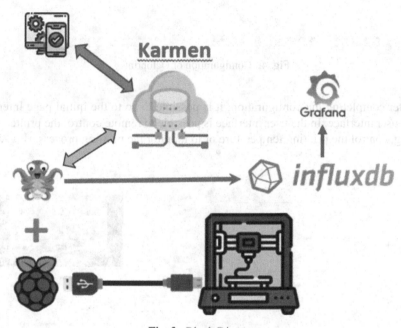

Fig. 3. Block Diagram

Before working with the Octoprint it is necessary to configure initial state, for instance it is mandatory to configure access (username and password), model of printer (creality cr-30), additional printer profile (print volume, print bed, print volume, axes, nozzle diameter, number of extruder and default extrusion length). (See Fig. 4).

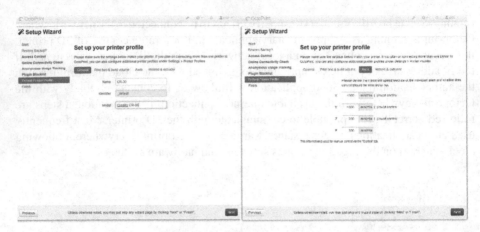

Fig. 4. Configuration of Octoprint

After completing the configuration, it is possible to go to the initial page intended for the user interface. In the user interface is possible to remote control the printer, start printing, control the printing temperature or to monitor the printing process. (Fig. 5).

Fig. 5. User interface of Octoprint

3   Research and Discussion

Research part of submitted study is dedicated to configured part of the Octoprint. Configured Octoprint enables to control 3D printer Creality CR-30, which is situated in laboratory, remotely. Octoprint is running on single board computer Raspberry Pi, which can be placed directly on 3D printer. Amendment between the basic shape of Octoprint and configured shape of Octoprint is in external additional modules. During the configuration were used six external modules to achieve the desired shape of Octoprint:

- Karmen Connector
- Octoprint-Influx DB
- Custom CSS
- Print Scheduler
- Dashboard
- PrettyGCode

Karmen Connector is cloud applications, from which is possible to communicate with the specific 3D printer remotely. Karmen Connector can be connected to the smart phone, which allows notifications to be sent and inform user about the printing process.

Octoprint-Influx DB is time series database, where the data for instance temperature are sent from the Octoprint. Collected data are sent only as a numbers to the selected database file, where they are subsequently stored. The octoprint itself does not store the specific data about the printing process, that is the reason why the database Influx DB is necessary.

Following Fig. 6 offers a view on Octoprint, which is running on Raspberry PI.

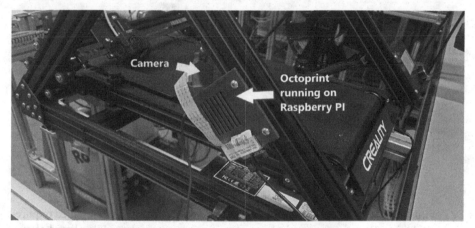

Fig. 6. Octoprint running on Raspberry PI

Custom CSS is additional external module used for customizing the basic user interface. Selected requirements are modified through the CSS programming language. For our needs, the base color of the user interface was changed from white to purple. Because the purple color represents our faculty of Manufacturing Technologies (Fig. 7).

Print Scheduler simplifies printing process because it enables to plan the printing forward ahead of time. This module is offering great help in situations, when it is not possible to be physically all day in laboratory, or when the factory has a commission, which has to be done in specific deadline as soon as possible.

Dashboard is module, which is used to configure the user interface of Octoprint. Basically, Dashboard enables to add commands, which user wants to have. For instance, if user wants to have a button on the user interface for temperature coming from an external sensor, it is necessary to click it in the dashboard.

PrettyGCode is visualization module, which displays colored lines to give you some idea, what the printer is doing and animates progress during the printing.

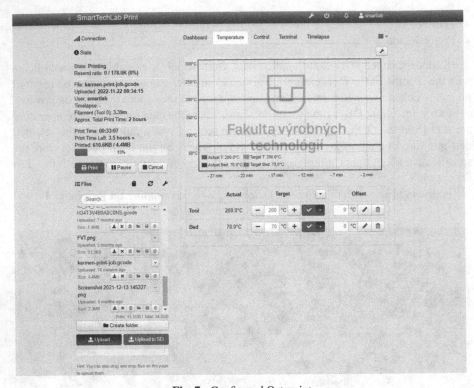

Fig. 7. Configured Octoprint

For this study was Octoprint configured and adapted according to the selected requirements. Additional configurations were made via using external modules listed above. The configured Octoprint was given a name SmartTechLab Print because 3D printer Creality CR-30, which can be controlled remotely by Octoprint, is situated in laboratory, which is called SmartTechLab. (See Fig. 6, Fig. 7, and Fig. 8). It is also possible to add more 3D printers, which can be connected remotely. For instance, this possibility is great for big laboratories, where employees have ten or more 3D printers. In order for remote control to be possible, the entire procedure explained above must be repeated for each printer separately. In large laboratories this possibility to remote control 3D printers is big advantage for employees, because they don't need to go the laboratory to simply turn on the 3D printer.

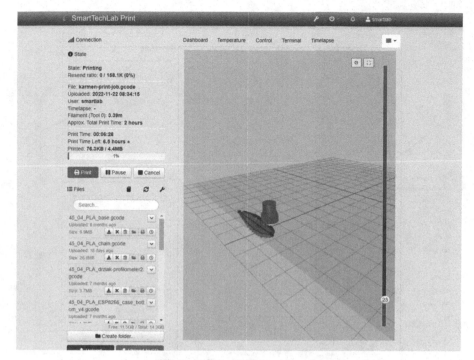

Fig. 8. 3D Visualization Octoprint

When the configuration of Octoprint is done, it is possible to start or pause or cancel the printing process. Octoprint dashboard displays information about printhead temperature, hot end temperature, total printing time. And it is also possible to control amount of filament needed for printing. On Fig. 7 is possible to see 3D visualization in Octoprint. This function of Octoprint dashboard is great for better imaginations of printed products. Following Fig. 9 displays bed temperature of printer Creality CR-30 and hotend temperature.

Displayed graph represents numerical data from printing process on 3D printer Creality CR-30. As we can see in the graph, the value of the measured temperature of hotend was 200,0 °C during the whole printing process and bed temperature was about 60,0 °C. Hotend temperature primary depends of type of filament, because every type of filament has different melting point. Presented graphs was download from visualization tool Grafana. (See Fig. 8).

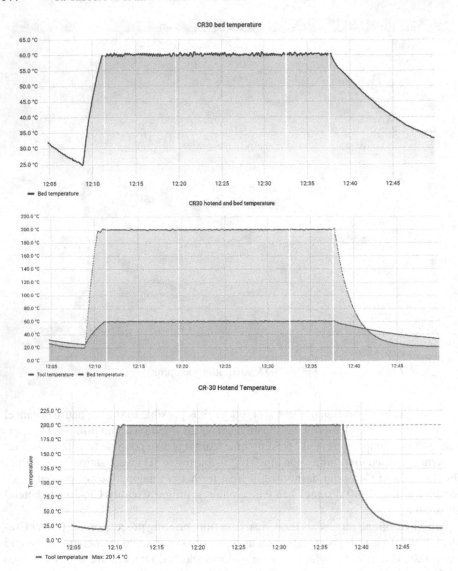

Fig. 9. Bed and Hotend Temperature of 3D printer Creality CR-30

Collected data are sent from Octoprint to the database Influx DB, which is saving them only as numbers. Influx DB is type of database, which is built specially for handling metrics, events, or measurements, that are time-stamped. For the statistical expression of the collected data is used Grafana. Grafana is popular open-source time-series data visualization and alerting tool. It has a data source model, which is highly pluggable and supports multiple time series-based data sources like Prometheus, Influx DB or SQL databases like MySQL. Regardless of where the data is stored, it allows you to visualize data through graphs. There is also possibility to measure the temperature in the laboratory, where specific printer is placed, but in this case, it is necessary to have some external sensors, which are fixed and cooperate with the 3D printer.

4 Conclusion

In the submitted study, the monitoring of FDM device is ensured by the open-source application OctoPrint, through which is possible to remote control of specific 3D printer. With the help of the use of available modern technologies is possible to start printing process from any place with accessible internet connection. Additive manufacturing is rapidly developing progressive technology, that is hiding number of potential possibilities, which has a great enforcement in the future. The primary focus of this paper is to reduce physical interaction between machine and human through the remote control of specific devices in additive manufacturing. Reducing physical interaction between machine and human can save time and human labor, that can be replaced. The proposed system is already implemented and verified in the laboratory at Faculty of Manufacturing technologies with a seat in Prešov. Future studies will be focused on working with the filaments, which are an important part of whole additive manufacturing processes.

Acknowledgment. This work was supported by the projects VEGA 1/0268/22, KEGA 038TUKE-4/2022 granted by the Ministry of Education, Science, Research and Sport of the Slovak Republic.

References

1. Zhang, X., Chu, J., Wei, S.: Design and simulation of remote monitoring system of 3D printer based on cloud platform. In: Institute of Electrical and Electronics Engineers (IEEE Xplore). 3rd International Conference on Automation, Electronics and Electrical Engineering (AUTEE), pp. 290–293 (2021)
2. Kakade, S., Mulay, A., Patil, S.: IoT-based real-time online monitoring system for open ware FDM printers. Mater. Today Proc. 363–367 (2022)
3. Naqvi, S.N.Z., Yfantidou, S.: Time Series Databases and InfluxDB. https://cs.ulb.ac.be/pub lic/_media/teaching/influxdb_2017.pdf
4. Chakraborty, M., Kundan, A.P.: Grafana. In: Monitoring Cloud-Native Applications, pp. 187–240. Apress, Berkeley, CA (2021)
5. OctoPrint.: PrettyGCode. https://plugins.octoprint.org/plugins/prettygcode/
6. Creality.: Creality CR-30. https://www.creality.com/products/creality-cr-30-3d-printer
7. OctoPrint.: Download & Setup OctoPrint. https://octoprint.org/download/
8. Ngo, T.D., Kashani, A., Imbalzano, G., Nguyen, K.T., Hui, D.: Additive manufacturing (3D printing): a review of materials, methods, applications, and challenges. Elsevier. Compos. Part B Eng. **143**, 172–196 (2018)
9. Rieder, H., et al.: Online monitoring of additive manufacturing processes using ultrasound. In: Proceedings of the 11th European Conference on Non-destructive Testing, pp. 2194–2201 (2014)
10. Rankin, K.: Hack and: what's new in 3D printing, Part IV: OctoPrint. Linux J. **2015**(257), 5 (2015)

11. Millon, C., et al.: Development of laser ultrasonics inspection for online monitoring of additive manufacturing. Weld. World **62**(3), 653–661 (2018)
12. Bhushan, B., Caspers, M.: An overview of additive manufacturing (3D printing) for microfabrication. Microsyst. Technol. **23**(4), 1117–1124 (2017)
13. Mohamed, O.A., Masood, S.H., Bhowmik, J.L.: Optimization of fused deposition modeling process parameters: a review of current research and future prospects. Adv. Manufact. **3**(1), 42–53 (2015)
14. Lishchenko, N., Piteĺ, J., Larshin, V.: Online monitoring of surface quality for diagnostic features in 3D printing. Machines **10**(7), 541 (2022)
15. Lishchenko, N., Lazorik, P., Demčák, J., Pitel', J., Židek, K.: Quality Control Monitoring in 3D Printing. In: Ivanov, V., Trojanowska, J., Pavlenko, I., Rauch, E., Peraković, D. (eds.) Advances in Design, Simulation and Manufacturing V. DSMIE 2022. Lecture Notes in Mechanical Engineering, pp. 31–40. Springer, Cham (2022). https://doi.org/10.1007/978-3-031-06025-0_4
16. Chung, S., Srinivasan, P., Zhang, P., Bandari, S., Repka, M.A.: Development of ibuprofen tablet with polyethylene oxide using fused deposition modeling 3D-printing coupled with hot-melt extrusion. J. Drug Deliv. Sci. Technol. **76**, 103716 (2022)
17. Kristiawan, R.B., Imaduddin, F., Ariawan, D., Arifin, Z.: A review on the fused deposition modeling (FDM) 3D printing: filament processing, materials, and printing parameters. Open Eng. **11**(1), 639–649 (2021)
18. Richardson, M., Wallace, S.: Getting started with raspberry PI. O'Reilly Media, Inc. (2012)
19. Phang, S.K., Ahmad, N.B., Aravind, C.V., Chen, X.: Internet of Things based architecture for additive manufacturing interface. Int. J. Grid Util. Comput. **12**(5–6), 460–468 (2021)
20. Shandilya, H., Kuchta, M., Elkaseer, A., Müller, T., Scholz, S.G.: Additive manufacturing: comparative study of an IoT integrated approach and a conventional solution. In: Arai, K., Kapoor, S., Bhatia, R. (eds.) Proceedings of the Future Technologies Conference (FTC) 2020, Volume 2 FTC 2020. Advances in Intelligent Systems and Computing AISC, vol. 1289, pp. 976–986. Springer, Cham (2021). https://doi.org/10.1007/978-3-030-63089-8_64

Possibilities of Applying Augmented Reality Elements in the Concept of Lean Management

Stella Hrehova[1]([✉]) [iD], Jakub Kaščak[2] [iD], Rebeka Tauberová[1] [iD], and Matúš Martiček[1,2]

[1] Faculty of Manufacturing Technologies with a Seat in Prešov, Department of Industrial Engineering and Informatics, Technical University of Košice, Bayerova 1, 080 01 Prešov, Slovak Republic
{stella.hrehova,rebeka.tauberova,matus.marticek}@tuke.sk
[2] Faculty of Manufacturing Technologies with a Seat in Prešov, Department of Computer Aided Manufacturing Technologies, Technical University of Košice, Štúrova 31, 080 01 Prešov, Slovak Republic
jakub.kascak@tuke.sk

Abstract. Increasing efficiency and reducing costs in production is currently a very desirable trend. In many areas, we can see the trend of introducing or improving lean techniques and tools, the task of which is to get as close as possible to achieving the ideal state in terms of customer satisfaction and the elimination of any losses. The fundamental benefit of introducing the lean production methodology into the corporate philosophy is the constant effort to achieve perfection and the periodic application of improvement. In this context, lean management is based on the condition that there is no level of perfection with which the company should be satisfied and which cannot be further developed. The introduction of the Industry 4.0 philosophy and the development of information technologies brought new possibilities for lean management. It offers new tools and options that can increase the efficiency of management and the achievement of set goals. In the presented contribution, we will focus on the possibilities of using augmented reality tools for selected areas of lean management. Augmented reality is a key technology enabling the implementation of the Industry 4.0 concept. This technology makes it possible to bridge the gap between the physical world and the increasingly important digital environment. We can see its application in many areas.

Keywords: Lean management · Augmented reality · Marker

1 Introduction

Lean management is a business management approach based on the Japanese example developed at Toyota [1]. The roots of Lean can be found in the relatively early stages of modern management. Already in 1910, Henry Ford promoted the ground-breaking theories of Frederick Taylor, Frank Gilbreth, or the founder of the Gantt chart, Henry

D. Perakovic and L. Knapcikova (Eds.): FABULOUS 2023, LNICST 542, pp. 147–159, 2024.
https://doi.org/10.1007/978-3-031-50051-0_11

Gantt. The common feature of these approaches was the effort to maximize the production process in the shortest possible time. James Womack, the author of the term lean production, or Taiichi Ohno can be cited as other exponents of the Lean philosophy. We can find several definitions of the term "Lean management" in the literature, e.g. [2, 3], in which the authors characterize the role of lean management as streamlining processes, reducing unnecessary activities, production times and minimizing the consumption of raw materials and energy, in [4] the authors characterize lean management as a system that includes the most efficient methods and techniques of production organizations with wide and successful applicability. The gradual introduction of the lean management principles into practice is carried out by applying small changes, which, however, have a large impact on the entire business system. In this context, the most descriptive definition of lean management [5] is the one that states that lean management is an approach to managing an organization that supports the concept of continuous improvement, a long-term approach to work that systematically tries to achieve small, gradual changes in processes in order to improve efficiency and quality.

The key principles of lean Management relate primarily to two elements [6]:

- value - is understood both in relation to the organization and the client. All activities carried out in enterprises should focus on creating value,
- efforts to eliminate waste - eliminating any activity or part of the process that does not create value.

The concept of lean management consists in continuous cyclical improvement of business management with the aim of reducing all possible operating costs, eliminating waste and increasing business performance [1]. The following figure (Fig. 1) shows the lean management history and development [7].

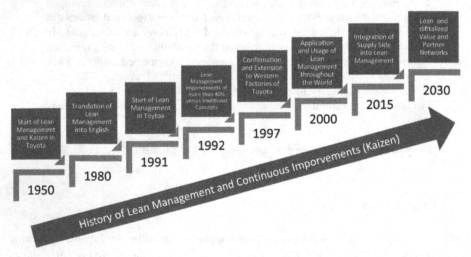

Fig. 1. History and development of lean management

Currently, managers have the opportunity to use digital information available in various IT (information technology) sources to make the right decisions and implement actions [1]. The concept of Industry 4.0. it has been implemented in various areas only in the last decade, but it has brought with it many tools and methods whose task is higher efficiency and digitization. However, the philosophy of "Lean" management was applied in some industries much earlier. These philosophies are currently influencing and intermingling, as shown in the following figure (Fig. 2) [8].

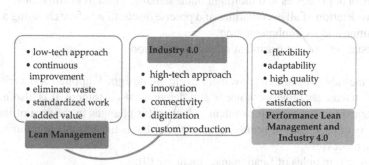

Fig. 2. Lean management and Industry 4.0 in mutual conjunction

However, the possibility of effective use of Lean tools rests on the shoulders of top and middle management, who need to have the necessary information and data at their disposal. This area could be covered by virtual reality technology, when it is possible to see and understand individual processes and workplaces in a short time and in real form. In the presented article, we will show the possibilities of using virtual reality technology in selected lean methods and procedures.

2 Methods and Tools

2.1 Lean Management

Lean management methodology represents [9] a philosophical approach promoted by top management through long-term strategic plans. This procedure is focused on the process as the bearer of the manufactured product quality or the service provided. Key functions in the enterprise related to the achievement of goals in this area include the following prerequisites:

- correctly designed process - the products will then achieve the required quality,
- the process is balanced and smooth - the costs resulting from maintaining stocks will be eliminated,
- production of what the customer requires and when he needs it,
- focus on quality in every single operation - costs resulting from repairs and complaints will be reduced.

Other features include:

- Intentional search for individuals through whom it is possible to implement the company's intentions in the area of quality improvement or cost reduction and supporting their personal development.
- Long-term support of self-educational processes and the prosperity of the company without exception:

  - control of processes and thorough understanding of address situations,
  - consideration of all eventualities and precise discussion before choosing a suitable solution and its implementation,
  - constant efforts for organizational self-reflection.

After the values of one improvement cycle are designed, applied and verified, it is necessary to reassess other, new needs and demands of customers. It is also necessary to pay attention to further improvement, whether it is changes in the area of increasing the capacity of processes or removing everything that is undesirable and unnecessarily burdening processes.

The basic principles of Lean management are [9]:

- Determination of value. The key point is that value can only be defined by the end customer and is truly meaningful when expressed as a concrete product that meets all of the customer's needs and wants;
- Identification of activities involved in value creation. A value stream represents a set of all specific activities required by an organization,

  - product development management – all problem-solving tasks from concept through detailed design and engineering to production launch,
  - information management - all information management tasks from product conception to product delivery
  - operational management - the entire physical transformation takes place from raw materials to the finished product in the hands of customers.

- Flow. Setting processes in motion. Ongoing processes cancel the idea of dividing the company into separate departments. All activities related to the completion of a product or service should be organized in a single, uninterrupted flow
- Pull. Processes are conditioned by the need to deliver a specific product or service. The product is produced only when there is real demand from the customer, and not to work on stock. This concept is called thrust and ensures that none of the eight areas of waste are created, or at least minimized
- Striving for perfection. The ability to strive for excellence from the customer's perspective is fundamental to the continuous improvement process. It represents an endless effort to reduce time, costs, errors and malfunctions in the production of products or the provision of services.

The following table presents a description of selected lean management tools for which augmented reality application options will be proposed (Table 1)

Table 1. Selected Lean management tools.

Tool	Description
Shop floor (SF)	Shop floor management (SFM) describes the supportive interaction among managers and employees. The emphasis is placed on the value creation process and the exchange of information is accelerated. Early meetings and problem analysis are held at the event location, i.e. in the workshop [10]
Value Stream mapping (VSM)	Value Stream Mapping is a lean tool that helps users see and understand the material and information flow as products move through the value stream. The value stream includes the value-added and non-value-added activities required to deliver a product from raw materials to delivery to the customer [11]
SMED	SMED Setup is a set of activities that prepare a system to produce a product, with setup time being the preparation period between the end of the last product produced and the first product produced in the next process [12]
5S	The 5S methodology is a lean philosophy that gives order and meaning to work dynamics and solves situations of disorganization in the workplace [13]

2.2 Augmented Reality

Augmented reality (AR) is among the leading technological applications in various fields. It is also part of the Industry 4.0 philosophy and has been among its fastest growing areas in recent times. AR is computer-generated virtual information that overlaps with a real scene. Virtual information is displayed in a realistic manner so that it appears to be part of the real environment. AR does not use a complete replacement of the real world with a virtual one, but complements or changes the perception of the real world. Thus, AR supplements the real world with elements of the virtual world. AR technology allows a person moving in a real environment to perceive objects made in the digital world [5, 14]. A typical AR application consists of three layers, as shown in Fig. 3 [15]. The bottom layer represents the real and material world. In the middle layer, digital information that is relevant and useful is added to the real world. The combination of these two layers creates a third extended world in which users have access to digital content. AR applications provide interaction between users and the augmented world in real time

This virtual content is displayed by devices such as tablets, smartphones or smart glasses. The user has the possibility to interact with both the real world and the virtual world and manipulate virtual content [16].

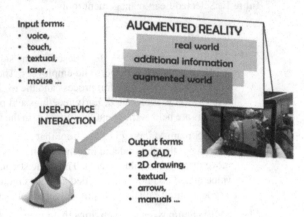

Fig. 3. AR application layers

AR application dividing is shown the following figure Fig. 4 [17].

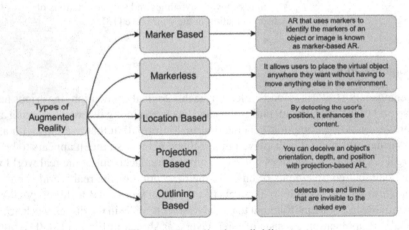

Fig. 4. AR applications dividing

Marker-based and marker-free methods are most often used in the creation of AR applications. AR marker-based methods rely on affixing a marker to a known location or object of interest to define the origin of the virtual world. However, this method has some limitations. Markings must be high contrast and non-reflective, occlusion may occur and the user must stay close to them. In addition, tags must be attached to all moving objects or the scene must remain static [18].

The success of introducing these principles and procedures is influenced by the quality of information about individual processes and workplaces. Individual management members can only have partial and incomplete or old data. This then leads to ineffective and partial solutions, which has a negative impact on achieving the set goals. An application that will use virtual reality can bring more detailed and complete information.

By using markers, problematic workplaces can be processed in detail and presented in a realistic form.

Based on the analysis of selected works [19], it is shown that systems based on markers are the most frequently accepted solutions in the creation of AR applications. In the following section, we focused on the application of this approach.

3 Possibilities of Applying Augmented Reality for Selected Methods of Lean Management

In the following section, selected lean management tools and the possible implementation of augmented reality applications using markers will be briefly described.

3.1 Shop Floor

One of the basic tasks of this approach is to obtain real data directly from the place where the process takes place. In many literary sources, the opinion is presented that entering the gemba and directly observing the process allows the best value flow analysis [6]. Such an approach brings measurable benefits. Working at the place where the process is performed allows managers to change their perspective and see the process exactly where it occurs. In small establishments, it is possible to obtain the necessary data by personally walking around the given establishment and writing down what is real. However, if teams of experts are involved in solving problems or optimizing processes, this is insufficient. For this reason, other methods with the use of modern information technologies began to be used [20, 21]:

- Simplified virtual Gemba walks – use hand-held cameras in a remote location to record or broadcast your walk live for other members.
- Extended walks Gemba – when wearable technologies such as Augmented Reality (AR) smart glasses are used. This method enables real-time IIoT-enabled "see and listen" (eg real-time performance data).
- Advanced Virtual Gemba Walks – when lean managers use digital technologies to "remotely interact" with intelligent, social machines and IIoT-enabled operators through digital twins, in a virtual environment (VR).
- Automated Guided Gemba Walks – when Gemba Walks are "automated and guided" by trend predictions based on data provided by IIoT (Industrial Internet of Things), social machines and operators in digital lean factories.

As part of augmented reality, it is possible to use the option of playing videos based on a marker. The workplace (or workplaces) will be photographed with a camera, or a virtual tour of the workplace will be created. The virtual tour can also contain a technical description of individual machines and devices that are adapted to the desired goals (Fig. 5). Command buttons can also be added within the application, which are used to override between possible individual scenes. The appearance of the marker can be a simple figure.

The created markers and the application saved in the tablet, or the mobile phone is portable, so it is always available.

Fig. 5. Virtual tour of the workplace with a technical description of the equipment

3.2 Value Stream Mapping

Optimizing the value stream of the process so that it brings the desired effect is a difficult task that requires the cooperation of several experts. The most important element of this method is the creation of a current state map, which should take into account the real state. In this activity, it is necessary to apply the already described shop floor method.

From the point of view of using the Unity and Vuforia environments options, we can propose two ways of displaying this map of the current state.

1. By using a marker - the corresponding marker is replaced by the corresponding map when it is used (Fig. 6)

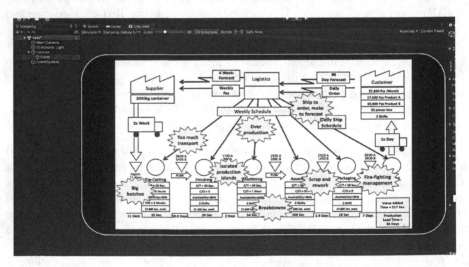

Fig. 6. Current state map with Kaizen

2. Using the scene itself, when the desired map is displayed based on pressing the appropriate button. In this case, however, it is tied to only one map for a specific operation. In the end, it can also be an advantage if a comprehensive application of augmented reality is created, which is managed, for example, by command buttons

Such a map can also show opportunities for improvement (Kaizen). The specific procedures to be chosen are usually determined by a team of experts. The necessary information can be obtained (supplemented) by displaying the map using the appropriate markers.

3.3 Single Minute Exchange to Dies

Switching to another type of product and subsequent machines setting up are necessary, but they do not add value. Therefore, the aim must be to reduce the time needed to perform these activities. SMED focuses on the identification of internal and external activities of the transition, the separation of internal and external activities, the transformation of internal activities into external activities and the streamlining of activities [22]. During analysis, the internal setup time is converted to an external setup time to reduce this time [4]. The main principle of the method recommends performing the maximum possible number of switching steps during the so-called external phase, which is the period of time when the machine or device is in operation. At the same time, the remaining internal operations are simplified and standardized in order to eliminate any unnecessary operations, downtime or waste of other resources [23]. Significant time losses can occur here, which are caused either by inexperience or poor preparation. The field of augmented reality tools application can be:

1. Reducing the time needed to find the appropriate tool, toolset, etc. To make it effective, it is advisable to use the 5S lean method, which will ensure the standardization of the individual tool location.

The basic 5S method is divided into five steps, which are: Seiri (Sort), Seiton (Set in Order), Seiso (Shine), Seiketsu (Standardize) and Shitsuke (Sustain) [24]. The workplace standardized in this way is then the basis for the application of augmented reality, when, based on the marker, the desired location is shown to individual workers [25] (Fig. 7). This will ensure the reduction of losses arising from the search for the correct location of individual tools.

The following image interprets an organized workplace in the Unity environment in simulator mode.

2. Training of necessary activities:
   a. One of the possibilities is to record a video, when an experienced operator performs all the necessary activities for an individual machine. Subsequently, based on the marker, the given video can be started, which will allow you to train and check the performed steps. This possibility illustrates next figure [26] (Fig. 8).
   b. Static option, when the sequence of individual steps is displayed based on the marker. In this case, the application may contain separate command buttons that will enable the transition to the next operation only after confirming the execution of the previous operation

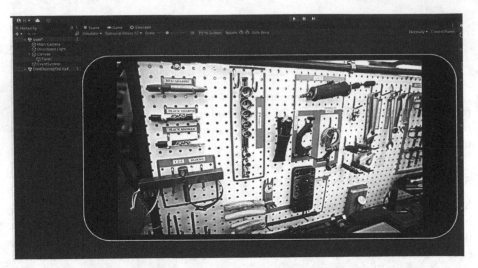

Fig. 7. The workplace after applying the 5S method in simulator environment.

Fig. 8. The possible approach to using AR for training.

The assumption is that the application will be intended for medium or top management. In this case, it should serve as a source of information, especially in cases of using the Shop floor and Value mapping stream methods. In the case of 5S methods and educational activities, it is determined by a specific user. However, the common denominator is the use of markers. A generalized application development procedure will be built based on the following steps:

- selection of the end user,
- creation of markers
- interface design
- selection of end device and application testing

Last but not least, it is possible to create an application that will contain both options, and by creating a user interface, the user will decide what to use.

4 Conclusion

Several years of implementation of Industry 4.0 principles and methods and the use of advanced information technology tools in the field of lean management can bring significant efficiency and flexibility of management in various areas. The connection of these approaches gives lean management the possibility of using many tools to improve and streamline processes in all parts of the material flow. Even if the use of a specific tool is conditioned by the company specificity and capabilities, there is always a tool that can be applied. Augmented reality is one such tool. It represents a tool that will allow better visualization and connection of the real world with the digital one. For managers, it can be a highly effective tool in decision-making and evaluation activities. It is possible to create different scenarios in a digital environment, simulations based on real data and thus flexibly manage individual processes.

In the submitted paper, some cases of the augmented reality use for selected methods applied in lean management are presented. These examples are based on the use of markers, which are used to the greatest extent in terms of augmented reality. The examples were designed to show the ease of their creation in individual environments.

In the future, the authors would like to focus on the possibilities of applying more advanced VR tools in the field of Lean, mainly for the needs of top management decision-making activities. By using this technology, individual members can achieve better results in managing and planning their activities.

Acknowledgements. This work was supported by the Slovak Research and Development Agency under the contract No. APVV-19–0590, by the projects VEGA 1/0268/22, KEGA 022TUKE-4/2023 granted by the Ministry of Education, Science, Research and Sport of the Slovak Republic.

References

1. Kościelniak, H., Łęgowik-Małolepsza, M., Łęgowik-Świącik, S.: The Application of information technologies in consideration of augmented reality and lean management of enterprises in the light of sustainable development. Sustainability **11**, 2157 (2019). https://doi.org/10.3390/su11072157
2. Orynycz, O., Tucki, K., Prystasz, M.: Implementation of lean management as a tool for decrease of energy consumption and CO_2 emissions in the fast food restaurant. Energies **13**, 1184 (2020). https://doi.org/10.3390/en13051184
3. Saxby, R., Cano-Kourouklis, M., Viza, E.: An initial assessment of lean management methods for Industry 4.0. The TQM Journal **32**(4), 587–601 (2020). https://doi.org/10.1108/TQM-12-2019-0298
4. Kiran, M.B.: Classical lean manufacturing philosophy–a review. In: Parwani, A.K., Ramkumar, P., Abhishek, K., Yadav, S.K. (eds.) Recent Advances in Mechanical Infrastructure. Lecture Notes in Intelligent Transportation and Infrastructure. Springer, Singapore (2022). https://doi.org/10.1007/978-981-16-7660-4_36

5. Balco, P., Bajzík, P., Škovierová, K.: Virtual and augmented reality in manufacturing companies in Slovakia. Procedia Comput. Sci. **201**, 313–320 (2022). https://doi.org/10.1016/j.procs.2022.03.042
6. Zdęba-Mozoła, A., Rybarczyk-Szwajkowska, A., Czapla, T., Marczak, M., Kozłowski, R.: Implementation of lean management in a multi-specialist hospital in Poland and the analysis of waste. Int. J. Environ. Res. Public Health **19**, 800 (2022). https://doi.org/10.3390/ijerph19020800
7. Helmold, M.: Lean management and kaizen, fundamentals from cases and examples in operations and supply chain management, Springer Cham (2020). https://doi.org/10.1007/978-3-030-46981-8
8. Florescu, A., Barabas, S.: Development trends of production systems through the integration of lean management and industry 4.0. Appl. Sci. **12**(10), 4885 (2022). https://doi.org/10.3390/app12104885
9. Charron, R., Harrington, H.J., Voehl, F., Wiggin, H.: The Lean Management System Handbook, CRC Press. Taylor&Francis Group, New Zourk (2015)
10. Bertagnolli, F.: Lean Management: Introduction and In-Depth Study of Japanese Management Philosophy. Springer Wiesbaden, ISBN 978–3–658–36086–3 (2022). https://doi.org/10.1007/978-3-658-36087-0
11. Star A., Sisay G. Application of lean tools for reduction of manufacturing lead time. In: 6th EAI International Conference, ICAST 2018, Bahir Dar, Ethiopia, October 5–7, Proceedings (2018)
12. Ribeiro, M.A.S., Santos, A.C.O., da Fonseca, G., de Amorim, C., de Oliveira, H., da Silva Braga, R.A., Netto, R.S.: Analysis of the implementation of the single minute exchange of die methodology in an agroindustry through action research. Machines **10**(5), 287 (2022). https://doi.org/10.3390/machines10050287
13. García-Alcaraz, J.L., et al.: Lean manufacturing tools applied to material flow and their impact on economic sustainability. Sustainability **13**, 10599 (2021). https://doi.org/10.3390/su1319 10599
14. Kaščák, J., Husár, J., Knapčíková, L., Trojanowska, J., Ivanov, V.: Conceptual use of augmented reality in the maintenance of manufacturing facilities. In: Trojanowska, J., Kujawińska, A., Machado, J., Pavlenko, I. (eds.) MANUFACTURING 2022. LNME, pp. 241–252. Springer, Cham (2022). https://doi.org/10.1007/978-3-030-99310-8_19
15. Reljić, V., Milenković, I., Dudić, S., Šulc, J., Bajči, B.: Augmented reality applications in industry 4.0 environment. Appl. Sci. **11**(12), 5592 (2021). https://doi.org/10.3390/app111 25592
16. Buń, P., Gapsa, J., Husár, J., Kaščak, J.: Mixed reality training in electrical equipment operating procedures. In: Trojanowska, J., Kujawińska, A., Machado, J., Pavlenko, I. (eds.) MANUFACTURING 2022. LNME, pp. 306–316. Springer, Cham (2022). https://doi.org/10.1007/978-3-030-99310-8_24
17. Devagiri, J.S., Paheding, S., Niyaz, Q., Yang, X., Smith S. Augmented Reality and Artificial Intelligence in industry: Trends, tools, and future challenges. Expert Syst. Appl. **207**, 118002, ISSN 0957–4174 (2022). https://doi.org/10.1016/j.eswa.2022.11800
18. Durchon, H., Preda, M., Zaharia, T., Grall, Y. Challenges in applying deep learning to augmented reality for manufacturing. In: Web3D 2022: Proceedings of the 27th International Conference on 3D Web Technology, No. 13, pp. 1–4 (2022). https://doi.org/10.1145/356 4533.3564572
19. Bottani, E., Vignali, G.: Augmented reality technology in the manufacturing industry: a review of the last decade. IISE Transactions **51**(3), 284–310 (2019). https://doi.org/10.1080/247 25854.2018.1493244

20. Romero, D., Gaiardelli, P., Wuest, T., Powell, D., Thürer, M.: New forms of Gemba Walks and their digital tools in the digital lean manufacturing world. In: Lalic, B., Majstorovic, V., Marjanovic, U., von Cieminski, G., Romero, D. (eds.) APMS 2020. IAICT, vol. 592, pp. 432–440. Springer, Cham (2020). https://doi.org/10.1007/978-3-030-57997-5_50

21. Syberfeldt, A., Holm, M., Danielsson, O., Wang, L., Brewster, R.: Support systems on the industrial shop-floors of the future – operators' perspective on augmented reality. Procedia CIRP **44**, 108–113 (2016). https://doi.org/10.1016/j.procir.2016.02.017

22. Garcia-Garcia, G., Singh, Y., Jagtap, S.: Optimising changeover through lean-manufacturing principles: a case study in a food factory. Sustainability **14**, 8279 (2022). https://doi.org/10.3390/su14148279

23. Malindzakova, M., Malindzak, D., Garaj, P.: Implementation of the single minute exchange of dies method for reducing changeover time in a hygiene production company. Int. J. Industr. Eng. Manage. **12**(4), 243–252 (2021). https://doi.org/10.24867/IJIEM-2021-4-291

24. Rodrigues, J., Sá, J.C., Silva, F.J.G., Ferreira, L.P., Jimenez, G., Santos, G.: A Rapid Improvement Process through "Quick-Win" Lean Tools: a Case Study. Systems **8**, 55 (2020). https://doi.org/10.3390/systems8040055

25. https://uttana.com/blog/free-lean-video-spotlight-intro-to-5s/. Accessed 25 Dec 2022

26. Thomas, M.: In the current remote and virtual environment, AR presents opportunities for learning. https://www.chieflearningofficer.com/2020/11/05/in-the-current-remote-and-virtual-environment-ar-presents-an-opportunity-for-learning/. Accessed 28 Dec 2022

Detection of Energy Consumption Cyber Attacks on Smart Devices

Zainab Alwaisi[1]([✉]), Simone Soderi[1,2], and Rocco De Nicola[1,2]

[1] IMT School for Advanced Studies, Lucca, Italy
{zainab.alwaisi,simone.soderi,rocco.denicola}@imtlucca.it
[2] CINI Cybersecurity Laboratory, Roma, Italy

Abstract. With the rapid development of the Internet of Things (IoT) technology, intelligent systems are increasingly finding their way into everyday life and people's homes. With the spread of these technologies, there is a growing concern about the security of smart home devices. Smart home devices suffer from resource-constrained problems, and these devices and sensors could be connected to unreliable and untrustworthy networks. Nevertheless, securing IoT technology is mandatory due to the relevant data handled by these devices. One of the critical tasks to be solved by the concept of a modern smart home is the problem of preventing energy attacks spread and the usage of IoT infrastructure. One of the possible approaches to abnormal behavior of IoT devices and IoT cyber-attack detection is monitoring energy consumption. Moreover, building a lightweight algorithm for securing IoT devices is essential to consider the limitation of its resources. This paper presents a lightweight technique for detecting energy consumption attacks on smart home devices based on analyzing the received packets by the smart devices. The proposed algorithm considers three different protocols, TCP, UDP, and MQTT, and different device statuses, like *Idle*, *active*, and when it is under attack. Moreover, it considers the resource constraints of the smart devices for detecting abnormal behaviors and sending an alert to the administrator as soon as the attack is detected. The proposed approach effectively detects energy consumption attacks by measuring the packet reception rate of the smart devices for different protocols.

Keywords: Smart Home (SH) · Internet of Things (IoT) · energy consumption · detection · security · resource constraint

1 Introduction

The Internet of Things (IoT) can incorporate many heterogeneous devices such as cameras, smart meters [3], vehicles, and others transparently while providing open access to various data generated by such devices to provide new services to citizens and companies [26]. The IoT paradigm can be extremely massive and complex. It may contain tens of thousands of sensors, actuators, and gateways. Devices can communicate with gateways via different protocols, whereas

D. Perakovic and L. Knapcikova (Eds.): FABULOUS 2023, LNICST 542, pp. 160–176, 2024.
https://doi.org/10.1007/978-3-031-50051-0_12

gateways may connect with the internet and cloud-based apps via a similarly diverse range of protocols [22]. IoT technology's services find applications in many domains such as automotive, medical aids, smart grids, and many others [9]. The relevant data exchanged between smart IoT devices are more vulnerable to attacks since they are often deployed in a hostile and insecure environment [5].

In this complex architecture, data can be processed by various heterogeneous entities. Data transmission, security, and integrity are key aspects to be considered. As a result, protocols and technologies are required to provide data security, access management, and flow data transmission [4]. Many recent studies have been conducted to cope with security issues in the IoT paradigm [2, 25]. Some of these studies concentrate on security issues at a particular layer, whereas other approaches aim at providing end-to-end security [16]. Several methods and protocols have been suggested, primarily concerned with reducing energy consumption and increasing the network lifetime [6, 21]. Therefore, security solutions are mandatory to protect IoT devices from intruder attacks. This paper aims to secure low-resource IoT devices, such as smart home devices, against energy consumption attacks [20].

In smart homes, detecting energy consumption attacks is required to protect the energy from vulnerability threats that could access the home network and attack the smart devices. Monitoring the energy consumption of IoT devices is a possible way to detect those performing attacks which require significant energy consumption. In addition, the energy consumption analysis-based approach is more secure when the device's kernel is already compromised. Data integrity cannot be guaranteed once the device has been compromised [7].

One of the most critical studies nowadays concerns the efficient use of energy resources. Almost a third of the total energy consumption comprises specific losses; for example, the energy is consumed not on purpose [10]. Additional growth in energy consumption is also expected. Increasing awareness of the problems of energy saving and energy efficiency also helps to develop the concept of a modern smart home. Furthermore, at first, this concept was to connect sensors and devices over a network for remote access, monitoring, and control of the living environment and provide the required services to users. While at the present stage, it also involves the optimal use of energy in buildings and malware and IoT cyberattack detection in smart home infrastructure. IoT devices' energy consumption monitoring is a possible way to detect those performing attacks which require significant energy consumption [21], for example, Distributed Denial of Service (DDoS) [24] and crypto-mining.

In this paper, we build a lightweight algorithm that considers the resource constraints for smart devices to detect energy consumption attacks. The algorithm is used to monitor the packet reception rate of the smart devices on different protocols. In this algorithm, we used the following protocols: Transmission Control Protocol (TCP), User Datagram Protocol (UDP), and Message Queue Telemetry Transport protocol (MQTT), as they are popular protocols used nowadays with IoT systems [15, 17]. We also consider different devices' statuses, such as *Idle*, *active*, and when they could be under attack. The algorithm automatically fetches the packets' reception rate and divides them into different behaviors, such as normal and abnormal, depending on the presence and absence of the energy consumption attacks. At the same time, the energy consumption of the smart devices is measured to determine the packet reception rate's behavior and to specify whether the packet reception rate's behavior is normal or abnormal. This algorithm successfully detected energy consumption attacks in smart home devices with a cost-efficient experimental setup (Fig. 1).

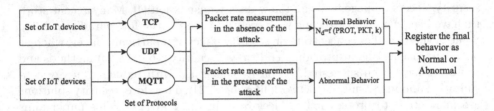

Fig. 1. Packet Reception Rate measurement in the absence and presence of the attack.

1.1   Motivation and Contribution

Security is the main issue that restricts the adoption of IoT in social life. Many researchers have been working to make the IoT a more reliable and secure technology so that it can be adopted in society to make some aspects of human life more manageable and convenient. Since researchers develop many schemes and methods, but due to the constrained environment, e.g., low computational power and low energy of IoT, these techniques are not feasible. Therefore, an added line of protection that considers resource constraints should be built into IoT devices and networks to defend IoT-based organizations from cyber threats. Our main contribution is building a lightweight algorithm to detect energy consumption attacks in smart homes deployed directly at sensors. It applies real-time packet rate measurement to discriminate between smart devices' normal and abnormal packet reception rate behaviors. In this work, we consider three different protocols such as TCP, UDP, and MQTT. We also consider the different device statuses, such as *Idle*, *active*, and when it is under attack, to evaluate the best detection of energy consumption attack. We simulate the detection algorithm and assess the results by applying the proposed algorithm to the smart devices themselves, such as the Raspberry Pi[1]. We measure the current consumption of the smart device to monitor the energy while measuring the packet reception rate to discriminate between normal and abnormal behaviors. Therefore, this algorithm design is a protection strategy for IoT devices to maintain their integrity, seamlessly make them available to legitimate users, and protect them from energy consumption attacks by considering their resource constraints.

---

[1] https://www.raspberrypi.com/documentation/.

1.2   Organization of the Paper

We organized our paper as follows. Section 2 presents a related work and background reading of energy consumption attacks in IoT systems. We describe our proposal, including metrics definition, methodology, and the detection algorithm, in Sect. 3. In Sect. 4, we show the results and discussions. Finally, Sect. 5 presents some concluding remarks and future works.

2   Related Work and Background

Energy-based attacks are often categorised as IoT sensing domain attacks, where the smart devices and sensors are the target [8]. Dabbagh and Rayes in [8] described the sensing domain attacks like vampire attacks, jamming attacks, sinkhole attacks, and selective-forwarding attacks. The vampire attack, among others is considered an energy-based attack because it aims to destroy the battery of sensors. The researchers also identified four types of vampire attacks based on the technique used to destroy power: Denial of Sleep, stretch attack, flooding attack, and carousel attack. Patil and Sharma in [19] also described several Denial of Service (DoS) attacks for wireless sensors. The authors mentioned two attacks that waste the energy of sensors, among others: Denial of Sleep and vampire attacks. Another category of attacks is related to DoS, but they can waste energy indirectly. These are jamming attacks, wormhole attacks, and path-based DoS attacks.

Different authors present detection techniques against energy consumption attacks. In [11], it is reported that the primary principle of the energy efficiency approach has been to encourage the use of more efficient smart devices. Home automation control plays a crucial role in efficient and sustainable operation by reducing and identifying energy losses and using energy only when and where it is needed; or by exercising effective control over the operational level of the system for correct application in the proper place. This study [13] evaluated well-known home energy management systems in order to identify key differences in functionality and quality by identifying possibilities for energy savings (both behavioral and operational) [18]. It is also observed that potential benefits related to comfort, convenience, or security can often determine the implementation of energy-efficiency scenarios. This work [23] proposed a detection framework for IoT systems based on energy consumption analysis. The suggested methodology analyzes the energy consumption of smart devices and classifies the monitored devices' attack status, e.g., cyberattacks and physical attacks. A two-stage approach is suggested, with a short time window for rough attack detection and a long time window for fine attack detection.

The authors in [12] introduced different techniques to control smart home systems to reduce energy consumption. Feed-forward control is the first approach. By monitoring interference factors in real-time to implement appropriate monitors based on known parameters, such a system directly compensates for interference factors like external wind, solar radiation, and internal heat gain. Another approach is Model-based Predictive Control (MPC) [12], which is used to predict the system's behavior in the future based on models and adjust the system accordingly. Fuzzy logic control does not require a complicated mathematical model to control the system and can be based directly on the quality of user experience. In this paper [14], energy consumption analysis approaches were considered, concluding that these approaches do not apply to such devices as smartphones because the typical energy consumption of such devices differs quite a lot in practice. In addition, the noise present in the system by the unpredictable user and environment interactions will lead to many false alarms. Also, practical tests were performed, showing that the additional power consumed by malicious applications is too small to be noticeable with the mean error rates of state-of-the-art measurement tools. However, it was noted that DDoS attacks could be detected by studying the energy consumption of similar devices.

The author of this paper [7] proposes a method for IoT attack detection based on analyzing the smart device's energy consumption, which considers the energy consumption-related user's preference modes. Moreover, it aims to enhance the accuracy of IoT cyberattack detection and localize the IoT malware on these smart devices. The IoT software opcodes sequences study is applied. The proposed technique allows the detection of the performance of the IoT devices, such as DoS and DDoS attacks.

To the best of our knowledge, our work is the first to detect energy consumption attacks in smart home devices, depending on measuring the packet reception rates by the smart devices.

3   Proposed Algorithm

In this section, we present the algorithm to detect energy consumption attacks in smart home devices by monitoring the packet rate received by the smart devices. The algorithm considers different protocols like TCP, UDP, and MQTT and different device statuses such as *active, Idle,* and *under attack.* The proposed algorithm is depicted in Fig. 2. In our previous work [1], we studied the effect of DDoS, energy consumption DDoS, and Fake Access Points (F-APs) attacks on the energy consumption of the smart healthcare devices.

The algorithm has three phases, 1) *collecting phase* where the algorithm collects samples of the number of received packets for different statuses when the device is Idle, active, or under attack; and divides the collected packets from different protocols, e.g., TCP, UDP, and MQTT, into normal or abnormal behaviors; 2) *calculating phase*, which calculates the collected samples and compares the final results of the fetching packets with the energy measurements to determine whether the state of packets measurements is caused by an energy consumption attack, then divides the final results into (normal, or abnormal behavior); and 3) *detection phase* where the algorithm applies different conditions to classify if there is an energy consumption attack or not.

We build the algorithm inside the Python scripts for automatically fetching the packets and analyzing the normal and abnormal behaviors.

In the detection stage of the proposed technique, the packet reception rate of IoT devices for different protocols is measured and analyzed. If the IoT device has abnormally high received packets, it may have carried out an energy consumption attack. Therefore, smart devices should stop listening to the received packets of such a port. Simultaneously, there should be a counter (x) on the total time that the smart device stops listening; if it exceeds (x) times, then the algorithm should register it as abnormal behavior. Our algorithm considers the $(x = 3)$ times.

Algorithm 1. A Technique to detect Energy Consumption Attack

1: $N(d) = f(PROT, PKT, k)$ ▷ *Normal packet reception rate*
2: $A = \overline{PKT}$ ▷ *Received packets in x minutes*
3: $y = N(d)$ ▷ *Normal received packets of smart device d*
4: Input: $PROT, d$
5: Output1: Normal($PKT, k, PROT, d$)
6: Output2: Abnormal ($PKT, k, PROT, d$)
7: Final Result: Output1 *or* Output2
8: **if** $A <= y$ **then**
9:     return to monitor packets rate
10: **else**
11:     Make the device stop licensing for x time
12:     $counter = counter + 1$
13:     **if** $counter > 3$ **then**
14:         register the device as abnormal behavior
15:         check energy consumption
16:     **else**
17:         return to monitor packets rate

3.1 Packet Measurements

To effectively build a technique to detect energy consumption attacks in IoT systems, it is necessary to take into account the different protocols used for different IoT devices. This algorithm considers three different protocols, e.g., TCP, UDP, and MQTT. Also, it considers different device statuses, e.g., *Idle*, *active*, and when it is under attack.

With the aim of IoT energy consumption attack detection at the learning stage, the packet reception rate of each IoT device in the IoT network in the absence or the presence of an IoT energy consumption attack is measured at a specific interval and at equal sub-intervals of time. Based on these measurements, the number of normal $N(d)$ received packets of IoT devices are constructed, part of them labeled as *normal behavior* and entered into the database (DB) to deal with them later on.

Let us describe the normal (N) packet reception rate measurement in the absence of energy consumption attacks.

$$N(d) = f(PROT, PKT, k) \quad \text{and} \quad k \in [0, 1] \tag{1}$$

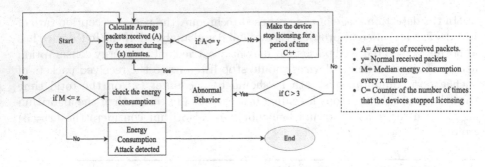

Fig. 2. A Technique to detect Energy Consumption Attack.

where $N(d)$ the normalized receiving packets of an IoT device (d) where d the certain smart home device, (PKT) received packets at a point in time in the absence of energy consumption attack for a specific protocol $(PROT)$, and K is the number of packets measurement in time interval, $n(d) = f(PROT, PKT, k) \in [0, 1]$ where 0 is the minimum received packets, and 1 is the maximum received packets by the smart devices for a specific protocol.

3.2   Energy Measurements

With the aim of IoT energy consumption attack detection at the learning stage, the energy consumption measurements of each IoT device in the IoT network in the presence or the absence of IoT energy consumption attacks are measured at a specific interval and at equal sub-intervals of time. Based on these measurements, the number of received packets of IoT devices on $N(d)$ are constructed, part of them labeled as *normal behavior* and others as *abnormal behavior* and entered into the DB to deal with them later on. The energy consumption measurement is essential at the first stage as it is used to determine the behavior of the packet reception rate as normal or abnormal.

With this aim, these IoT devices were infected with malicious attacks, which were able to carry out these types of IoT energy consumption attacks. After that, the energy consumption measurement of each IoT device for different statuses in the presence or the absence of IoT cyberattacks is measured at a specific interval and at equal sub-intervals of time. In this experiment, we designed a smart circuit using a non-invasive current sensor[2] with Arduino, capacitors, and other resistors to measure the current consumption of smart home devices. This smart circuit samples voltage, ampere, watt, and current per second. In our experiment, we use the Joule (J) values to calculate the energy consumption of smart devices, as shown in Fig. 5.

Let us describe the energy (E) measurement footprints considering the set of different device statuses in the absence or the presence of the attack.

$$E(d) = f(e(d), PROT, k) \quad \text{and} \quad k \in [0, 1] \tag{2}$$

---

[2] https://tinyurl.com/mrxyvr46.

where (e_d) the energy measurement (e) of the smart device (d) at a point in time in the absence or presence of cyberattacks for a specific protocol $(PROT)$, and K is the number of energy measurements in a time interval, $f(e(d), k) \in [0, 1]$ where 0 is the minimum energy consumption measurement, and 1 presents the maximum energy consumption measurement in the absence or presence of the attack (Fig. 3).

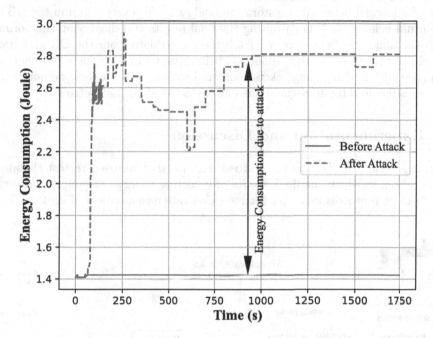

Fig. 3. Energy consumption measurement of normal and abnormal behaviors of the Raspberry Pi device.

Therefore, we calculated the energy consumption for every 3 min for a specific smart device; the time for each energy consumption measurement is also registered and entered into the DB.

3.3   Calculation of Normal and Abnormal Behaviors

In order to calculate the packet reception rate for each IoT device in normal and abnormal cases, we have divided the code into different parts:1) The first part is to fetch the packet reception rate for each protocol separately, depending on the set of protocols used in our system, 2) We measure the packet reception as shown in Eq. 1 for the active smart devices with the absence of the attack and for each protocol separately and register the final results as normal behaviors, 3) Then, we measure the current consumption of the smart device in the case of normal behavior as shown in Eq. 2 and monitor the packet reception rate with the energy consumption when the status of the smart device is *On* with the absence of the attack. The monitoring mode continuously fetches the packet, calculates energy for about 30 min, and stores the final results for every 3 min in the DB, 4) For calculating abnormal behaviors, we send malicious attacks to consume energy for about 30 min to the active smart devices. At this time, we start calculating the energy consumption and the packet reception rate for each protocol separately. Then, we compare the final results with the normal behaviors of such a device. In case of abnormal behavior, we store the final result for every 3 min in the DB as abnormal behaviors, 5) For printing the final results and displaying the normal with the abnormal behaviors, we fetch the stored data from the DB and start calculating the normal with abnormal behaviors, 6) In case there is abnormal behavior with fetching the packets compared to normal behaviors, we notify the system administrator to register the entire case as abnormal behavior.

4   Experimentation and Discussion

In this section, we describe the testbed scenario that we used to test the algorithm. Also, we show the final results of detecting energy consumption attacks for different protocols using packet reception rate measurement (Fig. 4).

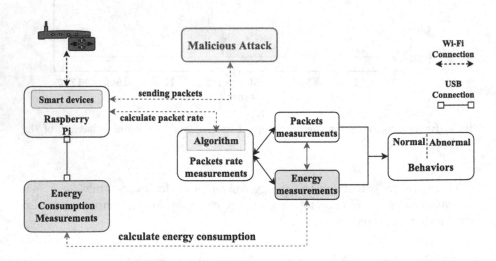

Fig. 4. Testing Environment.

4.1   The Testbed Scenario

We used Raspberry Pi as a smart home device in this experiment. We used different software tools for attacking data generation and collection. On the adversary side, we used *Nmap*[3] to launch a network scan and identify devices' status, such as *online* or *offline*, IP address, and MAC address. Different tools are used to generate malicious attacks on the victim side, such as *hping3*[4].

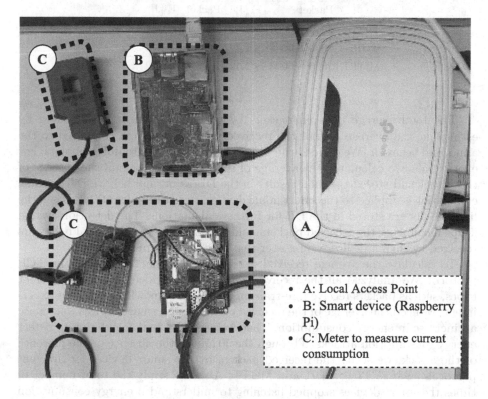

- A: Local Access Point
- B: Smart device (Raspberry Pi)
- C: Meter to measure current consumption

Fig. 5. Testbed scenario showing the devices used in our experiment and the sensor used to measure the energy consumption.

We designed a smart circuit using a non-invasive current sensor with Arduino, capacitors, and other resistors to measure the current consumption of smart home devices. This smart circuit samples voltage, ampere, watt, and current per second. In our experiment, we use the Joule (J) values to calculate the energy consumption of smart devices.

---

[3] https://nmap.org/.
[4] https://www.kali.org/tools/hping3/.

We analyze the packet rate received by the smart home device to detect energy consumption attacks. We built a program using *pyshark*[5] to sniff and fetch packets automatically and store the final results in the DB[6] (Table 1).

Table 1. Packets analysis depends on protocol type and energy consumption.

PROT	Normal Behavior		Abnormal Behavior	
	Packet	E [J]	Packet	E [J]
TCP	$2000 \div 6000$	≤ 1.42	>6000	>1.42
UDP	$2000 \div 6000$	≤ 1.42	>6000	>1.42
MQTT	$2000 \div 6000$	≤ 1.42	>6000	>1.42

The total average received packets by the smart devices is calculated by estimating the average rate of the received packets in 30 min compared to the abnormal behavior. We divided the packet reception rate into different slots. For every 3 min, we calculated the average of the received packets in the absence of the attack and stored the final results in the DB as normal behavior. The same calculation is applied to the smart home device when it is under attack. Then the final results are stored in the DB for further calculations. The detection system keeps monitoring the received packets, and in case there are abnormal behaviors received by such a device, we register that case as abnormal behavior.

To calculate the average received packets by the smart devices of the TCP protocol. We analyzed all the received packets and divided them into different types, such as packets received, re-transmission, and acknowledged. In our experiment, we need the average of the received packet by the smart devices that cause an increase in energy consumption. Then we used the final calculation to detect energy consumption attacks. Through the 30 min in the absence or the presence of the attack, we study the received packets by the smart devices for different protocols such as TCP, UDP, and MQTT. Also, we study the total number of times the smart devices stopped listening to understand if energy consumption attacks source the received packets. The normal average of the received packets for TCP protocol in 30 min fluctuates between 2 k and 5 k packets, as shown in Fig. 6.

In this experiment, for every 3 min, we calculated the normal and abnormal behavior. So, for the first 3 min, the normal behavior of the received packet is less than 5 k packets, while the abnormal received packets in the first 3 min in the presence of the attack are more than 6 k packets. The detection system registers the first case of the first 3 min as abnormal behavior. We also calculate the normal and abnormal behaviors for the total of 30 min by calculating the average of the packet reception rates of the normal behaviors and comparing

---

[5] https://pypi.org/project/pyshark/.
[6] https://github.com/developerZA/ATechniuqeToDetectEnergy.git.

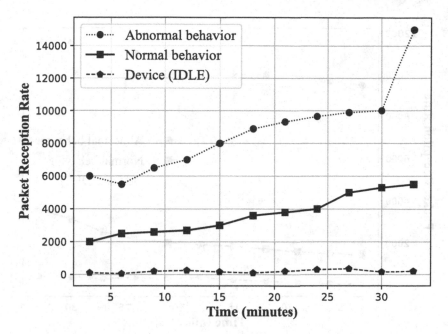

Fig. 6. Packet reception rate of normal and abnormal behaviors of the TCP protocol.

it with the average of the abnormal behaviors to register the entire case of the 30 min as normal or abnormal behavior.

In the case of UDP protocol, it is not easy to customize the actual receiving packet as the state of such a port cannot be confirmed by network scan using Nmap[7] because the port does not send any response. So, in our calculation, as shown in Fig. 7, we calculate the normally received packets of UDP protocol by the smart device. We monitor the packet reception rate of the smart devices for 30 min to check the normal and abnormal receiving packets of the Raspberry Pi. The normal behavior of the receiving packets is between 1 k and 3 k packets. In contrast, the abnormal behavior of the received packets by the smart device is between 9 k and more than 12 k packets.

Figure 8 shows the behavior of the subscribed packet's rate of the MQTT protocol. We study different behaviors of this protocol by registering the number of published and subscribed packets of the smart home device. To detect an energy consumption attack in the case of the MQTT protocol, we consider the number of subscribed packets as they affect the energy resources of the smart devices. Therefore, the normal behaviors of the MQTT protocol are registered to be less than 6 k packets, while the abnormal behaviors reached more than 8 k packets.

In this algorithm, we also consider the case where we do not have to specify the protocol; by calculating the average received packets for all the used pro-

---

[7] https://nmap.org/.

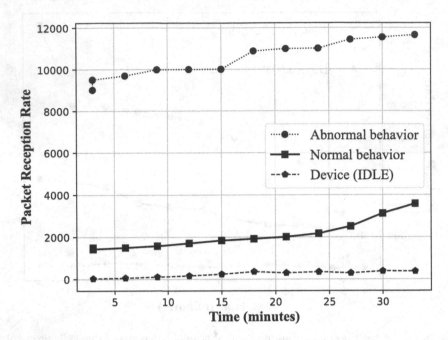

Fig. 7. Packet reception rate of normal and abnormal behaviors of the UDP protocol.

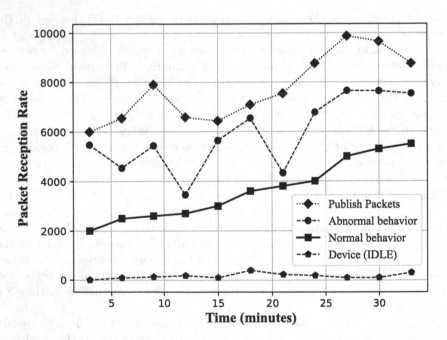

Fig. 8. Packet subscribed rate of normal and abnormal behaviors of the MQTT protocol.

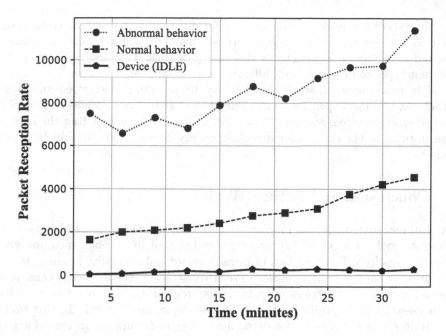

Fig. 9. General cases (Normal behavior Vs. Abnormal behavior) for TCP, UDP, and MQTT altogether, where the effect of each protocol in normal behavior is as follows: TCP effect is about 45%, and UDP effect about 30%, and the MQTT effect is about 20%. While the impact of TCP is about 40%, MQTT is about 40%, and 20% of UDP is in the presence of the attack.

tocols. We find that the normal behavior of the packet reception rate of the Raspberry Pi is between 1500 packets and less than or equal to 6 k packets. The abnormal behavior of the total received packets is between 7 k and more than 12 k packets, as shown in Fig. 9.

4.2 Experimental Results

The IoT device used in this experiment was infected with malicious software and used to carry out different flooding attacks on a target on an isolated network. During the experiments, the energy consumption footprints and the packet reception rate measurements of these IoT devices were obtained under normal operating conditions, as well as when these smart devices carry out cyberattacks. Each energy consumption footprint and packet reception rate were obtained by taking measurements after 5 s within 3 min when the smart device performs an attack and normal operation. A total of 30 min of calculation measurement of received packets and the energy consumption footprints of both in the presence of attacks and normal functioning smart devices were built.

The results of this experiment showed high efficiency of energy consumption attack detection based on the packet reception rate analysis. At the same time, the analysis of the packet reception rate for different protocols was considered. As it can be seen from Fig. 9, the abnormal behavior registered once the packets reached more than 6 k packets for different protocols. This analysis is done for different types of protocols and different devices' statuses.

This experiment shows high efficiency in detecting energy consumption attacks as it is not expensive to implement in a smart home device and considers the smart device's resource constraint. Compared to calculating the energy consumption of the devices for detecting energy consumption attacks in smart homes.

5   Conclusion and Future Work

The Internet of Things is an internet of smart objects where smart objects communicate with each other. IoT objects are deployed in an open medium with dynamic topology. Due to a lack of infrastructure and centralized management, IoT presents serious vulnerabilities to security attacks, such as energy consumption attacks, as smart devices suffer from resource-constraint. Therefore, security is an essential prerequisite for the real-world deployment of IoT. In this work, we propose a new technique for detecting energy consumption attacks in smart home devices based on the IoT devices' packet rate analysis. This technique considers the received packets related to the IoT devices for different protocols such as TCP, UDP, and the subscribed packets of the MQTT protocol. Therefore with the aim of energy consumption attack detection, the packet reception rate of the IoT devices is calculated and analyzed for each protocol separately or all the protocols simultaneously. In the algorithm, we consider different protocols and different device statuses. Our algorithm shows high efficiency in detecting energy consumption attacks in smart home devices compared to other algorithms that use the current energy consumption measurement for detecting this attack. As this algorithm is easy to use and not expensive to implement, it also considers the resource constraints of smart devices.

The key observations made from this work present a thorough understanding of the packet reception rate of IoT devices within a home wireless environment. And how the energy consumption attacks could be detected depending on measuring the packet rate received by the smart devices. In the future, we will try to detect the main sources that cause high energy consumption in smart home environments by detecting the attack type.

References

1. Alwaisi, Z., Soderi, S., Nicola, R.: Energy cyber attacks to smart healthcare devices: a testbed, April 2023
2. Ang, K.L.M., Seng, J.K.P., Ngharamike, E.: Towards crowdsourcing internet of things (crowd-IoT): architectures, security and applications. Future Internet **14**(2), 49 (2022)

3. Avula, R.R., Oechtering, T.J.: Privacy-enhancing appliance filtering for smart meters. In: ICASSP 2022–2022 IEEE International Conference on Acoustics, Speech and Signal Processing (ICASSP), pp. 9042–9046. IEEE (2022)
4. Barani Sundaram, B., et al.: Analysis of machine learning data security in the internet of things (IoT) circumstance. In: Jeena Jacob, I., Gonzalez-Longatt, F.M., Kolandapalayam Shanmugam, S., Izonin, I. (eds.) Expert Clouds and Applications. LNNS, vol. 209, pp. 227–236. Springer, Singapore (2022). https://doi.org/10.1007/978-981-16-2126-0_20
5. Bellavista, P., Cardone, G., Corradi, A., Foschini, L.: Convergence of manet and WSN in IoT urban scenarios. IEEE Sens. J. **13**(10), 3558–3567 (2013). https://doi.org/10.1109/JSEN.2013.2272099
6. Birajdar, D.M., Solapure, S.S.: Leach: An energy efficient routing protocol using omnet++ for wireless sensor network. In: 2017 International Conference on Inventive Communication and Computational Technologies (ICICCT), pp. 465–470. IEEE (2017)
7. Bobrovnikova, K., Lysenko, S., Popov, P., Denysiuk, D., Goroshko, A.: Technique for IoT cyberattacks detection based on the energy consumption analysis. In: CEUR Workshop Proceedings, vol. 2853 (2021)
8. Dabbagh, M., Rayes, A.: Internet of Things Security and Privacy. In: Rayes, A., Salam, S. (eds.) Internet of Things From Hype to Reality, pp. 211–238. Springer, Cham (2019). https://doi.org/10.1007/978-3-319-99516-8_8
9. Dawod, A., Georgakopoulos, D., Jayaraman, P.P., Nirmalathas, A., Parampalli, U.: IoT device integration and payment via an autonomic blockchain-based service for IoT device sharing. Sensors **22**(4), 1344 (2022)
10. (EIA), E.I.A.: Cisco visual networking index (VNI) (2019). https://www.eia.gov/outlooks/ieo/
11. Fabi, V., Spigliantini, G., Corgnati, S.P.: Insights on smart home concept and occupants' interaction with building controls. Energy Procedia **111**, 759–769 (2017). https://doi.org/10.1016/j.egypro.2017.03.238, https://www.sciencedirect.com/science/article/pii/S1876610217302680, 8th International Conference on Sustainability in Energy and Buildings, SEB-16, 11–13 September 2016, Turin, Italy
12. Felius, L., Dessen, F., Hrynyszyn, B.: Correction to: retrofitting towards energy-efficient homes in European cold climates: a review. Energy Efficiency **13** (2020). https://doi.org/10.1007/s12053-019-09838-3
13. Ford, R., Pritoni, M., Sanguinetti, A., Karlin, B.: Categories and functionality of smart home technology for energy management. Build. Environ. **123**, 543–554 (2017). https://doi.org/10.1016/j.buildenv.2017.07.020, https://www.sciencedirect.com/science/article/pii/S0360132317303062
14. Hoffmann, J., Neumann, S., Holz, T.: Mobile malware detection based on energy fingerprints a dead end, pp. 348–368 (2013)
15. Islam, M., Nooruddin, S., Karray, F., Muhammad, G., et al.: Internet of things device capabilities, architectures, protocols, and smart applications in healthcare domain: a review. arXiv preprint arXiv:2204.05921 (2022)
16. Khan, M.A., Salah, K.: IoT security: review, blockchain solutions, and open challenges. Futur. Gener. Comput. Syst. **82**, 395–411 (2018)
17. Kraijak, S., Tuwanut, P.: A survey on IoT architectures, protocols, applications, security, privacy, real-world implementation and future trends. In: 11th International Conference on Wireless Communications, Networking and Mobile Computing (WiCOM 2015), pp. 1–6 (2015). https://doi.org/10.1049/cp.2015.0714

18. Kumar, A., Sharma, S., Goyal, N., Singh, A., Cheng, X., Singh, P.: Secure and energy-efficient smart building architecture with emerging technology IoT. Comput. Commun. **176**, 207–217 (2021)

19. Patil, J., Sharma, M.: Survey of prevention techniques for denial service attacks (DoS) in wireless sensor network. Int. J. Sci. Res. (IJSR) (2016). ISSN 2319-7064

20. Pattewar, G., Mahamuni, N., Nikam, H., Loka, O., Patil, R.: Management of IoT devices security using blockchain-a review. Sentimental Anal. Deep Learn. 735–743 (2022)

21. Rahmadhani, M.A., Yovita, L.V., Mayasari, R.: Energy consumption and packet loss analysis of leach routing protocol on WSN over DTN. In: 2018 4th International Conference on Wireless and Telematics (ICWT), pp. 1–5. IEEE (2018)

22. Rondon, L.P., Babun, L., Aris, A., Akkaya, K., Uluagac, A.S.: Survey on enterprise internet-of-things systems (e-IoT): a security perspective. Ad Hoc Netw. **125**, 102728 (2022)

23. Shi, Y., Li, F., Song, W., Li, X.Y., Ye, J.: Energy audition based cyber-physical attack detection system in IoT. In: Proceedings of the ACM Turing Celebration Conference China. ACM TURC '19. Association for Computing Machinery, New York, NY, USA (2019). https://doi.org/10.1145/3321408.3321588

24. Tushir, B., Sehgal, H., Nair, R., Dezfouli, B., Liu, Y.: The impact of dos attacks onresource-constrained IoT devices: a study on the MIRAI attack. arXiv preprint arXiv:2104.09041 (2021)

25. Xu, J., Gu, B., Tian, G.: Review of agricultural IoT technology. Artif. Intell. Agric. (2022)

26. Zanella, A., Bui, N., Castellani, A., Vangelista, L., Zorzi, M.: Internet of things for smart cities. IEEE Internet Things J. **1**(1), 22–32 (2014). https://doi.org/10.1109/JIOT.2014.2306328

An Efficient Strategy for Deploying Deception Technology

Noora Alhosani, Saed Alrabaee[✉], and Ahmed Al Faresi

Department of Information Systems and Security, CIT,
United Arab Emirates University, Al Ain, United Arab Emirates
{202170216,salrabaee,ahmed.alfaresi}@uaeu.ac.ae

Abstract. This article introduces a methodology for maximizing the effectiveness of deception technology in detecting sophisticated cyber attacks and overcoming the limitation of intrusion detection systems' ability. The proposed methods implement multi-layered deception techniques at different network, system, and application levels to enhance coverage and improve attack detection by using decoys that mimic real systems to attract and identify potential attackers. The method proposes dynamic adaptation to changes in the network environment and employs obfuscation to maintain the effectiveness of the proposed techniques. Implementing this method can provide organizations with an early warning system to respond quickly and mitigate potential damage from cyber attacks, and we shall prove that by performing multiple cyber attacks towards a network with an intrusion detection system and decoys, then compare the detection capability on both technologies.

Keywords: Deception · Deception attributes · Network Attacks · intrusion detection system

1 Introduction

Deception technology is one of the security solutions that aims to distract and mislead attackers from their actual targets, such as critical systems and data [1]. It does this by deploying decoys, traps, or honeypots that imitate real systems or services and lure attackers into engaging with them. The decoys are typically configured to appear as legitimate targets with specific operating systems, applications, network attributes, and vulnerabilities that the security admin of the network has chosen. They are placed within a network of real servers, workstations, and devices, to blend in and increase the chances of attracting attackers [2] and detect them.

Once an attacker engages with a decoy by scanning, probing, or attempting to exploit it, the deception technology collects valuable data and alerts security administrators. This data may include the attacker's IP address, location, tactics, and the timestamps and sequence of events leading up to the engagement [3]. Deception technology can display all the activities reported from decoys, giving the security administrator insight into all the engagements. This can assist

D. Perakovic and L. Knapcikova (Eds.): FABULOUS 2023, LNICST 542, pp. 177–194, 2024.
https://doi.org/10.1007/978-3-031-50051-0_13

the security administrator to correlate and identify anomalies that traditional security systems can miss. In addition, security administrators can gain insights into the attacker's motives, methods, and potential targets and take appropriate actions to prevent future attacks or mitigate and encounter the attack that has been detected.

Security administrators' overall mitigation actions may include blocking the attacker's IP address, quarantining the infected systems, and patching the vulnerabilities [4]. Details of mitigation actions do not fall within the research scope. Deception technology has several advantages over traditional security mechanisms, such as intrusion detection systems (IDS), firewalls, or antivirus solutions. It is more proactive, flexible, and adaptable and can detect unknown or zero-day attacks that evade traditional defenses. Moreover, it provides a safe environment for researchers and penetration testers to simulate real-world attacks and enhance an organization's security posture.

Achieving efficient and adaptable cyber deception involves ongoing network monitoring to observe adversary activities, replace decoys based on strategic planning, and have feasible implementation without disrupting the integrity of existing system [5]. The primary goal is establishing an effective strategy based on best practices for maintaining deception technology. Due to the growing complexity of cyber attacks and their ability to evade numerous security measures, utilizing this technology can offer improved detection capabilities and align with a defense-in-depth approach, ensuring multiple layers of protection for information systems. This article aims to answer the following questions:

- What is an efficient method to define decoy attributes?
- What is the significance of network mapping in the deployment phase of decoys?
- How can we detect false negatives in logs?

Our proposed approach will help define realistic decoy attributes and fingerprints and identify the most suitable locations to deploy the decoys within the network for improved visibility and enhanced detection capabilities. Additionally, we will conduct lab demonstrations to simulate various types of attacks and demonstrate how deception technology can successfully detect them compared to intrusion detection system deception capability.

2   Background

2.1   Problem Statement

While the numbers and the sophistication of cyber attacks is increasing, improving detection and prevention mechanisms has become crucial to ensure higher security. Even with multiple monitoring devices and security controls such as web application firewalls, intrusion detection and prevention systems, and SIEM, sophisticated attacks can bypass these controls and result in significant losses.

To address this problem, researchers over time has developed deceptive methods including honey pots and deception technology, which adds an extra layer of defense to the network. honey pot and Deception technology is more of a strategy that needs to be tested, verified, and periodically changed to avoid exposure. It is crucial to establish clear set of objectives and prepare the prerequisites to ensure successful deployment.

2.2 Deception

Deception technology is a relatively new approach to cyber security that has gained much attention in recent years [6–8]. It is based on using deception to detect and prevent cyber attacks. The approach involves creating a controlled and monitored environment with decoys, traps, and honeypots that mimic real network assets and systems. Attackers are lured into engaging with these decoys, and their activities are monitored to gather intelligence on their tactics and techniques, and to detect malicious activity. One of the key benefits of deception technology is that it can provide an early warning system for detecting cyber attacks, allowing organizations to respond quickly and mitigate damage [9]. By creating a false sense of security for attackers, deception technology can also help gather intelligence on their tactics, techniques, and procedures, improving overall security posture. Additionally, deception technology can augment traditional security measures, providing an additional layer of defense against advanced threats that may bypass other security controls [9]. Deception technology is a comprehensive solution that has overcome some limitations of the traditional honey pot and honeynet technologies. It can create, customize, and manage decoys around the network to enhance the monitoring and detection of suspicious activities. The technology requires continuous network monitoring to observe adversary activities, optimal planning for feasible implementation, and safe deployment without breaking the system's integrity [5].

2.3 Honeynet

The project honeynet.org is a major source of information regarding honeynets [10]. The project's participants conduct research and run honeynets themselves, which serve as benchmarks for constructing and assessing honey nets [11]. They have also developed Open-Source honey net tools known as Honeywell [12]. Security enterprises, such as firewall/IDS manufacturers and antivirus manufacturers, maintain many honeypots in a honey net. These honeypots are distributed worldwide and provide threat information and an attack map. Organizations also use honeypots to hide their critical infrastructure and improve their security efforts with the obtained information. Honey nets are a type of honeypot, a security resource used to detect probes, scans, or attacks. Honey nets are more complex than honeypots and consist of multiple honeypots networked together to mimic a larger network. Deception technology is similar to honeypots but has several key differences.

2.4 Honeypot

Honeypots offer various capabilities and can mimic the operations of real systems, making them appear to be a part of the network. However, honeypots are actually isolated and closely supervised, allowing them to record the activities of attackers and gather information about their tools and operating procedures. Initially, honeypots were used as a trap method that is created and set up to be hacked to waste the attacker's resources and time on honeypots rather than attack real systems that actually exist [9]. Honeypots are classified based on the level of interaction they offer to the attacker, which results in low-, medium-, and high-interaction honeypots. The first two categories offer different levels of protocol emulation, while the high-interaction describes real-world systems. High-interaction honeypots are more expensive to maintain and are used significantly less than low/medium-interaction honeypots [13].

On a summary, honey nets, honeypots, and Deception share some similarities, there are also significant differences between them that are important to understand. Please refer to A comparison between Honey net, Honeypot, and Deception for comparing the main features of honey nets, honeypots, and deception technology (Table 1).

Table 1. A comparison between Honey net, Honeypot, and Deception

Feature	Honeynet	Honeypot	Deception
Scalability and administration	Honeynets utilize virtualization to create entire network topologies using pre-set or custom images on a single physical or virtual machine	Setting up a honeypot involves a separate physical or virtual system placed within the network, and administrators must access each honeypot individually for modifications	Deception technology solutions are prepackaged and scalable, allowing for rapid decoy deployment and central management without direct access to the decoy itself
Level of interaction	Decoys imitate active hosts, responding to basic network commands while sharing the same operating system and MAC address, but may not react to all packet types	- Low-interaction honeypots simulate specific services, such as FTP or web servers, with attacker interaction determining the emulation depth. - High-interaction honeypots offer real operating systems and services like FTP or web servers instead of just emulating them	High-interaction decoys on real operating systems gather extensive attacker information, enabling automated incident response, accurate alarms, and forensic reports
Risk of takeover/compromise	A compromised honeypot in a honeynet can become an attack source	It can be compromised	Modern deception platforms deploy out-of-band decoys to prevent attackers from launching network attacks
Logging capability and monitoring	They can be installed on the host system. However, there is no centralized dashboard to view logs and interactions	Honeypots don't have their own logs; they rely on capturing logs from the host OS. Logs can be forwarded to monitoring solutions or manually analyzed. There is no centralized dashboard to view honeypot logs and interactions	logs can be sent to the security monitoring tools like SIEM or viewed on the deception console's dashboard, without separate configurations for log forwarding or collection

3   Methodology

The research methodology will have three steps. First will explore and collect honeypot and decoy attributes/fingerprinting methods from different resources and summarize them in order to to apply test their efficiency using an open source deception technology. Second, the study will also explore effective network mapping techniques to locate existing network assets/components for optimal decoy placement. Third and last, the research testing shall conclude our methodology by performing multiple cyber attack scenarios, on a virtual lab, the lab will have an intrusion detection system, and we shall implement decoy attributes that we collected previously, then test the ability of deception technology to detect and alert about cyber-attack attempts compared to the installed intrusion detection system (Table 2) (Fig. 1).

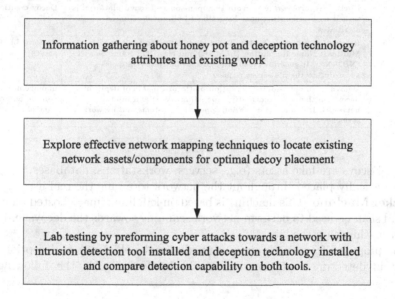

Fig. 1. Research methodology

3.1   Testing Lab Components

Our virtual testing lab consists of the following tools and components:

Each attack scenario will necessitate a unique network design and components tailored to the specific use case under examination and the type of cyber attack to be conducted. The following details the primary components that will be involved during the testing phase:

Central Management Console. The central management console provides a unified interface for configuring, managing, and monitoring the Dejavu system.

Table 2. A comparison between Honey net, Honeypot, and Deception

Tool name	Tool description	Usage for experiment
Oracle Virtual box	Oracle VM VirtualBox is a versatile virtualization software that operates across various platforms. It provides users the capability to expand their current computer system to simultaneously run multiple operating systems, such as Microsoft Windows, Mac OS X, Linux, and Oracle Solaris	Hosting on virtual machines
Snort (NIDS)	Snort is an open-source Network Intrusion Detection System that employs a set of rules to identify harmful network activities. It scans network packets to detect matches with these rules and subsequently triggers alerts for users	Testing detection capability
Kali Linux virtual machine	Kali Linux is a Linux distribution, based on Debian, specifically crafted for conducting digital forensics and penetration testing tasks	Performing cyber attacks and scanning activites
nmap	"Network Mapper," commonly known as Nmap, is an open-source tool that provides network discovery and security auditing capabilities for free	Network scanning
Docker	Docker, as incorporated within the open-source Dejavu platform, is tasked with generating new decoys based on our designated attributes	Decoy creation
responder	Responder, a built-in tool in Kali Linux, caters to Link-Local Multicast Name Resolution (LLMNR) and NetBIOS Name Service (NBT-NS). It generates responses to specific NetBIOS queries according to the file server request	Perform LLMNR attack
Dejavu	Dejavu is an open-source deception platform capable of deploying decoys on the cloud (currently supporting AWS) and internal networks. It can simulate various operating systems and network services	management console and decoy control

Decoy. Decoys are fake assets (e.g., servers, workstations, databases, etc.) that are strategically placed throughout the network to mimic the real assets.

Attacker Machine. This machine is based on kali linux image hosted on virtual box and shall be used to perform network scanning towards the decoys and other virtual machines on the lab.

The proposed framework aims to maximize the efficiency of deception technology in detecting sophisticated attacks by focusing on the following key aspects:

- Multi-layered Deception: The framework employs deception techniques at multiple layers of the network, system, and application to provide comprehensive coverage and increase the likelihood of detecting attacks.
- Strategic Decoy Placement: Decoys and honeypots are strategically positioned throughout the network to maximize their visibility to potential attackers and minimize the likelihood of accidental interaction with legitimate users.
- Dynamic Adaptation: The framework continuously adapts to changes in the network environment, modifying decoys and honeypots as necessary to maintain their effectiveness.
- Confidentiality: Ensuring the confidentiality of the deception process is crucial to prevent attackers from identifying and avoiding the decoys and honeypots. This can be achieved through obfuscation, encryption, and access control.

3.2   Phases

The virtual lab will simulate ten cyber-attacks, covering various decoy attributes and locations in the network to demonstrate the need for specific settings to enhance cyber-attack detection. The research will include the following phases:

- Phase one
  - Virtual lab setup and tool installation: We first choose Virtual Box to host kali linux and dejavu deception open source platform along with snort intrusion detection system which shall be inline mode to inspect all traffic on our internal network used for the lab.
- Phase two
  - Configure dejavu and deploy decoys: To configure DejaVu, we should install the software on a virtual machine. Then, we can follow the instructions provided by dejavu authors to set up the software and configure it to our network's requirements. Once DejaVu is configured, We shall determine the best deployment method based on our network's infrastructure and the type of decoys we want to use for testing.
  - Decoy customization and finger printing: Customization involves creating realistic decoy attributes such as open ports, services, and operating systems, and defining their behavior to appear as if they are legitimate.
- Phase three
  - Test cyber attack scenarios on decoys and perform result analysis: To test the effectiveness of the deployed decoys, various attack scenarios need to be simulated on them. During the simulation, we will compare the detection capability of deception technology and intrusion detection system and list the observations.

3.3   Steps

The following are the steps involved in deploying deception technology.

- Define objectives: Before implementing deception technology, map the network to help defining your objectives and desired outcomes.
- Identify the target areas: after network mapping, The next step is to identify the high-value areas in your network that need to be protected. These could include critical applications, databases, and other sensitive resources.
- Deployment: Deploy the decoys and honeypots in the identified areas of your network. Ensure they are configured correctly and blend in with the rest of your network to avoid detection.
- Monitor and manage: This includes collecting and analyzing data from the decoys, updating and refreshing them regularly, and integrating them with other security solutions if available.
- Incident response: In a breach or attack, deception technology can provide valuable insights into the attacker's tactics, techniques, and procedures. Ensure an incident response plan is in place to respond to such incidents effectively.

– Continuous improvement: Deception technology is not a one-time solution but requires continuous improvement and refinement. Regularly review and update your objectives, decoys to ensure that they remain effective.

3.4 Proposed Framework

Our proposed framework is based on covering multiple layers of attributes, including the network, system, and application, as well as the strategic positioning of the decoys. Most importantly, the entire process must maintain confidentiality:

Maintain Confidentiality

Security professionals should maintain the confidentiality of deception platforms, even from an organization's employees, such as IT staff. They ought to evaluate different solutions available in the market and may consult Gartner's [14] annual rankings for top choices. Furthermore, if a deception platform is acquired, its implementation shouldn't be broadly publicized or shared with IT companies. The involvement should be restricted, involving only government-approved companies with local offices who sign NDAs (Non-disclosure agreements) and have limited knowledge of the project and deployment.

3.5 Consider Data Ex-Filtration Detection Using Deception

During data ex-filtration, an attacker, whether an internal employee or an external threat, may gain unauthorized access to data and leak it externally. Determining the type of information leaked or the specific files targeted can be challenging. Placing honey files among sensitive files makes it possible to identify the source IP address when the file is opened in case of a leak, even if it is accessed outside the organization's network. This strategy enhances the detection and tracking of unauthorized data access and ex-filtration (Fig. 2).

Perform Network Mapping

To effectively integrate a deception platform into the network, comprehensive network mapping is crucial, covering all entry points like public websites and services across zones such as DMZ, VPN, webmail, and mobile apps. Decoys need to be tactically positioned in suitable quantities, offering diverse enticing services. Each decoy generates alerts, either false or true positives, which can be tracked and examined. Excessive decoys may lead to confusing and inundating log information [15]. Seek advice from the organization's network engineer or IT architect for a network diagram to aid in planning. Nonetheless, it's advisable to conduct independent mapping to confirm the accuracy of the provided network diagram. Take into account the following factors to maximize the benefits of this activity:

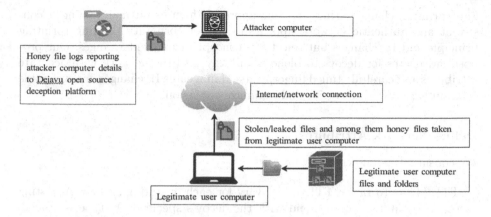

Fig. 2. Data Ex-filtration detection method

- Develop and uphold a list of essential active application servers: Organizations rely on particular services for maintaining their operations; for example, banks depend on payment systems, educational institutions on student and course registration systems, and healthcare facilities on patient databases. Each vital application comprises a list of servers and databases, with assigned IP addresses for incorporation into the information system/network. The list should connect the server to its respective IP address and outline the service it operates. It is best to designate an owner responsible for the routine upkeep of the server and application.
- To map the network, we can set up a host with full access from the organization's firewall, disable its internet connection, and scan the network using tools like nmap or masscan. These tools identify open ports in the IT system, which are then assessed for vulnerabilities. Nmap offers a wide assessment range, while Masscan focuses on quick, broad scans. For full network mapping with Masscan, use this command: masscan $0.0.0.0/0 - p0 - 65535$.

After obtaining the output, it will include all the hosts that responded to our host, allowing us to determine the number of subnets and live hosts, and gain further insight into the internal network.

Customization of Decoy Attributes

Deploying a decoy aims to make it appear realistic to mislead attackers into wasting their resources trying to compromise it. If a network contains HP devices, the decoy should mimic these with similar specifications, such as MAC addresses, default credentials, and hostnames. A Windows machine decoy should join the domain with a matching hostname. Periodically changing the decoy's IP address, vulnerabilities, and hosted services can increase its effectiveness. The CONCEAL research emphasizes anonymization through frequent decoy IP, attributes, and fingerprinting changes. However, our approach focuses on maintaining a consistent and authentic network appearance. We incorporate the fingerprinting principle and IP changes but reject the concept of frequent changes. Our proposal advocates for decoys to blend seamlessly into the network with accurate attributes and carefully tuned fingerprints. Manageable IP changes are preferable to maintain network integrity and minimize confusion.

Define Network Attributes

We consider the following attributes:

- TTL (Time to Live): TTL values vary for each operating system. Adjusting the TTL value to correspond with the decoy's specified OS type is crucial. For example, the TTL value for Windows OS is 128, whereas, for Linux, it is 64. When creating a decoy with a Windows operating system assigned, ensure the TTL value is modified to 128.
- MAC Address: When creating a decoy that mimics Fujitsu devices, it is essential to use Fujitsu-specific MAC addresses with their unique starting values (MAC prefix). According to CONCEAL, this principle applies to any device and operating system type; the MAC address prefix should correspond with the chosen operating system type. Simply copy and paste the appropriate prefix and complete the rest with random values.
- IP Address/Network VLAN: When deploying a decoy in user subnets, consider using a decoy with the same operating system as the users to make it blend in better. If you deploy a decoy in a server subnet, avoid using Windows 10 or Windows 7 (workstation operating systems), as placing a user workstation in a server subnet would be illogical. Such a strategy might raise suspicions among attackers.

After considering all these attributes, the likelihood of an attacker discovering the decoy on the network level is significantly reduced.

Define System Attributes

We consider the following attributes:

- OS: Select an operating system that is commonly used in your environment. If you primarily have Windows 10 machines, deploy a Windows 10 decoy rather than a Fujitsu decoy that stands out. If you have more Windows servers, use a Windows server decoy instead of RHEL. However, you can vary the decoy types if your environment includes a mix of operating systems. The main goal is to ensure the decoy blends in and doesn't stand out or appear unique among the other devices, as this could raise suspicion.
- Services: When deploying a decoy on a server subnet/VLAN, enable server-related services such as (but not limited to) FTP, SSH, and IIS. These services should also match the operating system type, as IIS service would not be

found on a RHEL server but on Windows-based hosts. Additionally, network administrators typically do not have user workstations with Apache or Tomcat within the regular users' VLAN, as they often separate the developers' environment.

Define Application Attributes

We consider the following attributes:

- Application protocols: When using deception technology, creating a fake webmail page with login capability is possible. However, such a decoy running on the intranet may be useless. It should be strategically placed on a target network, like the internet, to determine who is attempting to breach our network. Legitimate users are unlikely to use the fake page, as they already know the organization's main page.
- If we have a SWIFT network and decide to deploy a decoy within it, it's essential to ensure that all machines in this network are related to SWIFT and no other services. By doing so, an attacker roaming within this network will have difficulty distinguishing between legitimate devices and decoys.
- Consider enabling services such as Apache or Tomcat on application decoys, as application servers commonly use these services.

3.6   Network Scanning

When services are published online, attackers may compromise credentials and gain account access. Since these services generate large amounts of logs and users may lock their accounts accidentally, detecting attacks becomes challenging. To mitigate this, decoys can be used. These decoys, unknown to legitimate users, help to detect unauthorized attempts faster, as any login attempt indicates a possible security breach. Upon login attempts, users are looped back to the same page repeatedly. Meanwhile, the decoy reports to the Dejavu open source deception platform, triggering attack alerts.

Imagine an unknown, potentially compromised account within an organization in a realistic attack scenario. By placing a decoy of a webmail service, any login attempt becomes noticeable. Since internal employees are uninformed about this decoy webmail service, their chances of accessing or even seeking it are low because A) they already know how to access the organization's actual mail service and B) the organization may not even have a directly internet-accessible webmail service. Organizations with robust security controls usually avoid publishing their webmail services directly online, offering alternative access methods, thereby reducing their attack surface and limiting exposure. Entities considering deception implementation might opt to publish a decoy webmail service online without making any announcements. They can then monitor the type of traffic it attracts, which may alert them to an attacker's information-gathering activities. So considering one or both of the conditions, there is a high chance that an attacker is behind our network. To overcome the attack scenario, We shall place decoys on the internet replicating our online services, where it simulates a login page for employees. In the below section, we shall simulate the attacks on different services and how to detect them using deception and, test the ability of the intrusion detection system to detect the attacks, then compare the results (Fig. 3).

Fig. 3. Web mail decoy Log summary shown in dajavu open source deception platform console

4   Lab Testing Use Cases

Commonly, cyber attack phases include information gathering (reconnaissance), enumeration, and compromise of the system. We shall include recon and enumeration. The compromise phase is out of our scope. The test cases will be conducted via various cyber attack scenarios. The below table shows the tested attacks and their phases according to common cyber attack phases (Table 3):

Table 3. Test Cases

Use case	Attacker target	Security control
Scanning the network using nmap (two types of network scan: normal nmap scan and silent scan)	Reconnaissance	Decoy network positioning
Password spray was not identified by Snort IDS but got detected by Dejavu open-source deception platform	Enumeration	Decoy customization
LLMNR poisoning was not detected on Snort IDS but got detected in Dejavu open-source deception platform	Enumeration	Decoy customization and network positioning
Simulate the importance of decoy attributes	Reconnaissance	Decoy customization

4.1   Scenario 1: Scanning the Network Using Nmap (two Types of Network Scan: Normal Nmap Scan and Silent Scan)

Normal Nmap Scan. Port scanning is a method used to identify open network ports that may be sending or receiving data. By sending packets to specific ports on a host and analyzing the responses, vulnerabilities can be detected. Before port scanning can take place, it is necessary to first identify and map active hosts to their corresponding IP addresses. This process, called host discovery, starts with a network scan (Fig. 4).

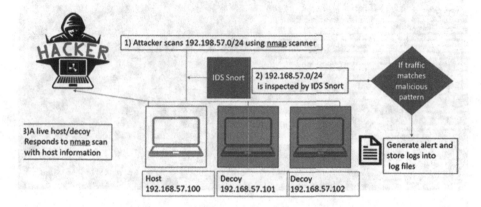

Fig. 4. Nmap Network scan

Port and network scanning is designed to identify the structure of IP addresses, hosts, and ports, enabling the detection of open or vulnerable server locations and assessing security levels. Network and port scanning can also uncover the existence of security measures to attackers. To identify port scanning activity, we can deploy a decoy on the internet that imitates a service (such as webmail) or a VPN service and then monitor the incoming traffic. Using kali linux machine we launched a scan towards the web mail service (Fig. 5).

On the other side, we open the Snort IDS log file and see the following logs that has been generated from the monitored network 192.168.57.0/24 and we can see that the scan has triggered alerts on NIDS side.

Observation: snort detected normal scan attempts on the subnet using Nmap, which has been presented in a series of logs. This was performed to confirm Snort is operating and inspecting the traffic (Fig. 6).

Silent nmap Scan. We prepared the following setup and used Nmap scanning tool. We added -ss to nmap command to enable the silent scan option and specified port numbers 80, 21, 443,22 for the scan. Nmap will scan 192.168.57.0/24 silently and search for the specified ports (Figs. 7 and 8).

Description: The log file is showing ipv6 traffic, which was generated from scenario 1.1 and not from the current silent scan. The screenshot shows that no

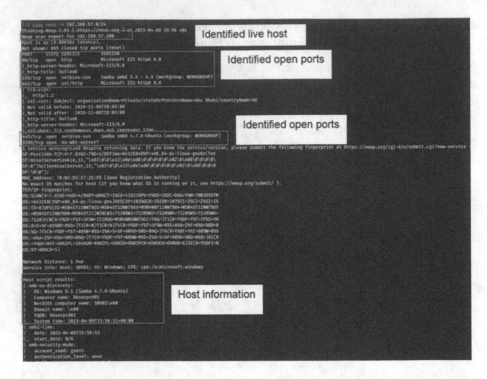

Fig. 5. Scan result from attacker side showing host information that has responded to nmap scan.

Fig. 6. scan result from IDS Snort side/terminal showing ping attempts and nmap scan traffic pattern which indicated as malicious

alerts have been triggered for this host, indicating that this is a false negative. On the other side, we can view the management console of deception technology to check if there were any alerts:

Description: We can see on the decoy IP, which is 192.168.57.101, has captured the scan attempt towards it, and it is showing the port numbers (on the

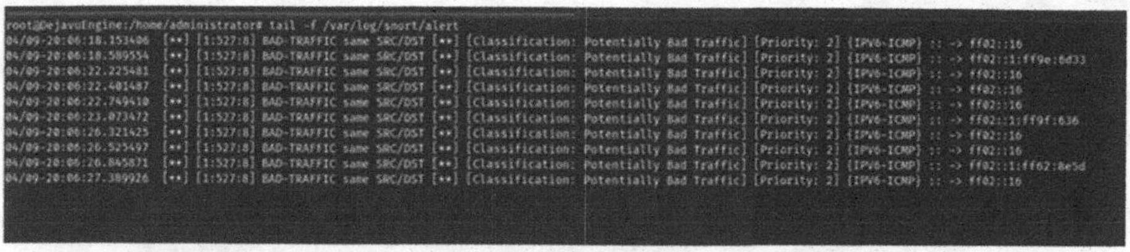

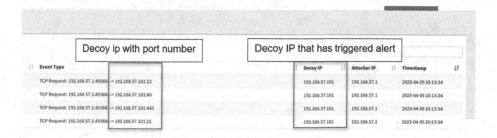

Fig. 7. Intrusion detection unable to detect silent scan

Fig. 8. silent scan detected on deception technology

event type) port 22, port 80, port 443, and 21, which we have specified on the
silent scan option (refer to Fig. 20: scan result from attacker side/terminal showing the nmap command along with the subnet, specified port numbers and silent
option (-ss)).

The console shows that alerts have been flagged for the targeted host of the
scan (Decoy). The alerts have been generated and reported from the decoy to
the management console.

4.2 Scenario 2: Password Spray Was Not Identified by Snort IDS but Got Detected by Dejavu Open-Source Deception Platform

67assword spraying is a type of brute force attack in which an attacker attempts
to gain access to multiple accounts on an application using a list of usernames
and default passwords. To avoid account lockouts that typically result from
repeatedly trying multiple passwords on a single account, an attacker uses a
single password (e.g., Secure@123) against numerous accounts on the application. This attack is common when an application or administrator sets a default
password for new users.

Creating a Decoy Without Setting Customized Attributes (Default):
Testing the case with no assigned attributes and relying on the default configuration of DejaVu as shown in Fig. 9.

**Credential Stuffing/Password Spray Not Identified by Snort IDS but
Got Detected by Dejavu Open Source Deception Platform.** In this
scenario, we have placed multiple decoys, and each runs a different service with

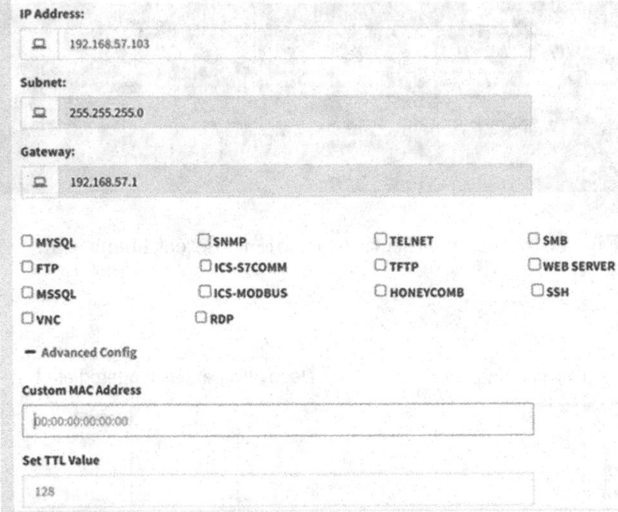
IP Address:
192.168.57.103
Subnet:
255.255.255.0
Gateway:
192.168.57.1
MYSQL
SNMP
TELNET
SMB
FTP
ICS-S7COMM
TFTP
WEB SERVER
MSSQL
ICS-MODBUS
HONEYCOMB
SSH
VNC
RDP
Advanced Config
Custom MAC Address
00:00:00:00:00:00
Set TTL Value
128

Fig. 9. Creating a decoy

login capability to test password spray detection. the created services (decoys) are below:

- Web mail login page decoy
- tomcat login page as a decoy
- Basic authentication application decoy

After attempting to login to the decoy services multiple times from the browser, we checked the logs on both IDS and Deception management console and identified that the attempt to login to the decoy from the browser had been alerted on deception technology and was not identified not alerted by IDS (Figs. 10, 11 and 12).

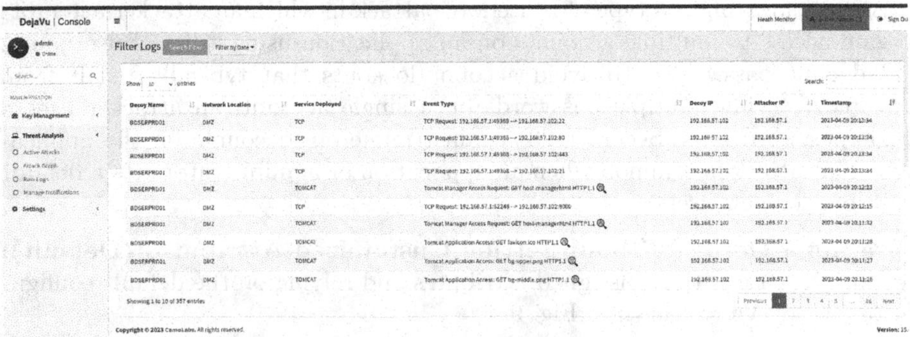
DejaVu | Console
Filter Logs
Decoy Name
Network Location
Service Deployed
Event Type
Decoy IP
Attacker IP
Timestamp

Fig. 10. Attack attempt detected on deception technology: example 1

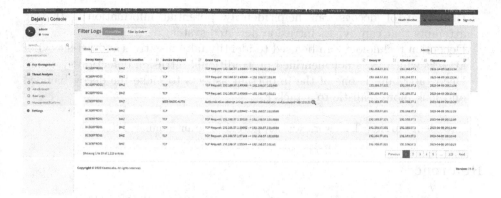

Fig. 11. Attack attempt detected on deception technology: example 2

On the other hand, we have the log file of the intrusion detection system that has not shown any attempt or alert:

```
root@DejavuEngine:/home/administrator# tail -f /var/log/snort/alert
04/09-20:06:18.253480  [**] [1:527:8] BAD-TRAFFIC same SRC/DST [**] [Classification: Potentially Bad Traffic] [Priority: 2] {IPV6-ICMP} :: -> ff02::16
04/09-20:06:18.589554  [**] [1:527:8] BAD-TRAFFIC same SRC/DST [**] [Classification: Potentially Bad Traffic] [Priority: 2] {IPV6-ICMP} :: -> ff02::1:ff9e:6d33
04/09-20:06:22.225483  [**] [1:527:8] BAD-TRAFFIC same SRC/DST [**] [Classification: Potentially Bad Traffic] [Priority: 2] {IPV6-ICMP} :: -> ff02::16
04/09-20:06:22.401487  [**] [1:527:8] BAD-TRAFFIC same SRC/DST [**] [Classification: Potentially Bad Traffic] [Priority: 2] {IPV6-ICMP} :: -> ff02::16
04/09-20:06:22.749410  [**] [1:527:8] BAD-TRAFFIC same SRC/DST [**] [Classification: Potentially Bad Traffic] [Priority: 2] {IPV6-ICMP} :: -> ff02::16
04/09-20:06:23.073472  [**] [1:527:8] BAD-TRAFFIC same SRC/DST [**] [Classification: Potentially Bad Traffic] [Priority: 2] {IPV6-ICMP} :: -> ff02::1:ff9f:636
04/09-20:06:26.321425  [**] [1:527:8] BAD-TRAFFIC same SRC/DST [**] [Classification: Potentially Bad Traffic] [Priority: 2] {IPV6-ICMP} :: -> ff02::16
04/09-20:06:26.525497  [**] [1:527:8] BAD-TRAFFIC same SRC/DST [**] [Classification: Potentially Bad Traffic] [Priority: 2] {IPV6-ICMP} :: -> ff02::10
04/09-20:06:26.865871  [**] [1:527:8] BAD-TRAFFIC same SRC/DST [**] [Classification: Potentially Bad Traffic] [Priority: 2] {IPV6-ICMP} :: -> ff02::1:ff62:8e5d
04/09-20:06:27.309928  [**] [1:527:8] BAD-TRAFFIC same SRC/DST [**] [Classification: Potentially Bad Traffic] [Priority: 2] {IPV6-ICMP} :: -> ff02::16
```

Fig. 12. Intrusion detection unable to detect password spray on the network

5   Conclusion

Overall, Deception technology is a comprehensive solution that has overcome some limitations of the traditional honey pot and honeynet technologies. It can create, customize, and manage decoys around the network to enhance the monitoring and detection of suspicious activities. The technology requires continuous network monitoring to observe adversary activities, optimal planning for feasible implementation, and safe deployment without breaking the system's integrity. This article summarized some of the best practices to follow to have a good implementation of the technology. We have tested multiple attack scenarios on a virtual lab and compared the results between a network with deception technology deployed and a network with a traditional intrusion detection system installed.

We conclude our observation on below:

- Placement of decoys can help identify potential information gathering attempts that can bypass intrusion detected system
- Deception technology can be used to identify false negatives and detect cyber attacks which were not identified on traditional intrusion detection systems.
- Decoy attribute is one of the important aspects to make the decoy blended and look more realistic to attacker.

Acknowledgement. This work was supported by grant number 12R170.

References

1. Dickinson, K.: Implementer's guide to deception technologies, SANS Institute Information Security Reading Room, P. 16 (2020)
2. Major, M., Souza, B., DiVita, J., Ferguson-Walter, K.: Informing autonomous deception systems with cyber expert performance data, arXiv preprint arXiv:2109.00066
3. Han, X., Kheir, N., Balzarotti, D.: Deception techniques in computer security: a research perspective. ACM Comput. Surv. (CSUR) 51(4), 1–36 (2018)
4. Chiang, C.-Y. J., et al.: Acyds: an adaptive cyber deception system. In: MILCOM 2016–2016 IEEE Military Communications Conference, pp. 800–805. IEEE (2016)
5. Srinivasa, S., Pedersen, J.M., Vasilomanolakis, E.: Deceptive directories and "vulnerable" logs: a honeypot study of the ldap and log4j attack landscape. In: 2022 IEEE European Symposium on Security and Privacy Workshops (EuroS&PW), pp. 442–447. IEEE (2022)
6. Andrews, K.T.: Deception techniques and technologies in the role of active cyber defense, Ph.D. thesis, Utica College (2020)
7. Bushby, A.: How deception can change cyber security defences. Computer Fraud Sec. 2019(1), 12–14 (2019)
8. Xu, Y., Chai, S., Shi, P., Zhang, B., Wang, Y.: Resilient and event-triggered control of stochastic jump systems under deception and denial of service attacks. Int. J. Robust Nonlinear Control 33(3), 1821–1837 (2023)
9. Melhem, H., Dayoub, Y.: A hybrid honeypot framework for ddos attacks detection and mitigation
10. Spitzner, L.: The honeynet project: trapping the hackers. IEEE Sec. Privacy 1(2), 15–23 (2003)
11. Stumpf, F., Görlach, A., Homann, F., Brückner, L.: Nose-building virtual honeynets made easy. In: Proceedings of the 12th International Linux System Technology Conference, Hamburg, Germany, Citeseer (2005)
12. Lackner, P.: How to mock a bear: honeypot, honeynet, honeywall & honeytoken: a survey. In: ICEIS (2), pp. 181–188 (2021)
13. Srinivasa, S., Pedersen, J.M., Vasilomanolakis, E.: Gotta catch'em all: a multistage framework for honeypot fingerprinting, arXiv preprint arXiv:2109.10652
14. gartner (2019). https://www.gartner.com/peer-insights/search?text=deception
15. Duan, Q., Al-Shaer, E., Islam, M., Jafarian, H.: Conceal: a strategy composition for resilient cyber deception-framework, metrics and deployment. In: 2018 IEEE Conference on Communications and Network Security (CNS), pp. 1–9. IEEE (2018)

The Use of Data in BIM Technology and Effects on Profitability of Construction Projects in Slovakia, Slovenia and Croatia

Tomáš Mandičák(✉), Peter Mésároš, and Lucia Zemánová

Technical University of Košice, Košice, Slovakia
tomas.mandicak@tuke.sk

Abstract. Current technologies can work efficiently with a large amount of data. Data and information can represent competitive advantage and are also necessary decision-making tools. BIM technologies are characterized by the ability to work with a large amount of data and thereby support decision-making in the management of construction projects. From an economic and investment point of view, the question is how these progressive technologies can contribute to achieving the financial results of construction activity. In other words, this research seeks to answer how these technologies help achieve selected KPIs. The parameters of profitability were investigated as part of the research. The research was carried out based on evaluating commercial projects from three countries, Slovakia, Croatia, and Slovenia. The aim of the research is to analyze the impact of using data in the BIM environment and their impact on profitability parameters.

Keywords: BIM technology · profitability · profitability index · construction project · data

1 Introduction and Problem Statement

Data and information nowadays have a lot of value in many cases [1]. Their value depends primarily on the degree of usefulness. In other words, to what extent they can be helpful for specific purposes, for example management or decision-making [2]. Effective work with data can bring added value in the form of support for decision-making. The effort to quantify results and manage based on facts is one of the main ideas of how data can be effectively used in management in any field [3]. Current technologies can work with a large amount of data, which leads to the facilitation of some management and the adoption of economic and financial decisions [4]. Therefore, smart technologies and information and communication technologies in general represent possibilities that can have a significant impact on the results and success of decisions based on this information [5].

BIM technologies represent a tool that largely works with a large amount of data and supports parametric modeling [6]. This results in fast data processing, visualization and

D. Perakovic and L. Knapcikova (Eds.): FABULOUS 2023, LNICST 542, pp. 195–207, 2024.
https://doi.org/10.1007/978-3-031-50051-0_14

simulations that can provide important information in the planning and management of construction projects [7].

From an economic point of view, it is an opportunity to plan and later implement construction activities and thereby ensure the success of the project from an economic point of view. Here it is important to define the success of the project from this point of view. In economic terms, this represents the fulfillment of the main essence of business activities and thus the achievement of positive financial indicators. Tracking key performance indicators can provide a quick way to evaluate the success of construction projects [8].

The success of construction projects from a commercial point of view can be assessed based on profitability indicators. Therefore, monitoring basic financial parameters and their evaluation is important and, in essence, it is a necessity [8]. The use of BIM technologies should contribute to better planning and, therefore, in the implementation phase, to the use of available resources (material, work, time, but also financial parameters). This view is the basis for investigating the impact of BIM technologies and the use of data in the planning and management of construction projects. The scientific assumption is that in the case of a higher rate of use of BIM technology and provided data in this environment, it can have a positive relationship with the profitability of these construction projects. Analysis of the correlation between these variables can provide an answer as to whether BIM technologies also bring benefit in achieving selected key performance indicators, in this case profitability indicators [9].

Development projects aimed at the sale of residential or commercial premises is one of the conditions for this assessment, primarily due to the time-consuming nature of the research. Considering the investigated impacts on profitability indicators, it is a condition of this research to ensure the measurement of comparable projects and parameters. From an investment point of view, it is therefore necessary to say that these projects must be sold, not rented, for easier comparison, and for an objective assessment it is important to determine the number of units already sold. From the point of view of profitability indicators, two indicators were considered: net income, which also considers the cost parameter, as a profitability index, which considers the size of the investment [10].

2   Data in BIM Technology and Profitability Indicators

BIM technology brings challenges and opportunities, as thanks to effective data management, it is possible to plan, manage and implement construction projects effectively. Data plays a significant role in the planning and management of construction projects. Digital technologies represent a tool that, according to several studies, can significantly make these processes more efficient. What is a significant advantage for any necessary changes in the model, it is easy to make changes in the planning and prepare multiple scenarios. It is especially suitable for investment evaluation of construction projects, where several variants can be simulated and modelled in advance, also from the point of view of economic and financial parameters [11] (Fig. 1).

Building information modelling in the construction industry plays an important role not only from the point of view of 3D modelling but also in a broader sense from the point of view of cost modelling, which significantly affects the profitability of projects,

Fig. 1. Dimensions of Building Information Modelling [12].

respectively, in the evaluation of investment intentions. Within the individual dimensions of BIM, i.e., 3D modelling, time planning, and cost modelling, i.e., 5D, also plays an important role. However, from the point of view of the life cycle of construction projects and thus also the phase of use, it is necessary to pay attention to the aspect of sustainability already during planning [12].

The current situation and the instability of the prices of building materials only confirm the necessity to work with data and use the possibilities of digital technologies to change them easily and the ability to quickly incorporate new information into plans, management processes and the implementation itself. BIM technology makes it possible to change input information quickly and thus promptly model new variants, eliminating possible time and financial losses. Another benefit can be maintaining the required level of quality, minimizing unexpected situations and the like [9].

Several studies have pointed out the benefits of using information and communication technologies and tools for working with data in planning, managing, and implementing construction projects. Considering the complexity of understanding the situation, it is also necessary to mention that there are several participants with often different goals within this process. The view of the developer, respectively the investor, is focused on financial indicators and economic benefit. In this way, he also tries to quantify the construction project's success. On the other hand, the pursuit of profit, which is based on the minimization of costs, is the pursuit of every participant in the construction project. This can sometimes be in contrast with the desired level of quality [13, 14].

From a business point of view, the success of construction and development projects is assessed primarily from the point of view of investment value and profitability. This is, of course, true if the discussion is focused on commercial projects, buildings to sell housing or commercial space.

One of the studies points to the fact that this process needs to be more standardized despite some contractors' adoption of BIM technologies in the construction industry, representing positive profitability and return results. Therefore, in this study, the proce-dure and standardization of the processes of not only implementation but also analysis of the costs that could have been increased if errors were not detected on commercial construction projects are proposed [15].

Another study compared BIM's impact on selecting an appropriate option in a resi-dential construction project in China and other alternatives from an LCA perspective. As part of this, environmental and energy requirements were assessed and analyzed from the point of view of profitability. However, this study worked with only one project and other alternatives that were not implemented [16].

Also, based on this study, BIM and working with data in this environment can be helpful for key performance parameters, which are part of profitability. BIM can also be used in the assessment of the so-called PPP projects. This was also pointed out by a study where, based on BIM modelling, PPP projects were assessed based on future performance indicators, primarily financial and assessment of the so-called value for money [17].

When implementing BIM technology, it is necessary to consider the benefits, diffi-culties and potential risks associated with this process and use. The study from Poland contained an analysis that also included the profitability of introducing BIM in Poland, specifically on the object of a military building. The result should be a standardized procedure and a recommendation that should recommend BIM technology even when assessing the profitability of construction projects [18].

Key performance indicators represent measurable indicators that reflect the results of creative activity and can be quantified. These indicators can be viewed from several perspectives. Since it is a management tool based on which it is possible to perform essential management functions, such as planning, monitoring and control of goals, the selection and monitoring of these parameters depend on the focus of goals and defining the success of construction projects. Several sources pointed to the segmentation of key performance indicators into several groups.

On the one hand, some indicators are focused on sustainability, primarily from an environmental point of view. It is an area where, within the life cycle of a construction project, there is an effort to achieve a minimum carbon footprint and to extend the life of the construction project. Within the framework of LCA, economic sustainability can also be perceived in this evaluation process [19]. Another view of the perception of key performance indicators talks about quality indicators as a measurable result of the performance and success of construction projects. Quality indicators, which also include the rate of failures, repairs, and complaints, but also partly the lifetime of the construction product, represent not only a qualitative indicator but also a quantitative indicator that quantifies and measurably.

From the point of view of the perception of the success of construction development projects, there is the perception of economic indicators. The group of economic key performance indicators belongs to the fundamental indicators from the point of view of setting and fulfilling the financial goals of construction projects. These indicators primarily include cost indicators. Planning and cost management makes much sense in connection with the use of BIM technologies. Several studies have pointed to the correct idea of the dependence on the use of BIM technology and cost optimization. Profitability indicators represent another group of indicators. Focusing on sales in planning, managing and evaluating the success of projects is not possible for all types of construction projects. Above all, construction projects where it is not a commercial interest but a public interest in the form of building infrastructure, non-profit projects for a public purpose, etc. they, represent a group where the use of this indicator is problematic. On the contrary, in development projects where there is an interest in constructing a building to rent or sell to end users, indicators of sales, revenues and overall profitability are very effective tools for planning and management.

Profit and sales represent the primary goal from a financial and business point of view. However, the volume of sales can depend on several factors, as well as the profit. When comparing these indicators are mainly used when comparing and analyzing construction projects of the same volume with the same purpose. Since the investigation of the impact of BIM technology and the use of data for planning and management of construction projects involves analyzing projects that differ in volume, scope and purpose, a better indicator may appear to be the profitability index or overall index indicators that also consider volume expenditure parameters. From this point of view, these indicators are more suitable for assessing the impact of data and BIM technology on the planning, management, and implementation of construction projects with a commercial purpose.

3 Methodology

3.1 Research Aim and Research Problem

This research is focused on analyzing the use of data and BIM technology in the planning, management, and implementation of construction projects to analyze the impact on selected performance indicators. Because these are development projects aimed at the sale of residences, and commercial and administrative premises, profitability indicators rebuild the possibilities of comparison and analysis of results for managers in this area. The research steps and methodological procedure can be seen in Fig. 2.

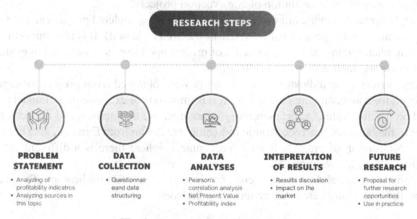

Fig. 2. Research flowchart and steps.

The aim of the research is to analyze the use of data and BIM technology and the impact on profitability indicators. The research is based on the basic idea and assumption that the use of data and BIM technology can positively improve the planning, management, and implementation of development projects. The result should be better performance indicators, the so-called key performance indicators. Performance indicators are among those based on the already mentioned reasons.

Comparing the results and analyzing profitability as a perception of the success of construction projects is an interesting perspective that should answer the consideration of BIM technologies as an aid to achieving the economic goals of the implementation of construction projects. Therefore, indicators such as profit from the sale or rental of residential and commercial buildings and premises are among those analyzed and researched. It should be mentioned that, to a large extent, this is the view of the developer, respectively, the investor. Another investigated indicator and relationship is the profitability index and the use rate of BIM technology in construction projects.

3.2 Data Collection and Data Processing

Data collection was carried out through an online questionnaire. Developers and investors of several construction projects from three countries (Slovakia, Slovenia and Croatia) were approached. The research was focused on commercial construction projects, the purpose of which was the sale of residential buildings and commercial and administrative premises. Respondents were approached to answer questions regarding using data in the BIM environment and BIM technology, primarily in the planning, management, and implementation of construction projects. The project manager, together with the finance department, answered these questions. Also, the goal was to obtain available economic performance indicators in the form of data such as project costs, profit, and profitability index.

To quantify the rate of data use in the BIM environment, a response scale from 1 to 5 was set. Based on the maximum use rate, 5 was set as the highest possible. On the contrary, 1 represents the lowest rate of use of Data and BIM technology in the planning, management, and implementation of construction projects.

Fundamental economic indicators were provided for completed projects and already in the advanced sales phase (that is, at least 80% sold or leased). It is also important to note that when renting, at least five years of project operation is considered to evaluate the projects and their economic results.

Key performance indicators, such as costs were obtained from project managers. However, from an economic point of view, it is important to examine these impacts also based on the time value factor; therefore, for an objective comparison and evaluation of the data, fundamental macroeconomic indicators are drawn from Eurostat, also because it is a comparison of projects from three countries where there is a different rate of inflation and some conditions.

Profit and profitability index were examined, among other indicators. To a large extent, these indicators are basic economic indicators.

$$PI = \frac{\sum_{n=1}^{N} \frac{NCF_n}{(1+r)^n}}{\sum_{n=1}^{N} \frac{I_n}{(1+r)^n}} \equiv \frac{NPV}{I_0} \tag{1}$$

where [20]:

CFn – net discounted cash flow in the n period,

In – initial investment in the n period (or total investment),

r – discount rate,

NPV net discounted (present) income.

These indicators were entered as variables. The dependence between these indicators and the utilization rate was investigated. This was done through Pearson's correlation analysis. The level of significance was set at $p = 0.1$.

3.3   Research Sample

The research sample represents enterprises that participated in the planning, management, and implementation of construction projects for administrative and commercial premises and residential buildings. From the point of view of examining and analyzing the profitability of indicators, this represents commercial projects where the primary goal of the developers is the profit generated by the sale and rental of buildings and premises - construction projects.

Most of the respondents represented micro-enterprises. However, many of the respondents also represented medium and small businesses, and 13% of the respondents were large businesses. Therefore, from this point of view, it is the composition of the research sample that represents the situation on the construction market in the mentioned countries.

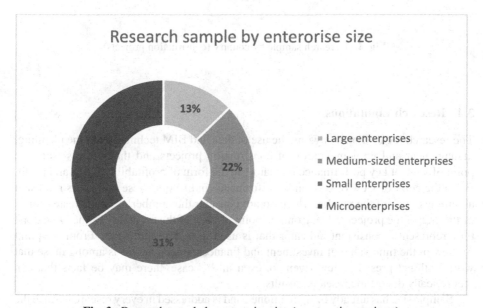

Fig. 3. Research sample by enterprise size (construction projects)

It is interesting to look at the research sample of respondents according to the implementation of construction projects in individual countries. The research was implemented on projects in Slovakia, Slovenia, and Croatia. Individual representation can be seen in Fig. 3, which reflects the representation of respondents by country. Projects implemented in Slovakia have the most significant representation. Croatia is second in the number of projections, followed by Slovenia (Fig. 4)).

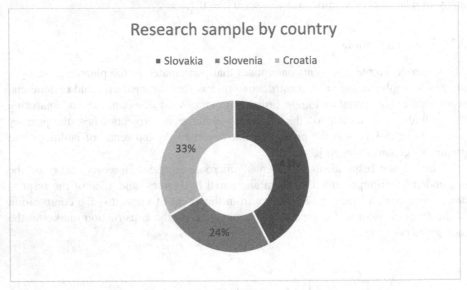

Fig. 4. Research sample by country (construction projects)

3.4 Research Limitations

The research focused on analyzing the use of data and BIM technology in the planning, management and implementation of construction projects and their results from the point of view of key performance indicators in the form of profitability index and profit. From the point of view of economic performance indicators, these indicators represent a complex view of the results, which do not consider the number of overinvested funds or the size of the project. Also, from the point of view of the neutrality of the indicators, they represent a consistent indicator that is used in several industries. From the point of view of the time value of investment and finances, this indicator is among those that work with net present value. Even so, even in this case, there may be facts that can theoretically distort the research results.

Sample size has already been mentioned and is addressed in every research. Since the distribution and geographical location of the projects are comprehensive, these results should reflect a comprehensive sample of respondents despite the smaller number of respondents.

Another possible conflict is the focus of projects. Based on the selection and determination of the research problem, only commercial projects focused on residential buildings and commercial and administrative spaces were selected. Since, in terms of investors' interest, this represents the most common construction projects in the research countries, these results cannot be generalized to all construction projects. Above all, not for those in the field of infrastructure and so on.

4 Results and Discussion

The analysis of the relationship between the use of data in the BIM environment and selected key performance indicators in the form of profitability indicators points to the trend of the positive impact of BIM technology and the use of data in favor of effective planning, management and implementation of construction projects. Figure 5 shows the relationship between data and BIM technology use in construction project management and the average profitability index. The profitability index represented high values for the companies that reported the highest use rate. This value was 2.06, representing a high return and profit rate when considering the investment. Acceptable values were also recorded for companies that use BIM technologies at levels 3 and 4 to plan, manage and implement construction projects.

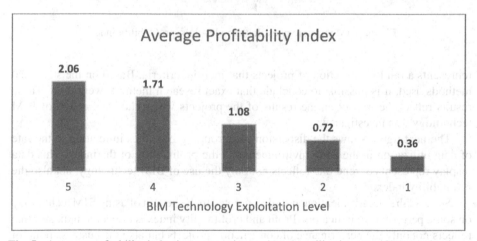

Fig. 5. Average profitability index in construction projects by utilization rate of BIM technology

On the contrary, for projects where the rate of data and BIM technology use was at level 2 and 1, i.e. of low intensity of use, the average profitability index did not even reach level 1, which represents an investment that is not suitable from the point of view of profitability in the examined period. Figure 6 describes this situation better. Cases of construction projects where the profitability index is higher are associated with a higher intensity of using BIM technology. Based on these values, a trend line was constructed to describe the dependence.

From the point of view of the limits of the research, it is possible to discuss whether it is a significant statistical phenomenon or not. As already mentioned, the research sample

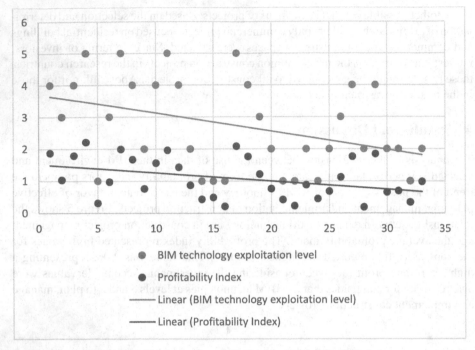

Fig. 6. BIM technology exploitation level vs. profitability index.

represents a random selection of projects that met the criteria. Based on the statistical methods used, it is possible to conclude that exact research methods were used. These results reflect the impact on the results of the projects where the level of use of BIM technology was investigated.

The next figure shows the dispersion and grouping of values in relation to the rate of data utilization in the BIM environment and the profitability of the index. This data display represents a trend that reflects not only the use of BIM technology, but also the profitability index.

Some of the already mentioned studies pointed to the benefit of using BIM technology on some performance indicators. Profit and profitability index is a specific indicator that reflects not only the performance of construction projects but also the business point of view. Since the primary goal of business a. implementation of business activities (Fig. 7).

In the context of examining the correlation and relationship between the rate of data use in the BIM environment in the planning, management, and implementation of construction projects in the context of examining the progress of profitability indicators. In the following graph, the curves show a high degree of correlation. This is also confirmed by Pearson's correlation, which shows values of $r = 0.96501$.

The following picture talks more about it. The following plots show a high degree of correlation, which only confirms the assumption that was the subject of the plot (Fig. 8).

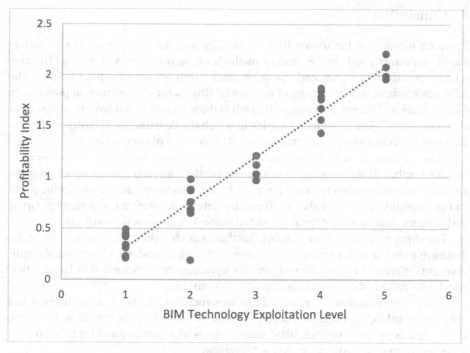

Fig. 7. Intervals between the profitability index and the use of BIM technology

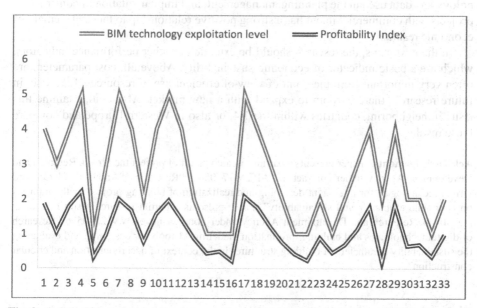

Fig. 8. Relationship and correlation between the profitability index and the use of BIM technology

5   Conclusion

Research focused on the use of BIM technology and data in relation to key perfor-mance indicators points to the modern methods of analyzing project results. The cor-relation pointed to a significantly positive relationship between the use of data in the BIM environment and the results of the profitability index of construction projects. In three countries. This research was carried out in three countries that have several similar characteristics. These are small countries in which the construction industry represents an important component of the creation of GDP and thus of the economy.

This relationship was investigated by Pearson correlation analysis. Despite the smaller number of respondents, who still represented the reference group of projects, an important relationship between the use of BIM technology and results in the profit and profitability index was shown. These indicators represent an important group of performance indicators that speak about the success of construction projects.

The strength of this study is the fact that the research results reflect several countries that have a similar construction industry, but on the other hand, the geographical condi-tions are different. The investigated projects were mainly implemented in larger cities, which also reflects the focus of the construction projects.

This research pointed to the strengths of construction projects where the investor had the goal of making a profit. This economic goal was set as a clear intention. However, achieving this goal was difficult. BIM technology as a progressive tool for achieving set goals has become a medium for their achievement.

The research, based on empirical methods, confirmed the assumption that BIM tech-nology and data used in the planning, management, and implementation of construction projects with commercial intent has a strong positive relationship to the achievement of economic results.

In the next steps, the research should be extended to other performance indicators, which are a basic indicator of economic sustainability. Above all, cost parameters are often very important from the point of view of efficient use of resources. Likewise, in future research, there is room to expand with a new market. Above all, examine this issue in neighboring countries within the V4, or also in Western Europe and compare these results.

Acknowledgements. Paper presents a partial research result of project the Slovak Research and Development Agency under contract no. APVV-17–0549, "Research of knowledge-based and virtual technologies for intelligent designing and realization of building projects with emphasis on economic efficiency and sustainability". Paper presents a partial research result of project the Slovak Research and Development Agency under contract no. APVV 22–0576 "Research of digital technologies and building information modeling 11 tools for designing and evaluating the sustainability parameters of building structures in the context of decarbonization and circular construction".

References

1. Sudzina, F., Kmec, P.: The technological paradox and evaluation of the benefits of informatization. Ekonomický časopis **54**, 281–293 (2006)

2. Johansson, B., Sudzina, F., Pucihar, P.: Alignment of business and information strategies and its impact on business performance. J. Bus. Econ. Manage. **15**(5), 886–898 (2016)
3. Johansson, B., Sudzina, F., Newman, M.: ERP system implementation costs and selection factors of an implementation approach. Int. J. Bus. Inform. Syst. **8**(1), 87–105 (2011)
4. Dugas, J., Seňová, A., Kršák, B., Ferencz, V.: Implementation of business intelligence tools in companies. New trends in process control and production management. In: Proceedings of the International Conference on Marketing Management, Trade, Financial and Social Aspects of Business. – Leiden, pp. 93–95 (2018)
5. Behún, M., Knežo, D., Cehlár, M., Knapčíková, L., Behúnová, A.: Recent application of Dijkstra's algorithm in the process of production planning. Appl. Sci. **12**(14), 7088 (2022)
6. Mayer, P., Funtík, T., Gašparík, J., Makýš, P.: Analysis of the current state of automation of hazard detection processes in BIM in Slovakia. Appl. Sci. **11**, 8130 (2021)
7. Dasović, B., Klanšek, U.: Integration of mixed-integer nonlinear program and project management tool to support sustainable cost-optimal construction scheduling. Sustainability **13**, 12173 (2021)
8. Jackson, T.: Key performance indicator (KPI) examples defined. Retrieved November 3 (2019). https://www.clearpointstrategy.com/18-key-performance-indicators/
9. Mellado, F., Lou, E.C.W.: Building information modelling, lean and sustainability: an integration framework to promote performance improvements in the construction industry. Sustain. Cities Soc. **61**, 1–13 (2020)
10. Korytarova, J., Hromadka, V.: Building life cycle economic impacts. In: Proceedings of the International Conference on Management and Service Science, Wuhan, China, 24–26 August 2010
11. Kravanja, S., Klanšek, U., Žula, T.: Mass, Direct Cost and Energy Life-Cycle Cost Optimization of Steel-Concrete Composite Floor Structures. Appl. Sci. **11**, 10316 (2021)
12. Kiritharan, A., Dimensions of BIM. LinkedIn (2021)
13. Juricic, B., Galic, M., Marenjak, M.: Review of the construction labour demand and shortages in the EU. Buildings **11**, 17 (2021)
14. Biolek, V., Hanák, T.: LCC estimation model: a construction material perspective. Buildings **9**, 182 (2019)
15. Bocksteal, D., Issa, M.: A methodology for contractor clash detection using building information modelling on commercial construction projects. J. Inform. Technol. Constr. **21**, 233–249 (2016)
16. Dauletbek, A., Zhou, P.G.: BIM-based LCA as a comprehensive method for the refurbishment of existing dwellings considering environmental compatibility, energy efficiency, and profitability: a case study in China. J. Build. Eng. **46**, 103852 (2022)
17. Ren, G.Q., Li, H.J., Zhang, J.S.: A BIM-based value for money assessment in public-private partnership: an overall review. Appl. Sci. **10**(18), 6483 (2020)
18. Wojtowicz, M.: Design and execution of building investments using BIM technology for facilities subject to the polish military administration. computational technologies in engineering (TKI'2018). In: 15th Conference on Computational Technologies in Engineering (TKI) Jora Wielka, Poland (2019)
19. Blichova, Z., Vilcekova, S., Kridlova Burdova, E., Katunský, D.: Life cycle assessment of residential buildings and scenarios for prolonged life span. IOP Conf. Ser.: Mater. Sci. Eng. **1252**(1), 012006 (2022). https://doi.org/10.1088/1757-899X/1252/1/012006
20. Strategic Line: profitability index – PI (2022)

Author Index

Printed in the United States
by Baker & Taylor Publisher Services